The
Obstructed
Path

French Social Thought in the
Years of Desperation 1930-1960

The
Obstructed
Path

H. Stuart Hughes

with a new preface by
Stanley Hoffmann

Transaction Publishers
New Brunswick (U.S.A.) and London (U.K.)

Library of Congress Catalog Number: 2001027200
ISBN: 0-7658-0850-1
Printed in the United States of America

Library of Congress Cataloging-in-Publication Data

Hughes, H. Stuart (Henry Stuart), 1916-
    The obstructed path : French social thought in the years of desperation, 1930-1960 / H. Stuart Hughes ; with a new preface by Stanley Hoffmann.
        p. cm.
    Includes index.
    ISBN 0-7658-0850-1 (pbk. : alk. paper)
    1. France—Intellectual life—20th century. I. Title: French social thought in the years of desperation, 1930-1960. II. Title.

DC33.7 .H844 2001
944.081—dc21   2001027200

For Judy

Plus tost seront Rhosne, et Saone desjoinctz
Que d'avec toi mon coeur se désassemble. . . .
MAURICE SCÈVE, "Delie"

Contents

Preface to the Transaction Edition

How difficult it still is to write a study of the French intelligentsia in the years of turmoil and torment which were also years of tremendous literary and philosophical exuberance—1930 to 1960! So much was indeed going on, so much talent was on display. The observer of the period is torn between putting all these figures into the camps that ideological battles and political choices determined, with the risk of reducing their originality as writers or thinkers, and focusing on the latter (and on their contribution to the old French cleavage between Cartesianism on the one had, faith and romanticism on the other), at the cost of underestimating the effects of their political and ideological commitments. Compare, for instance, H. Stuart Hughes' book, published in 1967, with Tony Judt's *Past Imperfect* published in 1992: Judt's reads like a brilliant indictment of the political stance, the (left-) totalitarian temptations, the parochialism and the posturing of a generation whose illiberalism he deplores. Hughes deliberately focuses on what this generation produces that was "work or high seriousness and universal scope", on the "disinterested study of society" rather than on the sound and fury of the ideological battlefield. Judt's is a prosecutor's brief, rather unconcerned with nuances; Hughes is the explorer of a fascinatingly diverse and fertile continent. Judt tends to reduce it to St. Germain des Prés and the strident *Temps Modernes*. Hughes blends his constant concern for the many ways in which historians define and practice their

ix

craft, his lifelong interest in literature, his fascination with
the influence of Marx and Freud, his empathy with the
varieties of Christian thought, and his delicate grasp of
singular personalities.

The result is a book whose main and enduring value
lies in the superb portraits of such writers as the great,
tragic Bernanos, the "artist-adventurer". Malraux (who,
in my opinion but not in Hughes', remained faithful to
his "death-defying heroism" even when he served as
"France's official purveyor of culture"), the elusive, brilliant, and badly known Merleau-Ponty, and that formida-
bly gifted *mélange* of profundity and abundance, intellectual *démesure* and political naiveté, Jean-Paul Sartre.
The story of Marc Bloch's relation with Lucien Febvre
has been told several times, but Hughes remains the fair-
est. He pays attention and tribute to thinkers whose stars
have faded, such as Maritain, Marcel and Teilhard du
Chardin (but leaves aside such other Catholics as Mauriac
and, except very briefly, Mounier— less important as
thinkers). His sketch of Levi-Strauss' deep contribution
to anthropology does justice to a powerful and pessimistic mind.

Even for a man as subtle and thoughtful as Hughes,
predictions are a slippery business. Martin du Gard (whose
grand series of novels, *Les Thibault*, he judges more
harshly than I do) did not "give up completely" his final
project: *Maumort* is a fragment, but like Camus' *First Man*,
a masterly and fascinating one. After the abrupt end, ca.
1975, of French fascination with the Soviet Union and
Marxism, Camus' reputation has soared again, while
Sartre's has fallen (there is more justice in the former's
posthumous fate than in the second's). The rather drab
vision Hughes leaves to his readers at the end of his book,
that of a structuralism that "banned both humanism and
the starker attitudes that had issued from it", was soon to
be dispelled by the new burst of spontaneity and romanticism of 1968. Foucault himself turned out to be an odd

mix of "objective" anthropology and highly subjective, and very traditionally French, rebellion against social constraints and coercion.

In so rich and perceptive a book, I find two pieces missing. Greater attention might have been lavished on *"L'esprit des années 30,"* on that intellectual revolt against the political and social status quo whose champions ended up divided between Fascism or Vichy, and the Resistance. French Fascist literature is barely mentioned: Brasillach (and his trial) don't appear, Drieu la Rochelle gets a couple of sentences. In French intellectual as well as political history, the confrontation of Fascism and anti-Fascism, after 1934, was of great importance. The other element that isn't given the place I think it deserves is the incredible effervescence of French intellectual and literary life in "the years of desperation", when French films, the plays of Giraudoux, Anouilh, Sartre, and Camus, the public quarrels among famous minds, the blend of philosophy and show business on the Left Bank, the presence of brilliant stage directors, and a mass of magazines proved how much vitality, curiosity, and excitement there was in an otherwise lamentably weakened nation.

We should nevertheless be grateful to Hughes for his constant empathy and for the range of his concerns. Unlike Judt, he is willing to "comprehend" the reasons why Marxism and philo-Communism marked many French intellectuals after the war—without whitewashing them. Also, he understood that "most of the time between 1930 and 1960 French social thought had had poetry at its core", that "writers who had thought of themselves as rigorous theorists had been poets without knowing it". This is a profound insight, both into the flimsiness of many elaborate philosophical constructions, and into the core of deep emotions, bold images, and searing passions that were often hidden in them, and keep us close to these thinkers.

Stanley Hoffmann

Preface

For a long time I was perplexed as to what kind of sequel I should write to my *Consciousness and Society*—published ten years ago—or indeed, as to whether I should follow it with any sequel at all. Certain major tendencies of European social thought in the four decades (1890–1930) covered by that volume had established themselves clearly in my mind: the succeeding era seemed to lack a comparable focus.

As the years passed, matters gradually sorted themselves out until it became apparent that more than one sequel was required. It was only by dividing the intellectual generation 1930–1960 into two distinct groupings that I could make sense of it. The first was limited to the French. The second consisted of the anti-fascist émigrés from Central Europe and Italy who settled in England or the United States. The reasons for treating these two themes separately should emerge from a reading of the first chapter of the present study.

This book forms, then, the second volume of a trilogy, which, after a further pause for reflection, I hope to complete before another ten years have gone by. I should hasten to add that it is a free-standing work in itself and that it is not necessary to read *Consciousness and Society* in order to understand it. It is intended as a contribution both to European intellectual history in the contemporary era and to the study of the culture of modern France. In the latter guise, it marks my first effort to deal explicitly with a French theme. Although I have been acquainted with France for more than forty years and have taught its history, I have

refrained until now from putting on paper any extended
reflections about it; I can only speculate on the origins of
this curious *pudeur*.

Certain portions of the book have previously figured in
the following forms: Chapter 1 was delivered as a lecture
on the occasion of Cornell University's centennial celebration
in April 1965; selections from Chapters 2 and 3 constituted
the Stephen Allan Kaplan Memorial Lectures which I gave
at the University of Pennsylvania in March 1966; parts 1–4
of Chapter 3 were published in *The American Scholar*,
XXXV (Fall 1966), and part 4 of Chapter 5 in *Ramparts*, V
(March 1967). There are also a few echoes of phraseology
from reviews I wrote of Simone de Beauvoir's *The Mandarins*, of Camus's *The Rebel*, and of Lévi-Strauss' *The
Savage Mind*, when these books first appeared in English
translation.

To maintain a consistent tone, I have uniformly employed
the past tense, even when dealing with authors whose work
at the time of writing was far from finished. The footnotes
are designed to make a bibliography unnecessary. Although I
have almost invariably used the original French version of
the works cited, and I begin each footnote with this version,
I have referred the reader to the pages of the English translation, where such exists, taking care when necessary to
correct the passages I have quoted.

Among those to whom I should like to express my grati-
tude, I should first mention François Crouzet and René
Rémond, professors of history at the University of Paris
(Nanterre), who arranged for me to teach at Nanterre as
Bacon Exchange Professor from Harvard University in the
second semester of the academic year 1966–1967, and thereby
to complete my book in the appropriate atmosphere of Paris.
I have also profited from conversations with Jean-Marie
Domenach, Claude Lévi-Strauss, Edouard Morot-Sir, and
Paul Ricoeur. Two of my PhD students, David L. Schalk

and Dominick La Capra, contributed respectively to my understanding of Martin du Gard and Durkheim, while Stephen A. Schuker undertook, on a wholly volunteer basis, the tedious and indispensable task of serving as my representative at home base in Widener Library while I was away in France. I am particularly indebted to Stanley Hoffmann for giving the entire manuscript a reading that was both discerning and heartening. Of my wife, to whom the book is dedicated and who combed it over for errors of fact and logic, I can only say that without her stimulation and encouragement it would have been neither conceived nor carried through to completion.

CHAPTER

I

Introduction:
The Obstructed Path

IN HIS NOVEL *Le Grand Meaulnes*, Alain-Fournier speaks of a search for an "ancient obstructed path, the path to which the weary prince could find no entrance. It is found at last at the most forlorn hour of the morning, when you have long since forgotten that eleven or twelve is about to strike. . . . And suddenly, as one thrusts aside bushes and brier, . . . it appears in sight as a long shadowy avenue, with at its end a small round patch of light."[1]

The words are from 1913—but the sentiment might have been expressed with equal fervor at almost any time over the next forty years of French cultural history. In itself no more than a literary metaphor, it may serve to forecast the insecurities of the decades ahead. The *motif* of an "obstructed path," of blind alleys and blocked vistas, of faltering and stalemate, and of an increasingly desperate search for a way out, pervades the thinking of Frenchmen of all types and intellectual interests through nearly a half century following the outbreak of the First World War. It is as though Alain-Fournier had divined, one year before the conflict, the life-

[1] Translation by Françoise Delisle as *The Wanderer* (Boston and New York, 1928), p. 156.

1

long obsession of his contemporaries who, more fortunate
than he, were to survive the terrible year 1914: the sense of
one's world as a dark tunnel, beset with vague threats and
of uncertain exit.

Besides the wound of the war itself—more grievous in
France than elsewhere, since here the loss of youth was
irreparable—the four years of bloodshed prompted a wider
questioning of traditional French values. Yet this came only
slowly: the delayed-action effect that postponed to the 1930's
France's social and political examination of conscience was
also apparent in the cultural sphere. An Indian summer of
glory bedazzled Frenchmen and foreigners alike with an
image of primacy that was already threatened on all sides.
On the international scene, the first flush of illusion was
quickly over: the ambiguous outcome of the Ruhr occupation and the electoral victory of the Left in 1924 marked the
beginnings of abdication as a great power and a turning inward of the national energies. But from the narrower standpoint of the assumptions on which social and political life
rested, the next half decade remained one of substantial
self-satisfaction and self-esteem. It took the great depression
and the advent of Hitler to shake the French loose from
their inherited securities.

So much is familiar to any student of the period. What is
less readily apparent is the extent to which this delayed realization of the war's effect had its parallel—indeed, was reinforced—by a corresponding overestimate of France's cultural situation. The military and diplomatic illusions of the
years 1919–1924—the conviction that the French had regained the leadership of Europe and were once more the
grande nation to which others would defer—appeared confirmed by the general esteem which France's artists and
writers enjoyed. In painting, the prestige of the school of
Paris remained unchallenged; in literature, such writers as
Proust and Gide and Valéry had suddenly come into their
own as the precursors of the avant-garde; in philosophy,
Henri Bergson seemed without a rival. Subsequently, from

the middle of the decade on, as the French withdrew from foreign commitments to the cultivation of their own garden, the nation's sense of cultural primacy became, if anything, still more pronounced. For an assertion of artistic or philo- sophical pre-eminence served as psychic compensation for the relinquishment of an active international role. The rest of the civilized world might no longer follow France's diplo- matic leadership, but it continued to pay tribute to its cre- ative achievements. Paris might have lost its position as the hub of international doings, but it still ranked as the cultural capital of the West.

Even the more perceptive French were usually unaware of the extent to which their country's artistic and literary primacy rested on an accumulation of past glories. While they realized perfectly well—perhaps overestimated—the bene- fits they enjoyed from a classical tradition extending in un- broken, orderly succession from the seventeenth century, they did not appreciate how close they were to that tradi- tion's end. By 1930, the original avant-garde experiments had spent their force. Proust was dead, and Gide and Valéry beyond the period of their greatest creativity and influence. With this passing of masters, the perspective on them began to be subtly altered. Their works now figured less as the great innovations of the early twentieth century than as contemporary classics. And as the 1930's passed, and writers of similar scope failed to appear, people began to suspect that theirs might be the last generation for which the classical tradition would be a living reality.

In France, classicism had greater continuity than in other comparable European countries; it also pervaded the national culture more completely. In England, the classical tradition was associated with particular phases of literary history— and those not necessarily the most tenacious or influential. In Germany, it meant the legacy of one great era of achieve- ment whose products had subsequently been embalmed by the schools and the official purveyors of ethical values—and which in the process had become more and more remote from actual behavior. Neither among the English nor among the Germans did the classical tradition prompt the dominant style of thought. England had no single "official" philosopher; Germany had Kant, but by the twentieth century the Kantian tradition had been interpreted so variously as to remain only the vaguest point of reference—and besides, few pedagogues aimed to teach children to write like Kant. In France, in contrast, Descartes had for nearly three centuries supplied a ready-made style of thought and of expression; here Cartesianism suffused the intellectual atmosphere so thoroughly that much of the time it went unnoticed. The French not only possessed an official philosopher; they had in the Cartesian tradition a pass-key that did service for literature and social thought alike. Across the Rhine, "high" culture might go one way and social science quite another—with both of them for the most part irrelevant to the country's public life. In France, all these endeavors shared a common ancestor and found in Cartesian categories the guide to the orderly style of thought and the felicity of expression which had long been assumed to constitute the special excellences of the Gallic mind.

By the 1930's, this ancient confidence was flagging. Or at the very least a few Frenchmen of particular discernment were beginning to discover the fragility of their country's cultural prestige abroad. Claude Lévi-Strauss has related how on his arrival in Brazil toward the middle of the decade he found the products of French social science still enjoying almost universal esteem. But the names held in highest honor were of a generation that had passed or was passing; their successors had become the generalizers or popularizers of earlier discoveries. The national talent had been canalized toward synthesis and ready explanation; it excelled in exposing with clarity and grace the larger outlines of theories, which was all that the general public wanted or needed to know.[2] In broader terms, the French were maintaining a cult

---

[2] *Tristes tropiques* (Paris, 1955), translated (and slightly abridged) by John Russell under the same title, Atheneum paperback edition (New York, 1963), p. 105.

of the spoken and written word which might impress the remoter reaches of the Latin world but which was becoming outmoded elsewhere; in France people still tended to assume that an elegant verbal solution to a problem would suffice to settle it. Such was the special vulnerability of the French classical tradition as the second quarter of the twentieth century began.

So it seems to us in retrospect: with the experience of a further generation behind us, we find confirmation for the contemporary suspicions that classicism had reached its end. In this perspective, authors like Proust and Valéry rank as the last of the French classicists (to whom some might add Albert Camus in the role of a dutiful grandson). And we can see the next generation as an era in which one writer after another strove to break the classic mold—not so much in technical experimentation (for that had been the work of the previous quarter century) as in the moral assumptions on which their work was based. The classical tradition had assumed a common psychology and a common standard of artistic excellence; even at its end, when it enlarged the criteria of conscious time, when it discovered the inconsequence of personal motivation or made room for the sexual deviant within the circle of a recognized humanity, it did so with a universal aim and in accordance with a rigorous canon of literary craftsmanship. By the 1930's and 1940's such a purist definition of the writer's aim seemed dated; indeed, the métier as such came under question as ethically insufficient for an apocalyptic era.

Hence the literature of engagement: this also is an old story. In the present context, what is significant is that in the literary as in the political and social field the real reckoning with the First World War arrived a decade late. The end of the classical tradition—and with it the ebbing of the flood of innovation, in the novel, in painting, in music, that the years immediately preceding the war had witnessed—came accompanied and reinforced by the great depression and the fascist onslaught. The result was a crisis of confidence on all sides. Just as the grave malfunctioning of

France's economic and administrative machinery was becoming generally apparent, the foundations of pride in the
country's cultural tradition were beginning to be sapped.
The years of political and social despair were also years of
aesthetic and moral rethinking. What wonder that the prewar era figured in retrospect as the belle époque—that nostalgia for a time of facile pleasures and national confidence
should have had its parallel in regret over a waning of cultural self-assurance.

It was to be another generation before both types of confidence were regained. After the Second World War, as in
the aftermath of the First, the full social and moral effect
of the military ordeal was a long time on the way. Not until
the mid-1950's were the tempos and manners of a new kind
of society in general evidence. And it was about the same
time that the signs of innovation in intellectual and aesthetic
interests became widespread. Hence for cultural study, the
conventional division of contemporary French history into
an interwar and a post-Second World War period makes
little sense. The more natural order is to continue the effects
of the pre-1914 currents down to the late 1920's, and then
to delimit another era—the years of desperation—from the
1930's to the early 1960's. It is this latter era that now needs
to be defined.

With the liberation of Paris from Nazi occupation and
the end of the Second World War, France seemed once
more to have become the cultural center of Europe. The
old primacy had apparently been regained—one could even
say that it had been reinforced by the almost total abdication of Germany. In the late 1940's, Paris was the focus of
general curiosity and attention: the existential philosophy of
Jean-Paul Sartre figured as the most discussed intellectual
movement in the Western world. Superficially the situation
looked much as it had been following the First World War,
with the cultural pilgrims returning to France as numerous
and as eager as before. But this time their worship at the

shrine had a crucial difference: in the 1920's the Parisian novelties had been in evidence for more than a decade—they were extensions before a wider audience of what had previously been the concern of coteries; after 1944, foreigners came to Paris on true voyages of discovery—they wanted to find out what the French had been up to during their years of enforced isolation.

What the Englishman or American discovered often disconcerted him. For it was both novel and curiously familiar; it was both new and at the same time very old. In literature and philosophy, the merging of previously antagonistic systems and a calculated crudity in diction might shock or amuse. But the elements that went into the process were familiar enough. Marxism and phenomenology were far from new—it was only their marriage that came as a surprise. Likewise the modes of thought of men like Sartre and Merleau-Ponty were not as strange as they at first seemed—whether Cartesian or Hegelian or a combination of the two, their antecedents had been the common property of the European educated public long before the occupation of 1940 had cut off the French from intellectual circulation.

Had their imposed isolation been only four years long? This was what the foreign observer began to wonder as he noticed a perplexing provincialism in French cultural responses. Perhaps the separation of France from a wider intellectual exchange had started a good deal earlier, as early as the beginning of the 1930's. It was then that French concentration on indigenous values had assumed a character of prickly defensiveness. In the military sphere, it came to be called the complex of the Maginot Line. From the intellectual standpoint, it bore no such clear label. Yet the phenomenon was obvious enough: as the French had gradually found themselves outclassed in arms, bereft of economic expedients, ideologically torn asunder, and diplomatically beleaguered, their assertions of cultural superiority had quite naturally become more insistent. And this cultural pride was one of the intangible forces that sustained them through the long ordeal of military occupation. Those who knew the French on the morrow of victory can recall the patronizing tone they frequently took toward their American or British liberators—a tone brought to a perfection of unruffled assurance in the greatest literary classic of the Second World War, the memoirs of General de Gaulle.

After 1933, the French had been more and more alone. The only great nation of the Western European continent that resisted a fascist takeover had paid the price in an increasing isolation of its intellectuals from a wider exchange of ideas. What had earlier been the misfortune of Italy and Germany and Austria by the mid-century had revealed an unsuspected positive aspect. It would be absurd, of course, to suggest that the exile or death of so many Italian or German writers during the years of fascist tyranny had been in any sense a cultural gain; on the contrary, this sort of persecution impoverished the cultural life of their nations— and in a fashion which in the German case seemed almost irremediable. But such a vast displacement of intellectual personnel could not fail to confer a number of side benefits. In the case of the emigration of the 1930's and 1940's the chief gain was a breaking down of the provincialism of national cultural frontiers. The fact that so many German and Austrian writers (and to a lesser extent Italians) passed a decade or more in Britain or the United States was of immeasurable value to both sides in the exchange. The universe of discourse of the Anglo-Saxon and the Central European worlds were for the first time brought into close contact, and each was enriched in the process. Indeed, this near-symbiosis of two widely contrasting traditions appears in retrospect as the most important intellectual event of the era.

There was no reason for the French to emigrate before 1940. After then it was too late—and besides, there was the deep-seated prejudice, going back to the 1790's, against the whole idea of self-exile. So the French stayed at home. Only a handful of leading writers such as Jacques Maritain and

Antoine de Saint-Exupéry lived for any length of time in the United States. Thus the French shared scarcely at all in the great exchange of ideas going on in Britain and America. Their own tradition—which they had always assumed to be the central one—was suddenly cut off from the world outside.

We are back to the theme of confinement, of breaking out of an impasse. Let us turn now to define this process of turning inward in the specific field of social thought.

For the Americans and the émigrés from Central Europe, the masters of twentieth-century social thought were Sigmund Freud and Max Weber. Neither of these was honored in France as he had been in Germany before 1933 and subsequently in the United States. The French were far from being ignorant of what Freud and Weber had taught. But their application of Freudian doctrine was largely confined to imaginative literature or semi-intellectual conversation— the clinical practice of psychoanalysis was far less widespread in France than in Central Europe or America—and it was only a rare French scholar, like the young Raymond Aron, who had fully digested Weber's criteria for a methodology of social science.

The reasons for the French resistance to Freud are not far to seek. Psychoanalysis has always prospered less in a predominantly Catholic milieu than among Protestants or Jews; in this respect Italy in the interwar years was even more resistant than France. But among the French there was a special reason for reluctance to take up Freudianism and for dismay at the appearance of a discipline that claimed to have made a science of introspection. France was, after all, the classic home of the examination of conscience. For three and a half centuries since Montaigne a succession of French moralistes had been subjecting human motivation to a scrutiny that was both precise and disabused. Into this traditional national preserve the foreigner ventured only at his peril; even Freud had experienced his first glimmerings of insight in the hospital of a Frenchman, Charcot. What had

a people that had produced Stendhal to learn further about
the evasions and prevarications of the human heart? There
was presumption in the claim of a mere physician from
Vienna that he could reduce to a system what the classics
of French literature had left on the level of aphorism or
aperçu.

In the interwar years competent French studies of Freudian
theories were readily available. As early as 1923 Raymond de
Saussure had produced an account of psychoanalytic method
which satisfied Freud's close associates (and concomitantly
ran afoul of the French police). But in France even a professional understanding of psychoanalysis had a way of turning
into something else. The French distrusted Freud's schemati-
zations; they wanted more poetry in their psychology, and
they were constantly smuggling in a voluntarist note at
which the master would have bridled. Thus beginning in
the late 1930's the leading philosopher of science Gaston
Bachelard was using the term "psychoanalysis" in a new
sense that included the reflective observation of such natural
elements as fire and water, and was criticizing classic psychoanalytic theory for converting protean symbols and images
into precise concepts; Bachelard envisaged a therapy of return to direct contact with nature and "things," of emotional restoration through work in the world of matter.[8]

Besides all this, the French had produced a contemporary
of Freud who before 1914 had been far better known than
he and who seemed to have said many of the same things
in a more graceful and palatable form. As an explorer of
the unconscious, Henri Bergson was in no sense Freud's
equal; the adepts of psychoanalytic theory did not even consider him a precursor. But in liberating the study of human
behavior from the tyranny of rationalistic, ready-made explanations, he had performed much the same function.

Thus the French possessed on their home ground a

[8] See François Dagognet, *Gaston Bachelard: sa vie, son oeuvre* (Paris,
1965), pp. 29-35, and among Bachelard's own works, *La psychanalyse
du feu* (Paris, 1949).

Weltanschauung that was the deceptive mimic of Freudianism. Yet even as such it was far from satisfactory. By 1932, when Bergson's last major work finally appeared, its effect was muted by a protracted delay in its publication and by the fact that its author had been virtually silent during the previous decade. Outside France, *Two Sources of Morality and Religion* evoked little response: Bergson's way of thinking had gone out of fashion. Within France, the book's restrained reception revealed the extent to which the "Bergsonian revolution" in philosophy and social thought had long ago spent its force.

By the 1930's, although Bergson was still held in honor as the French philosopher laureate, it was difficult to find many full-fledged Bergsonians among his country's intellectual elite. The tendency, rather, was toward a selective Bergsonism; each writer chose the particular aspects of the doctrine that fitted his own needs and temperament. And Bergson himself seemed to invite eclectic treatment. He was "one of those philosophers who will always have progeny, because they sow seeds in the mind eternally—but almost no pupils; their system cannot be transmitted."[4] Such was the situation in the literary world. In the lycées and the universities, the official teaching had for the most part fallen back into the familiar neo-Kantian mold.

The failure of the Bergsonian revolution is a perplexing topic: its full explanation would demand a probing into countless individual biographies. At the very least one can say that the slaughter of 1914–1918 had taken the bloom off the philosophy of the élan vital. Tens of thousands of educated young Frenchmen who in the immediate prewar years had intoxicated themselves on Bergson's heady prose had marched off to battle trusting in spiritual fervor to see them through. The ghastly reality had borne almost no resemblance to what they had imagined. Bergson, of course, had not meant his notion of an élan to be taken in an exclusively

[4] Henry Bars, *Maritain en notre temps* (Paris, 1959), p. 197.

or even predominantly military sense. But that was the way
the greater part of his young followers had interpreted it.
From this standpoint, the Bergsonian ideal was simply another casualty of the First World War.

Beyond that, those who had understood the ideal with
the greatest depth and sympathy were nearly all practicing
Catholics or converts to Catholicism. At their hands what
was left of Bergson's message—and the quiet undercurrent
descending from Pascal of which it was the most prominent
contemporary manifestation—had passed into the revival of
specifically Catholic thinking that distinguished the interwar
years. As early as 1913 the young Maritain had published a
critique of the Bergsonian philosophy which marked his personal shift toward an allegiance to St. Thomas Aquinas. Two
decades later, the cultivation of Thomism was at its peak
in Catholic intellectual circles. Neo-scholastic precision had
dimmed the prestige of Bergson's anti-intellectualist philosophy. And for those who—as in one aspect of Bergsonism
itself—drew sustenance from the American pragmatic tradition, there was a younger Catholic teacher, Gabriel Marcel,
to guide them.

Yet enough of Bergson's style of thought lingered among
French students of society, more particularly among historians, to make them still aspire to an immersion in the flux
of reality. When nearly all the rest had been discarded, this
yearning toward a close embrace of social and historical experience remained intact as the core of the Bergsonian inheritance. It implied the rejection of any schematic understanding of the social universe. So far as the concepts of
social thought were concerned, it was incompatible with
Weber's ideal-type method.

This was one reason why Weber was not accepted in
France, as he had been in Germany and was later to be in
the United States, as a methodological guide. A more important reason was that in this field also the French already
possessed their own master—a contemporary of Bergson's
whose influence had held up far better than his.

Emile Durkheim had died in 1917, and many of his ablest young followers had perished in battle. Yet had he lived into the 1930's, he could scarcely have had a prestige greater than that already enjoyed by his students and intellectual heirs. In the interwar years, the systematic study of society in France—and more particularly the linked disciplines of sociology and anthropology—were dominated by Durkheim's precepts. These methodological principles were not always mutually consistent: Claude Lévi-Strauss has complained of their oscillation "between a dull empiricism and an aprioristic frenzy,"[5] and several others have noted how far they traveled in the course of Durkheim's life from their simple positivist origins. The range of Durkheim's interests can be held responsible for some of this diversity of emphasis. The fact that he was starting almost from scratch and that he died before he had time to spell out the final—and more idealist— stage of his thought also help to explain it. But the really troubling aspects of Durkheim's work—and those that created the most difficulty for his heirs—were his philosophical assumptions and the moral view of human society which he had derived from two quite distinct nineteenth-century traditions.

Kant was his master in philosophy, and Comte his great precursor as a systematic sociologist. The wedding of these two in Durkheim's mind already suggested one intellectual problem—a nostalgia for an abstract scheme of ideas which was in implicit contradiction with the empirical labors to which he devoted himself and which he urged on his disciples. Beyond that, it meant a constant search for a moral imperative in the study of society. To the intellectual historian, Kant and Comte may seem to have little in common, but at least they were in agreement in their ethical goal. Kant was unashamedly a moral teacher; Comte believed in a science of morality. Neither would have understood a social theory that aspired to freedom from commitment to specific

[5] "French Sociology," *Twentieth Century Sociology*, edited by Georges Gurvitch and Wilbert E. Moore (New York, 1945), p. 528.

values. Such a "value-free" sociology was what Weber had
proposed and what his German and American disciples were
trying to cultivate. Here, quite apart from differences in
technical methodology, lay a substantial ground for the
divergence of French social thought from the Central European–Anglo American exchange in the 1930's and 1940's.

Durkheim believed with Comte that a moral philosophy
could grow out of "positive science." He himself and the
intellectual tradition he founded were living manifestations
of such a conviction. The values they espoused were secular
and "enlightened"; they were a modernized version of an
eighteenth-century faith. Durkheim and those like him cherished an intense loyalty for the Third French Republic,
which in their minds incarnated the great abstractions of
freedom, democracy, tolerance, and humane behavior.

Hence the school of Durkheim found a reassuring con-
gruence between public values and private morality. The
state in whose educational system they served was also one
to which they could give ethical endorsement. This close
association with the values of the Third Republic presented
no particular problem in the years of growing national confidence before the First World War—although it reduced
critics like Sorel and Péguy to impotent fury. But in the
war's aftermath the Republic's virtues were less apparent;
here also the bloom had disappeared. And by the 1930's—
when nearly every writer of perception, left or right, found
some grievous fault in the Third Republic—a school of social
thought that was so intimately tied to it could not fail to
be threatened also. At the very least, the value system of
Durkheim and his heirs now seemed morally shallow. Indeed,
it sometimes appeared indistinguishable from the "bourgeois
morality" of the ordinary philistine. One cannot understand
the rage—the nausea—of a young philosopher like Jean-Paul
Sartre at France's intellectual establishment on the eve of
the Second World War unless one appreciates how smug
and fatuous the entrenched dignitaries of the Sorbonne
looked to those outside.

Once more the stress is on intellectual confinement and the need of breaking out. French social thought had its own native masters, but they were not the same as those who were held in highest esteem abroad, and their teachings were becoming increasingly irrelevant to the efforts of the younger French thinkers. The ways out of the impasse took a long time to find, and they had little in common with what contemporary writers were doing elsewhere. Neo-Thomism, neo-Marxism, existentialism—these were the paths most frequently followed. No one proved entirely satisfactory: each soon took on specifically French contours which made for difficulties in translation or understanding beyond the confines of French culture. By the 1950's, the modes of thought that had originally been devised as avenues of escape were themselves becoming culs-de-sac.

The 1930's have conventionally been depicted as an era of almost unparalleled squalor in modern French history. The focus has been on diplomatic defeat abroad and on irresponsible partisanship at home—and on that vague complex of unsavory features grouped under the heading of "moral decay." Without question there was much in French politics and society in this decade that was extremely disquieting, and the collapse of 1940 had a long and unhappy prehistory. More especially, the customary warfare among ideological schools mounted to an unprecedented shrillness, as rival intellectual clans threatened to devour each other whole. This merciless, this near-suicidal struggle among France's cultural leaders has been repeatedly chronicled, and with both verve and discernment.[6] While it is an astonishing and en-

---

[6] See, for example: Jacques Chastenet, *Histoire de la Troisième République*, VI: *Déclin de la Troisième* (Paris, 1962), Chapter 13; David Caute, *Communism and the French Intellectuals 1914–1960* (New York, 1964); Raoul Girardet, "Notes sur l'esprit d'un fascisme français 1934–1939," *Revue française de science politique*, V (July-September 1955), 529–546; Stanley Hoffmann, "Aspects du régime de Vichy," *Revue française de science politique*, VI (January–March 1956), 44–69, "Paradoxes of the French Political Community," *In*

grossing story, it is not the whole record of what French intellectuals were doing in these years of growing despair. Nor does the ideological aspect of the succeeding decade—the schism within France's writers between the Resistance and the adherents of Vichy, and the apotheosis of the former at the war's end—exhaust the interpretive possibilities of that era. An almost exclusive ideological focus on the 1930's and 1940's has made the French intellectuals appear rather worse than they actually were in the first of these decades and rather better in the second.

A different perspective emerges if one tries to locate and analyze what the French wrote in the generation after 1930 that transcended the warfare of ideological schools—the more lasting achievements of French social thought in these decades when the voices of disinterested investigation came so near to being stifled in a cacophony of abuse. Those who tried to lift the level of the debate did so under circumstances of unprecedented difficulty, and their work is all the more impressive for the obstacles it encountered along the way.

Such obstacles were not only the perils of partisanship. They were inherent in the French literary tradition and French educational practice. Here once again the tendency to take words for actualities is crucial to our understanding of the epoch. It helps explain why most of the ideological rhetoric of the 1930's rings so hollow today: besides its inflation and its striving after literary effect, it seems to hover beyond reality in a special atmosphere of its own. In earlier decades the French knew how to decode the rhetorical flights of their statesmen and publicists; sometime in the interwar years they lost the knack. One by one, the honest and rigorous social thinkers began to realize that a new kind of discourse was necessary—a discourse which would give a surer grasp on reality and would translate more easily into

Search of France (Cambridge, Mass., 1963), pp. 21–60; Eugen Weber, *Action Française: Royalism and Reaction in Twentieth-Century France* (Stanford, Calif., 1962).

the vocabularies in use outside France. In this perspective, the task of purifying the language from ideological bombast was simply another aspect of the general effort to cast off what was confining in the traditional patterns of thought and expression.

Thus regarded, the activities of intellectuals single-mindedly committed to a political cause must take second rank. The apologists for the extra-parliamentary Leagues or the Popular Front of the 1930's, even the writers who in the next decade were Resistance figures and nothing besides, begin to recede into the background. Yet this background is by no means irrelevant to the wider story. Only a bloodless—and hence uninteresting—writer could remain totally un-affected by the clash of rival doctrines around him; every in-tellectual of stature necessarily had some moral commit-ment which could not fail to become more articulate as external threats closed in upon it. The fact that the disin-terested study of society was pursued in an atmosphere so charged with ideological passion gave it a particular re-sponsibility of tone. The very isolation under which French intellectual life labored, suffused it with a special intensity, as in the case of a tormented Catholic spokesman like Georges Bernanos or in the thought emerging from the Resistance experience.

In this light, the period from 1930 to the early 1960's appears as one in which desperate and fratricidal passion could in a few privileged instances be harnessed to work of high seriousness and universal scope. The arc of such writing extends all the way from the new social history of Marc Bloch and Lucien Febvre to the imaginative creations of novelists as diverse as Martin du Gard and Malraux—or, at the end of the period and at the farthest reaches of "re-spectable" inquiry, the cosmological speculations of Teilhard de Chardin. Examples like these mark the range and bold-ness of French thought in this era; they also suggest its tenta-tiveness and its fragmentary character. The literature and the social thought of some periods bear the stamp of classical self-assurance: this had earlier been the French norm. In contrast, the work of the 1930's and 1940's appears shot through with self-doubt. Such was its special vulnerability, and such its special claim to our esteem. The way out of the impasse could never quite be found; the obstructed path still glimmered only obscurely ahead.

CHAPTER

2

_____

The Historians
and the Social Order

I N 1929—the year of Poincaré's retirement and the stock-
market crash in the United States, the year in which (as
it appeared in retrospect) France's renewed time of troubles
began—two French historians, already established scholars
in their middle years, inaugurated a journal that in the next
decade was to become the single most important forum for
the revitalization of historical studies in the Western world.
The foundation of the _Annales d'histoire économique et
sociale_ by Lucien Febvre and Marc Bloch showed that a new
generation of historical thinkers had come to maturity—that
the neo-idealist precepts of men like Croce and Meinecke no
longer remained unchallenged in the imaginative investigation of the past. And for the first time since the eighteenth
century, this newly constituted school of economic and social
research put France in the forefront of European historical
scholarship.

It was characteristic of Bloch and of Febvre that they
should have launched their experimental venture at a time
when so many of their countrymen were either gripped or
about to be gripped by skepticism and despair. They were
robust-spirited men, confident of themselves and of the pro-

fessional discipline they served. Both sons of professors, they
had come to their calling with an assurance derived from
hereditary familiarity with France's academic elite. Although
scarred by four years of combat service, they had suffered
from the shock of the First World War less profoundly
than had men a few years their juniors; Febvre was thirty-
six when the conflict began, Bloch twenty-eight. Their values
were already formed: the war stimulated their historical
imaginations by making them aware of an incipient new
society, but it did not threaten their own moral certainties.
These remained "enlightened," democratic, and strictly
secular—Third Republican in the most favorable meaning
of the term. Something of this ethical security—this good
conscience—passed over into their professional labors to
sustain them with a happy sense of scholarly integrity and
a mountainous volume of work well done.

Such are the reasons for dealing with the historians of
society at the very start of the present study. Among their
contemporaries in other pursuits, they were the closest to
the generations of France's past. In their inmost being, men
like Febvre and Bloch lived in a pre-catastrophe world. They
also lived rooted in French patriotism, deep and unquestioned—just as they taught their pupils to seek in France's
soil and in the tangible evidence of France's monuments the
key to the riddles of historical interpretation that had eluded
their predecessors. Febvre and Bloch never pretended to
know all the answers: they emphasized again and again that
the historian was more a "searcher" than a propounder of
explanations. But in their restless search they were sure at
least of their own point of departure—and in this they were
more fortunate (or more limited) than those in other fields
who took years or decades to find a solid footing. At the
hands of a Febvre or a Bloch the study of history became
more flexible, more pluralist, more self-questioning than it
had ever been before—and it became so partly because its
practitioners lived both in the old universe of certainty
and in the new universe of flux, and could exploit the dis-

continuities between the two to the maximum benefit of their historical understanding.

1. From Michelet via Durkheim to Henri Berr

At the death of Lucien Febvre, his leading academic successor referred to him as "since Michelet . . . the greatest, perhaps the only great historian writing in the French language."[1] Outside France such an accolade may sound odd. In Germany or the Anglo-American world until very recently Michelet did not rank as a great historian at all. He seemed too careless, too "literary"—too romantic in style and spirit. The first to rehabilitate Michelet was Edmund Wilson, who discovered in him the heir of Vico and the precursor of historical writing harnessed to revolutionary ends. But even for Wilson he remained primarily a littérateur, a man with a "novelist's social interest and grasp of character," a "poet's imagination and passion."[2]

For the French—and particularly for French professional historians—the polemical stimulus to exhuming Michelet was rather more pointed. To hold up as an example the writer whose most celebrated pages were hymns to the vast anonymous force of the French people was to assault head-on the established cult of Germanic methodology. Lucien Febvre knew exactly what he was doing when he claimed Michelet as his master. "Do you know Michelet?" he asked his readers, with his characteristic verve and irony. "We know him all too well," he had them answering:

> Between you and me he wasn't that good at history!
> He didn't get to the bottom of his sources. Far better
> scholars than he . . . have proved it. His bibliography,
> . . . not worth speaking of: he didn't even keep his

[1] Fernand Braudel, "Lucien Febvre et l'histoire," *Cahiers internationaux de sociologie*, XXII (1957), 15.
[2] *To the Finland Station* (Garden City, N.Y., 1940), p. 13.

notes in a filing box. And his history, rotted through
with errors . . . : one can't trust it. Besides, an old
fogey, a humanitarian, a professional patriot, a liberal.[3]

Such criticisms were no news to a man like Febvre: for two
generations they had been the staples of French historical
scholarship. He knew Michelet's weaknesses—what he wanted
to do, as an older associate interpreted his aims, was to be
"another Michelet—but better equipped, with a more critical spirit, . . . intuitive like him, yet not letting himself be
carried away by his creative genius."[4]

As opposed to the dominant fetish of the "documents and
nothing but the documents" and its accompanying emphasis
on strictly political history, Febvre and his associates saw in
Michelet the historian who had tried to "resurrect" the past
in all its variety and complexity, who had viewed a civilization like that of France as the work not merely of its kings
and statesmen but of the untutored strivings of its entire
people. For Michelet all realms of thought and action had
been continuous and all types of historical evidence worthy
of examination; the historian's task was to understand and
describe the "common climate" that underlay them.[5] Most
of these lessons had been forgotten since Michelet's death.
The last quarter of the nineteenth century had witnessed the
triumph of professional scholarship on the Teutonic model;
the study of history offered a prime example of the prestige
of German methods of scientific investigation that had followed France's defeat in the War of 1870.

Yet one of Michelet's precepts stood fast as a basic tenet
of French pedagogy. In the preface to the 1869 reissue of his
History of France, he had warned of the indispensability of
geographical knowledge to historical study: "Without a geo-

[3] Introduction to a volume of selections entitled *Michelet* (in the
series *Les classiques de la liberté*) (Geneva and Paris, 1946), p. 11.
[4] Preface by Henri Berr to Febvre's *Le problème de l'incroyance au
XVIe siècle: la religion de Rabelais* (Paris, 1942), p. viii.
[5] Lucien Febvre, "Vivre l'histoire. Propos d'initiation" (1941),
Combats pour l'histoire (Paris, 1953), pp. 25–26.

graphical basis, the people, the makers of history, seem to be walking on air, as in those Chinese pictures where the ground is wanting. The soil, too, must not be looked upon only as the scene of action. Its influence appears in a hundred ways, such as food, climate, etc."[6] The eighteenth-century philosophes had already argued the practical merits of the linked disciplines of history and geography as antidotes to an exclusive diet of the classics. The educational reformers of the Third Republic had reinforced the association of the two. Just as in Germany philosophy was considered the natural ally and support of historical studies, so in France a geographical foundation for such endeavors came to be assumed. In addition, the alliance of history and geography had a republican flavor; the classics were associated with reaction.[7] By the twentieth century, the characteristic French university professor of history was a convinced republican; a historian of conservative or royalist bent was far more likely to be an amateur man of letters.

At the turn of the century, the masters of French historical scholarship were professional universitaires whose interests were overwhelmingly political and institutional—Charles Langlois for the Middle Ages, Ernest Lavisse for the seventeenth and eighteenth centuries, Charles Seignobos for the contemporary period. Men like these might in a loose sense be called "positivists"; that at least was how Febvre and Bloch referred to them when they made their own appeal for a "broader and more human" definition of historical studies. In an unsophisticated understanding of scientific method and a conviction that "the facts" of history could speak for themselves without the intrusion of hypothesis or theory, Langlois and Lavisse and Seignobos ran true to form

[6] Quoted by H. C. Darby in "Historical Geography," *Approaches to History: A Symposium*, edited by H. P. R. Finberg (London, 1962), pp. 152–153.

[7] Felix Gilbert, "Three Twentieth Century Historians: Meinecke, Bloch, Chabod," *History*, edited by John Higham (Englewood Cliffs, N.J., 1965), p. 367.

as children of the late nineteenth century. But their particular brand of positivism proved comparatively benign. Aided
by the grace and fluency of the language in which they wrote,
the French professional historians of the early twentieth century were far from being pedants or antiquaries: they organized their works impeccably, and their style ran with a bright
clarity. Bergsonians before the fact, they had a talent for
working themselves into the historical movement they were
studying, for "recapturing the rhythm of this movement by
an act of imaginative sympathy."[8] It is noteworthy that the
eighteen-volume history of France to the Revolution which
Lavisse directed maintained its authority longer than any
similar collaborative work of national history published in
another country; it was also characteristic of the French historical tradition that the introductory volume to the series,
which appeared in 1903, should have been a "tableau" by
France's leading geographer, P. Vidal de la Blache.

Such are some of the reasons why a revolt against positivism in historical studies came later in France than in
Germany and Italy and in rather different form.[9] The professional landscape in France gave less cause for radical dis-
satisfaction. Hence the neo-idealist movement associated
with such names as Croce and Meinecke largely passed the
French by. When the revolt did materialize—a generation
after it happened in Germany and Italy—it was less explicitly
idealist in tone and less afraid of scientific terminology and
associations.

Two further peculiarities of the French historical scene
contributed to the scientific cast of methodological innovation. The first was the prestige of Emile Durkheim. Febvre
respected Durkheim—and feared the imperialist aims of a
school of sociology that threatened to "annex" the study of

[8] R. G. Collingwood, The Idea of History (Oxford, 1946), p. 189.
[9] For an analysis of this revolt, see my Consciousness and Society
(New York, 1958), Chapter 6.

history for its own purposes.[10] But Febvre had already completed most of his professional training before 1902, when Durkheim began to teach in Paris; the direct sociological influence never dominated his thought. Bloch, eight years younger than Febvre, came to his historical training when Durkheim's fame was at its height. He was powerfully attracted to the reigning school of French sociology. Three decades later he was still citing Durkheim, along with Michelet, as one of the masters who had taught him that in order to understand his own time he must avert his eyes from it and look to the past.[11]

The second special feature of the French historiographic configuration was the quiet but tenacious work of Henri Berr. Now nearly forgotten, Berr left behind him a lasting monument in the form of the multi-volume series entitled *L'évolution de l'humanité.* If it is unquestionable that the French have excelled all others in such collaborative historical enterprises, it is also clear that among the French collective studies Berr's was the very best. Two generations after the work of Lavisse and one generation removed from that of Berr, it is instructive to contrast the two. The former kept severely to a chronological ordering of data; its sections were demarcated by the reigns of kings; within the sections the bulk of the chapters were devoted to politics, war, and diplomacy, with social and cultural life relegated to "topical" chapters tacked on to the end. Berr's series established society and culture as the central focus: although the author of each volume had license to proceed as he chose, most elected an analytical scheme in which the emphasis was on transnational comparisons and the integration of the various aspects of a given period into a comprehensible synthesis.

[10] "Vers une autre histoire" (first published in *Revue de métaphysique et de morale,* LVIII [1949]), *Combats,* p. 422.
[11] "Que demander à l'histoire?" (address to the *Centre polytechnicien d'études économiques,* 1937), *Mélanges historiques,* edited by Charles-Edmond Perrin (Paris, 1963), I, 12.

L'évolution de l'humanité, originally planned for a hundred volumes, began appearing in 1920; by 1954—at the
death of Berr, past ninety in age—the number published
stood at 65. Among them were works of Marc Bloch and
Lucien Febvre that had become historical classics overnight.
The series continues—in this sense Berr is still a living
presence, more than a century after his birth. *L'évolution de
l'humanité*, however, was the product of his already established influence. What had originally set him in polemical
opposition to his colleagues—and profoundly appealed to a
handful of younger men like Febvre—was the foundation
two decades earlier, in 1900, of the *Revue de synthèse historique*.

The aim of the new review, in its founder's words, was to
overcome the fear of "premature generalizations" that had
narrowed the range of French historical scholarship since the
1870's, and to induce specialized scholars in the various
branches of history "to be of greater mutual assistance
through a clearer conception of the common task." Struck
by the sudden popularity of sociology in the Durkheim manner, Berr argued that this had come about through a default
on the part of the historians; in renouncing the task of
philosophical synthesis, they had left a void that the sociologists had been eager to fill. Among these latter, the example
of Durkheim had proved the most helpful; his "great merit"
was "to have applied a precise, experimental, comparative
method to historical facts." Yet sociology, for all its "importance and legitimacy," was not "the whole of history." Beyond it, Berr found still greater significance in the psychology
of individuals and of groups. "The comparative study of
societies," he explained, "must lead to social psychology and
to a knowledge of the basic needs to which institutions and
their changing manifestations are the response." And this
study would in turn direct attention to "the psychology of
great men of thought and action, of ethnic groups, and of
historical crises." At the end of his injunction, Berr urged
his colleagues to grapple with the "delicate psychological

problem" of arriving "at a clear picture of the role of the intellectual element in history"—an early warning signal of the pitfalls that lay in wait for the twentieth-century historian of ideas.[12]

Such, in schematic outline, was the program to which Berr's friend Lucien Febvre, a half generation younger than he, was to devote nearly fifty years of scholarly endeavor. At the turn of the century the ground had been already staked out that would be formally occupied two or three decades later. In this sense one can equate Berr's projected revolution in French historical studies with the contemporary efforts of the neo-idealists in Germany and Italy. But in this sense alone: although Berr was of an age with Croce and Meinecke, his mentality was very different. His epistemological canon might be idealist—he held that the historical past existed "only to the extent" that it was "re-created by the mind"— but he was far more science-oriented than the historians who usually bore that label. Much of his language carries the ring of nineteenth-century positivism. In his long life Berr began his studies with the scientific certainties of the first positivist age; he closed them in the more sophisticated idea-world of contemporary neo-positivism; the high-flown philosophizing of the idealists apparently left him cold. In reading the nearly octogenarian Berr's introduction to Febvre's masterpiece, published in 1942, we can clearly detect the disparities in historical temperament between the two: more sanguine than the author himself, Berr gently chides his younger friend for claiming less than his due as a reinterpreter of the sixteenth century.

This contrast makes it difficult to assess the part of each in the summary article on history that they jointly wrote for the *Encyclopaedia of the Social Sciences* in the early 1930's. (That the American editors should have chosen two insurgent Frenchmen for this assignment was of historical

[12] The program of the *Revue de synthèse historique* has been translated by Deborah H. Roberts for *The Varieties of History*, edited by Fritz Stern (New York, 1956), pp. 250–255.

significance in itself.) The prose sounds more like Berr than like Febvre. There is a pat, positivist tone to the discussion of historical causality, which, the authors claim, "may be divided into three categories: contingency, necessity and logic." A similar easy confidence seems to underlie the assertion that "the laws of history will most certainly eventually be established." Yet in the same breath Berr and Febvre hasten to inform us that "laws" must be understood rather differently from the way they have been "conceived by some who have pretended to formulate them or by others who deny such a possibility." They should not be thought of as "necessarily universal and eternal"—they should be treated, rather, as "generalities, similarities, uniformities." What begins as an echo of a late nineteenth-century faith ends in a formulation that is impeccable from the standpoint of the up-to-date scientific method of the interwar years. Such is the character of the article as a whole: it suffers from a split personality, as though Berr had written the original draft in a mood of sweeping self-assurance and Febvre had subsequently added the qualifications and sophistications that professional scruple prompted. And so the essay promises more than it performs: the crucial discussion of the place of sociology and psychology in historical study peters out in little more than a general typology. At the end, of course, comes the anticipated call for universal, comparative history. But with an unexpected twist—this new type of historical study will solve the age-old problems of "bias" and "objectivity":

> The ideas of discipline, of subordination of individual view in a general direction, of internal organization of the work—these ideas inherent in every efficacious work of science will penetrate in their turn into history, will . . . assure its gradual transformation into a science conscious of its goal and of its means and notably will solve a capital problem, that of the objectivity of the historian. The various studies, all tainted . . . by an important coefficient of error, of illusion and of personal blindness,

will constantly control each other; the "involuntary
biases" too will correct each other and to a large measure cancel out.[18]

We shall of necessity return to these formulations. As
answers to the perennial question of value judgments in
history, they are transparently inadequate. Meantime it may
suffice to suggest that the very inconclusiveness of this effort
marks it as a transition document. When the *Encyclopaedia
of the Social Sciences* commissioned the article on history,
Berr was an elderly man and Febvre only just arrived at a
position of mastery in the French historical profession. His
foundation of a school of historians in his own image still
lay in the future.

In an affectionate memoir of Henri Berr composed for his
eightieth birthday, Lucien Febvre traced the qualities that
had made the older man so effective a propagandist—
cordiality, grace of manner, respect for the ideas of others,
above all, an unfailing optimism.[14] Febvre himself was less
ingratiating: his own notion of advancing his intellectual
cause was unremitting struggle—as "combats" was the title
he chose for his collected essays. He and his younger ally
Bloch saw Berr as their precursor. There was a hint of
patronizing in the way they spoke of him and his work—
customarily referring to the *Revue de synthèse historique* as
their "Trojan horse" in the enemy's camp. At the end of the
1920's they decided that the era of caution had come to an
end: they were now ready for a full-scale assault on the
citadels of French historiography.

ii. *From Strasbourg to Paris: The Collaboration of Lucien Febvre and Marc Bloch*

The two first came together in the autumn of 1920 in newly
liberated Alsace. The conversion of the University of Stras-

[18] The article is in volume VII of the *Encyclopaedia* (New York,
1932), pp. 357–368.
[14] "Hommage à Henri Berr" (first published in *Annales: économies—
sociétés—civilisations,* VII [1952]), *Combats,* pp. 339–342.

bourg from a German to a French institution had created a
unique opportunity for the recruitment *de novo* of a faculty
of distinction. Febvre arrived as professor of history, Bloch as
a maître de conférences soon to receive a regular chair. Both
had attained the rank of captain in the war—both had won
the citations and decorations that were "the required baggage
of a French gentleman in these years." The mood was of
"joyous spontaneity": the exhilaration of their unprecedented
venture broke down the barriers of distrust and rivalry
ordinarily characteristic of French faculty life.[15] Febvre and
Bloch quickly became friends: they began a collaboration
whose untroubled intensity was to surprise them both. As "a
human achievement"—the younger man put it—in which
they could justly take pride, they "succeeded in pedaling
their tandem together, thanks to the major ideas they held
in common and the great affection they had for each other—
despite strong contrasts in temperament and little taste on
either side for diplomatic cunning."[16]

The senior partner was already a fully accredited historian
when he came to Strasbourg. The French historical profession is well-known for its extended incubation period, and it
was a sign of rapid advance that Lucien Febvre should have
received his doctorate in 1911, at the age of thirty-three, a
safe margin of time before his long years of combat service.
Born in the Franche-Comté, Febvre had spent his childhood
and youth in Nancy, the capital of Lorraine. Both of these
much-fought-over border provinces appealed to the young
man's feeling for the French past, but it was the Franche-
Comté that he considered his "vraie patrie." As a boy he had
discovered in the rugged Jura the sights and sounds and
smells of an earlier era which here lingered on until the close
of the nineteenth century; such direct contact with the
countryside and its living history fired his imagination and

[15] Lucien Febvre, "Souvenirs d'une grande histoire: Marc Bloch et
Strasbourg," *Combats*, pp. 391–393.
[16] Letter of Bloch to Febvre, March 11, 1942: "Marc Bloch:
témoignages sur la période 1939–1940," *Annales d'histoire sociale*,
VII (1945), 27.

distinguished his childhood from the more usual atmosphere of confined bookishness in a French intellectual upbringing. As a mature man, Febvre escaped as often as he could from the exhaustion of Paris to the therapy of pastoral life at his country home in the Jura.

In Nancy, a longing to wipe out the shame of 1870 suffused the atmosphere; it was not easy to forget that Metz and the other half of the province lay in German hands. Born eight years after the catastrophe, Febvre came to his historical studies in a mood of patriotic insurgency; the scholarly caution of his older colleagues he saw as a specific case of the more general timidity of the vanquished. Yet to be a historian was not his original intention: his father was a grammarian, and the young Febvre's earlier bent was toward literature. At the same time, he had a historian uncle, and his father read history as an avocation; it was in his father's library that he first came across Michelet.

Much later he added Jacob Burckhardt and Jean Jaurès as masters of imaginative history—and Stendhal, less as a novelist than as a guide to the urban charms of Italy. Meantime Febvre had gone to Paris to seek his intellectual fortune. And this was the best that the capital offered—the elite Lycée Louis-le-Grand and, in 1898, that forcing-house of French academic talent, the Ecole Normale Supérieure. But as opposed to the younger Lorrainers in Barrès' *Les déracinés* —published the previous year—Febvre did not let the blandishments of Paris sap his native ruggedness and rectitude. However sophisticated he later became, he remained a provincial by temperament. His own memories of his early Paris years were of constant discovery—of Wagner and Zola and Rodin at the start, and then, at the turn of the century, the vast explosion of political passion in the Dreyfus Case, and the Exposition of 1900, with its sudden revelation to the young historian's dazzled eyes of the glories of French Impressionist painting. Throughout his life Febvre tried to keep abreast of aesthetic innovation, and he had among his friends the painter Adrien Marquet.

After Normale, the agrégation, and four years of research

under the auspices of the Fondation Thiers, Febvre completed his doctoral thesis on *Philippe II et la Franche-Comté*. This work established his intellectual direction for the future: its major theme was social conflict, and its framework a detailed analysis of the geography of the region. It was fitting that Febvre's first teaching position should have been close to the Franche-Comté in the old Duchy of Burgundy, at the University of Dijon. It was from here that he set out in 1914 to show through four years of armed combat how "passionately French" he was.

Febvre's intellectual heir, Fernand Braudel, has written of him that he was launched into historical scholarship with three exceptional advantages—first, a home in which the classics and humanist culture became so familiar to him that as a mature man he could speak about someone like Montaigne in as informal a tone as he would use in discussing a good friend; then, the "erudite accumulation" of the generation of historians between himself and Michelet, who, however he might rail against their example, taught him to balance the latter's literary "ardor" with patience and documentary care; finally, his arrival on the French academic scene in the "springtime" of the social sciences, and with it the chance to profit by all of them and to develop his faculties along with them.[17] Febvre knew Durkheim's successors as intellectual colleagues; he was also well acquainted with the work of Weber and Sombart—and Marx. His own attitude, however, was always less solemn than theirs. He liked association with younger men, and identified not with

[17] "Lucien Febvre et l'histoire," pp. 16–17; see also by Braudel, "Présence de Lucien Febvre" in the volume of essays written by his friends entitled *Hommage à Lucien Febvre: éventail de l'histoire vivante* (Paris, 1953), I, 1–7; further biographical information may be found in two essays by Febvre himself: the preface to his *Combats*, pp. v–ix, and "La Vie, cette enquête continue" (originally published as the Conclusion to the *Encyclopédie française*, XVII [1935]), *Combats*, pp. 44–49; in Robert Mandrou, "Lucien Febvre 1878–1956," *Revue universitaire*, LXVI (January–February 1957), 3–7; and in Palmer A. Throop, "Lucien Febvre 1878–1956," *Some Twentieth-Century Historians*, edited by S. William Halperin (Chicago, 1961), pp. 277–298.

the generation of Croce and Meinecke, born in the 1860's, and whose intellectual course had been established before 1914, but with those such as Bloch who found their way only after the war was over.

Marc Bloch, on the contrary, identified "up" with those slightly older than he. (This in itself offers one explanation for the harmonious relationship between the two.) He and his classmates at Normale considered themselves "as the last of the generation of the Dreyfus Affair."[18] In so doing they parted company with what came to be called the "generation of 1905"—the post-Dreyfusard youth which inclined toward religion, scorned the parliamentary republic, and preached the mystique of action.[19] Although only twelve years old when the Affair erupted, Bloch had good reason to take it to heart: he sprang from the assimilated Jewish intellectual milieu which discovered to its grief and horror the anti-Semitic hatred that had lain barely concealed under the polite surface of French society. Such people thought of themselves as just as good Frenchmen as any others: the conflict of 1914 gave them a chance to prove it. The fact that he was a Jew is relevant to our appreciation of why Bloch risked his life for his country once more in the second war and why he finally lost it under circumstances of exemplary heroism.

As a young man, however, Bloch scarcely seemed cut to heroic dimensions. The more robust Febvre recalled having encountered him one day in 1902 at his father's house in Paris: "a slender adolescent, his eyes bright with intelligence, his face timid, a bit overshadowed by his older brother, who was to be a physician of distinction."[20] The father, Gustave Bloch, professor of ancient history at the Ecole Normale

[18] *Apologie pour l'histoire ou métier d'historien* (Paris, 1952), translated by Peter Putnam as *The Historian's Craft* (New York, 1953), p. 186.
[19] See my *Consciousness and Society*, pp. 337–344.
[20] "Marc Bloch et Strasbourg," *Combats*, p. 392; see also the essay on Bloch by Febvre in *Architects and Craftsmen in History: Festschrift für Abbott Payson Usher* (Tübingen, 1956), pp. 75–76.

Supérieure, was one of the stern masters who had done their
best to discipline Febvre's youthful enthusiasm. He also
taught his son, who entered Normale in 1904. "I owe to my
father," Marc Bloch wrote, "the best part of my formation
as a historian."[21] The tribute suggests both intellectual grati-
tude and deep affection. It also shows that the younger Bloch
fully realized what a privileged upbringing he had enjoyed:
in later years he was to give "particularly attentive care . . .
to young researchers who had reached . . . intellectual
heights despite the handicaps of commonplace circumstances
in their youth, as though he wanted . . . to compensate for
the favor fate had granted him."[22]

His own early professional career had proceeded with swift,
untroubled efficiency—the agrégation in 1908 was followed by
a year of study at Leipzig and Berlin, where he attended the
courses of the great historian of religion Adolf von Harnack.
Then after three years at the Fondation Thiers and two of
teaching in provincial lycées, the war caught Bloch in the
midst of research for his doctorate. In this case for once the
French educational system showed itself compassionate: a
special provision for doctoral candidates who had served in
the war allowed him to submit as a thesis only a fragment of
the large work he had originally planned. The result—a study
of the enfranchisement of royal serfs in the Ile-de-France,
completed in 1920—was sufficient to establish Bloch as a
recognized medievalist. It also led him toward the research
topics that were to occupy him for the next two decades,
rural history and the psychological basis of kingship.

The latter interest proved the more transitory. Among
Bloch's three major books, the first, *Les rois thaumaturges*,
published in 1924, initially seems unrelated to the others. A
study of the power of touch—the miraculous ability to heal
scrofula attributed to the kings of France and England—the
book grew directly out of conversations with the author's

21 Preface to *Les rois thaumaturges*, new edition (Paris, 1961), p. vii.
22 Charles-Edmond Perrin, "L'oeuvre historique de Marc Bloch,"
Revue historique, CXCIX (April–June 1948), 162.

physician brother. Hence the medical expertise it displayed: Bloch very sensibly pointed out that scrofulous infections were by nature intermittent; a diminution, even an apparent cure of the disease was completely admissible from a scientific standpoint. But to explain in terms of modern science what had earlier passed as a miracle was not Bloch's chief concern. He was interested, rather, in the aspect of folklore, of popular belief, of what the men of the Middle Ages and early modern times meant when they spoke of the miraculous. In the nineteenth or twentieth century, people held all-or-nothing views of such an event; they asked for unambiguous results—and witnessed few, if any, miracles. The men of an earlier age were not so "intransigent"; they did not expect a constantly reliable performance from their thaumaturges; a quasi-miracle from time to time sufficed. Thus they were psychologically prepared to stretch their belief as circumstances required: "What created faith in a miracle was the idea that a miracle was going to take place"—in short, a "collective illusion."[23]

The phrase sounds like Durkheim, and *Les rois thaumaturges* quite apparently springs from Durkheim's spirit and method. Bloch shared with the master of French sociology the quality of being a Jew who had lost the faith yet remained fascinated by religious experience. More particularly they had in common a concern for religion as the source and primary manifestation of social cohesion. This intellectual absorption Bloch never forsook; while his subsequent work was cast primarily in the framework of economic history, his economic interpretations—as in the case of Weber—were constantly illuminated by material drawn from the history of religion. Still more, the second and major focus of his mature scholarship—the historical sociology of the peasantry—bore directly on the class in which traditional religious values had proved most tenacious.

As early as 1913 Bloch had published a little study of the

[23] *Rois thaumaturges*, pp. 19, 420–423, 426–429.

Ile-de-France in a series of provincial monographs initiated by
the ever-active Henri Berr. (Febvre had quite naturally
written the corresponding book about the Franche-Comté.)
Thus when in the mid-1920's Bloch turned his attention to
rural history, he was not a total stranger to the subject. But
this early work, like his doctor's thesis, had been based on
conventional documentary sources, primarily legal in character. By origin and upbringing, Bloch was anything but a
country dweller: although born in Lyons, he had been taken
to Paris as a small child, and a Parisian he remained. Even
his rural monograph dealt with the region immediately sur-
rounding the capital!

All this began to change when he moved to Strasbourg.
Perhaps it is not too farfetched to suggest that here he began
to discover some long-buried provincial roots. His family had
originally come from Alsace, and Bloch was not above tracing
his unquestioning patriotism to a great-grandfather who had
fought against the Prussians in 1793. In any case, beginning
with the Strasbourg years, we hear of excursions to the
country and tramps in the Vosges. Here Febvre possessed the
previous experience that could "open windows . . . onto the
living countryside." The older man strenuously encouraged
the younger along the path toward which he was already
groping his way. And—whether through self-abnegation or
need of mental change, it is hard to say—Febvre in effect
turned over to Bloch the rural department of their common
enterprise and directed his own future researches toward
religious and psychological history.[24]

A curious game of musical chairs ensued: Bloch took over
Febvre's assignment; Febvre pushed forward the work that
Bloch had begun in his *Rois thaumaturges*. This double
change once again suggests their harmonious working relations. It also suggests self-understanding on both sides: the
cooler-headed Bloch was the better suited to economics and
the history of technology; the fiery Febvre was more at home
in the theological battles of the Reformation.

[24] Febvre, "Marc Bloch et Strasbourg," *Combats*, pp. 394–395.

The first fruit of Febvre's new interest was the study of Luther he published in 1928. Avowedly written for the general public, it was brief, discursive, and in the animated, contentious style that had become his hallmark. Yet it was more than a summary of earlier writing on the subject: as he was to do so often in the future, Febvre took off from the work of a previous scholar, in this case the Catholic historian Father Heinrich Denifle, and then went on to stake out his own interpretation. While welcoming the thoroughness with which Denifle had demolished the conventional image built up over the centuries by Protestant hagiographers, Febvre was far from satisfied with his polemical conclusion—that the Reformation had sprung from Luther's emotional weakness, from "the sorry predicament . . . of a soul so evilly disposed, so wholly a prey of concupiscence that, confessing defeat, it threw down its weapons and evolved a new system of thought from its own undoing." To Febvre all this sounded dangerously simple—"reductive," to use the contemporary expression. In placing the emphasis almost exclusively on Luther's sexual obsessions, Denifle had composed a "pre-Freudian" work of fiction. The truth was rather less sensational: in his early life as a monk Luther's conviction of guilt betrayed no actual transgression but rather an excessive scrupulousness in the performance of his religious duties.[25]

Unquestionably Febvre was on the right track in rejecting his predecessor's work of denigration. Page after page of his *Luther* shows the touch of a master: in the swift sketch of a German society racked with pent-up grievances, ready to break forth into open protest once the word is spoken; in his delineation of Luther's literary style and the way it crystallized a new German language; in his analysis of the great reformer's failure to convey his own vision to the church founded in his name and how that church became the vehicle for what was routine and submissive in his countrymen's mentality. Febvre was at his best in tracing the inter-

[25] *Un destin: Martin Luther* (Paris, 1928), translated by Roberts Tapley as *Martin Luther: a Destiny* (New York, 1929), pp. 28–29.

play of social conflict with religious and metaphysical ideas;
he handled both elements as independent variables, treating
neither as a function of the other. But in respect to what was
becoming his major aim—psychological history—Febvre's
Luther remained embryonic. Its author saw the potentialities
of a psychological biography whose implications would extend beyond the career of a single great figure; he also
recognized that the discipline of psychology in France in the
1920's was not yet equipped for such an assignment. "Later,"
he surmised, "when the science of psychology is sufficiently
developed to be applied without hesitation, it will doubtless
be possible to discern in the individual whose personal effort
precipitates a revolution the clearly and strongly marked representative of a group or family of like yet diversified minds
recurring again and again down through the ages."[26]

Febvre predicted better than he knew. Thirty years later—
and two years after his own death—a psychiatrist widely read
in history and with a long experience of talented and troubled
young men produced the psychological biography in depth
that Febvre had foreseen.[27] Its tone was Freudian—but
Freudian in a sense that Febvre could scarcely have imagined.
Like most cultivated Frenchmen of his day, he understood
psychoanalytic theory in terms of unidimensional sexual explanations. From this standpoint he was quite correct in
questioning Father Denifle's reduction of a great man's
inspiration to despair at his ungovernable lust. What Febvre
was unprepared for was a post-Freudian canon of interpretation, as flexible and perceptive as his own, in which sexual
drives and ideal aspirations would be seen as tightly bound
together in an overwhelming longing for divine forgiveness.

The year following the publication of *Luther*, Febvre and
Bloch founded their *Annales*. The new review had precisely
the effect that its editors had hoped for. Encouraged by the
advice of the leading Belgian historian Henri Pirenne and by

[26] *Ibid.*, pp. 73–74.
[27] Erik H. Erikson, *Young Man Luther* (New York, 1958).

the cooperation of a few contemporaries in France itself, such as Georges Lefebvre, soon to become the greatest of the historians of the French Revolution, Febvre and Bloch made the *Annales* the forum for a broadly-based history that was economic and social, geographical and psychological, all in one. The times were menacing: a review which stressed economics and the historian's concern for his own era fitted the public atmosphere of mounting crisis. Lefebvre in particular offered an example of meticulous scholarship in alliance with social commitment that gathered around him an unusually gifted generation of left-oriented students of the Revolution. Already by the turn of the decade the *Annales* group had begun to exert a perceptible influence within the closely-knit structure of French university life. The external rewards were on the way—for Febvre and Bloch were of that peculiarly fortunate breed of innovators who know how to work inside the established system and attain official recognition while they are still alive to enjoy it. By the early thirties, Strasbourg was becoming too small for their talents. The inevitable move was to Paris.

In 1933, Febvre was called to a newly established chair of the history of modern civilization at the Collège de France. This position provided exactly the setting he needed—prestigious, centrally located, yet outside the regular degree-granting faculties. (We may recall that the Collège de France had similarly given Bergson a platform for reaching a public far beyond the professional confines of philosophy.) Moreover, the chair itself, as Febvre interpreted its stipulations, seemed designed to fit his talents. In his inaugural address, he called attention to the fact that it was in effect a restoration of the professorship which Michelet had held and which had been abolished in 1892. The lesson was manifest: four decades of compartmentalized, "positivist" history had come to an end; France was ready once more to listen to the voice of the "general" historian.[28]

[28] "De 1892 à 1933. Examen de conscience d'une histoire et d'un historien," *Combats*, pp. 3-4.

The move to Paris drew Febvre into a maelstrom of public activities. He served as general editor of the *Encyclopédie française*, he repeatedly lectured abroad, he harried his colleagues and urged on the young with a cascade of short articles and book reviews. Of necessity his major writing proceeded more slowly. Although Febvre's capacity for work was awesome, he was in the classic situation of the scholar who has taken on too much. The completion of his greatest endeavor had to await the dismal quiet of German occupation.

A few years after Febvre, Bloch also came to Paris as professor of economic history at the Sorbonne. Here his working time was rather better protected. Economic history lay outside the mainstream of French academic historiography—indeed, economics as a whole was in a retrograde and neglected state. In another country, it might have occasioned surprise that a medievalist like Bloch should have been named to such a chair with so little previous preparation. In France it was only to be expected: no one else was better qualified.

Moreover, ever since Febvre had spurred him in the direction of rural history, Bloch had been laboring to give himself the technical equipment he required. He had studied land allotments, crop rotation, the different methods of plowing and of harvesting—the realities of traditional agrarian life that one could still detect by observation on the spot. Nor did he limit himself to France. Inspired, like his older friend, with a vision of comparative history, he tried to become equally proficient in the rural techniques and sociology of other Western countries. He plunged into the study of foreign languages; he added Scandinavia to England and Germany as areas whose history he knew at first hand. On a visit to Oslo in 1928 he had sketched the possibilities of the comparative method. The following year he was invited to return for a series of lectures that firmly established his international reputation.

The book that resulted from them, *Les caractères originaux de l'histoire rurale française*, ranks as the first of Bloch's two classic works.[29] Blessedly brief and clear, its scope was wider than its title indicated. Although the focus was on France, the comparative material it presented was drawn from the whole of Western Europe. Beyond that, it marked the first major application of what its author called the "regressive method" in the study of the European countryside. Here, Bloch argued, it was impossible to proceed in the usual chronological fashion. Since the history of rural societies did not enter the written record until the eighteenth century, its investigation demanded that one begin with the present, or perhaps with "a past very close to the present," and then work one's way backward toward the primeval mist. The countryside changed only very slowly; much of its outline remained as it had been in the Middle Ages; the task of the historian was to extrapolate into the past from the direct observation he could make in his own day. Here place names, the look of the fields, folklore—even aerial photographs—showed the historian how to go about his work of reconstruction.

The result was a masterpiece of historical detection. *Les caractères originaux* combined meticulousness in procedure and phraseology with a rare self-assurance in generalization. Bloch's primary effort was directed toward the geographical delimitation of two basic areas of contrasting technique, neither exactly coextensive with the other, each remarkably stable through the centuries—the area of triennial rotation of crops as against regions on a two-year cycle, the area of the wheeled plow as opposed to that of the plow guided by hand —the former in each pair associated with the plains of the north, the latter with the Mediterranean. Distinctions such as these bore no relation to national frontiers; France lay in both areas, which in each case extended far beyond its

[29] Originally published in Oslo in 1931, *Les caractères originaux* was reissued in Paris in 1952, with a supplementary volume of Bloch's subsequent notes and expansions on the same theme. An English translation by Janet Sondheimer, entitled *French Rural History: An Essay on its Basic Characteristics*, was published in Berkeley, Calif., in 1966,

borders. And the same transnational sweep characterized
Bloch's subsequent analyses of community solidarity, the
structure of the family, and the changing nature of the
seigneurie. With *Les caractères originaux* Bloch rescued the
study of rural history from the clutch of antiquaries and
legalists and made it a model of imaginative deduction from
scanty and unorthodox evidence.

Throughout the 1930's Bloch kept at work on the theme
that had emerged as central to his rural investigations—the
relation of popular mentality to technological change. The
example of the water mill became his favorite: the ancients
had known the principle of this invention, but they had
given it little practical application; then, with the decline of
the Roman Empire and a manpower scarcity deriving from
the Christian Church's injunction against holding fellow
Christians as slaves, such mills became an economic necessity; finally, as medieval seigneurs began to enforce a monop-
oly for their own mills, the primitive hand implements of
the peasantry were driven from use. The entire sequence
could be called a triumph of technology—that and much besides: "In a word, a very old invention which from the start
had almost reached its highest point of perfection secured
. . . its conquests only through the successive action of
factors quite alien to its intrinsic merits: the defeat of an
Empire; a religious belief; a new structure of public authority."[30]

Bloch's writings "are most illuminating when they analyze
the sensitive point at which purposeful, rational action is
limited by accepted customs and beliefs."[31] Just as Febvre
brought his talents to bear at the intersection between religion
and social class, so Bloch sought out the popular attitudes
and practices, the vestiges of an earlier rationality, that put
technical and emotional constraints on innovation. As a

---

[30] "Technique et évolution sociale: réflexions d'un historien" (first
published in *Europe: revue mensuelle*, XLVII [1938]), *Mélanges*, II,
838.
[31] Gilbert, "Three Twentieth Century Historians," p. 369.

medievalist by training, Bloch had a thorough acquaintance with the literature of community sentiment; in his later role as an economic historian, he had learned how to make the crucial demarcations and distinctions in the realm of technology. The conjunction of these two lines of investigation produced the second major book for which he was subsequently to be remembered, his study of feudal society.

Bloch's work of synthesis quite naturally took its place in Berr's *L'évolution de l'humanité,* a first volume appearing in 1939, a second volume a year later.[82] In its discussion of feudal relationships alone it outclassed its predecessors. Where these had been legal and schematic, Bloch tried to retrace the medieval pattern of authority in all its sprawling inconsistency. Nor was he so much concerned with an "organization chart" of how the feudal system worked as with the spirit in which its institutions had been understood. Hence what was most original in his book was not about feudalism at all in the usual meaning of the term. It consisted rather of the most curious inquiries into such topics as place names, difficulties in overland communications, fluctuations and uncertainties in the sense of time, the role of "collective memory" in distorting the image of the past to suit present needs, and the ambiguities with which the bilingualism of the educated afflicted the discussion of feudal arrangements. Such apparent preliminaries—which Bloch grouped under the title "the milieu"—in fact gave the key to his whole interpretation. And he could cope with them only because, in addition to the method of direct observation which he had applied to so good effect in his agrarian studies, he had exploited a variety of unconventional sources—epic poems, works of theology, and the like—to enrich his account.

By the time the second volume of his *Feudal Society* was published, Bloch was once more in military service and his country in desperate peril. During the years in which he had

[82] A translation of *La société féodale* by L. A. Manyon, entitled *Feudal Society,* was published in London in 1961.

been bringing this work to completion, his friend Febvre was making slower progress. Febvre knew exactly what he wanted to do with his new program of psychological history, but his multiple distractions kept postponing its realization. Meantime he made a number of programmatic statements which showed where he was heading.

By now the rubric "economic and social history" under which the *Annales* had been launched had become too confining for the type of work at which he aimed. "Properly speaking," Febvre argued, there was no such thing as economic and social history; there was only history tout court, in its full "unity"—that is, "the study, carried out in scientific fashion, of the various activities and various creations of the men of another day."[33] Such a study was by definition "social" in character. Febvre never wavered in his attacks on the chroniclers of politics and diplomacy who wrote of the high policy of rulers as though it bore no relation to the deeper and more permanent needs of the ruled. He was almost equally severe with the historians of ideas: these too handled abstract concepts in a vacuum without reference to the emotional climate in which they had originated. "Milieu," "mentality," "climate"—such were the umbrella terms under which Bloch and Febvre gathered both their impatience with the work of their predecessors and their specification of the task ahead.

By Febvre's definition, then, "psychological history" was not a specialized branch of historical study. It was rather his particular way of getting at history tout court—just as another might have chosen an economic or sociological approach. At the same time Febvre stressed psychology because he found here the biggest gap in the historian's knowledge of the past. "We have no history of Love," he complained. "We have no history of Death. We have no history of Pity nor of Cruelty. We have no history of Joy." The whole realm of man's "sensibility" lay virtually untouched by scholarly hands.

[33] "Vivre l'histoire. Propos d'initiation" (lecture to the students of the Ecole Normale Supérieure, 1941), *Combats*, pp. 19–20.

Febvre himself guessed that the best way to proceed was by tracing the pulsations of emotion—the alternations, gradual or violent, between the predominance of love over hate, or of intellect over affect—in a given era of the past. Every human sentiment, he surmised, was of necessity ambivalent; each was both "itself and its opposite." For the historian, such a line of investigation was at once "extremely enticing and frightfully difficult." But he was not totally without resources: etymologies, iconography, the close study of works of literature—these were some of the instruments at the historian's command in charting the course of human sensibility.[84]

During the war years Febvre finally published in quick succession three studies of religious and intellectual life in the sixteenth century which gave tangible evidence of the new method in practice. The chief of these, *Le problème de l'incroyance au XVIe siècle,* is generally known as his finest achievement. It had been a decade in the making, and its author was over sixty when it appeared. Into it he had poured his rich humanistic scholarship, his almost professional understanding of theology, and the sense for emotional "climate" that he had been cultivating and refining ever since the publication of his book on Luther.

Like Bloch's *Feudal Society,* Febvre's volume on sixteenth-century "disbelief" found a place in *L'évolution de l'humanité.* At first glance, however, it did not look like a work of synthesis. As its subtitle, *La religion de Rabelais,* suggested, its narrower theme was the attitude of François Rabelais toward the Christianity of his day. The idea of such a study had first occurred to Febvre in the Strasbourg years when he had encountered in the work of a certain Abel Lefranc the assertion that Rabelais was an atheist. The accusation sounded odd: total disbelief in the modern sense, Febvre knew, was scarcely conceivable in the idea-world of the six-

[84] "Comment reconstituer la vie affective d'autrefois? La sensibilité et l'histoire" (first published in *Annales d'histoire sociale,* III [1941]), *Combats,* pp. 228–236.

teenth century. And so, as he had earlier done with Luther, but this time more explicitly and thoroughly, he set out to correct the work of a predecessor. His specific purpose was to put the record straight on Rabelais; his wider goal was to determine the limits of credulity and skepticism within which the speculations of Rabelais's contemporaries were confined.

The initial question, then, that Febvre asked himself was not the conventional "Is it true?" but rather "Is it possible?"[85] The answer proceeded in three stages. First came an examination of the evidence against Rabelais—the innuendoes of fellow humanists—which on closer inspection proved to be contradictory and inconclusive. Then Febvre took up the question of what Rabelais himself had said about Christianity—and here he discovered that the attitudes expressed by the good-humored giants Gargantua and Pantagruel, far from being rationalist or freethinking, were actually more acceptable to the Catholic Church than those of the Reformers. Moreover, that the "creed of the giants" was Rabelais's own emerged from a study of his letters and occasional writings: in the early stages of the Reformation he had found himself close in spirit to Luther's followers, but as Calvin turned the movement toward guilt and gloom, Rabelais had broken with him and taken his stand with the aging Erasmus. The conclusion was inescapable: Rabelais was no *libertin*, two centuries ahead of his time; he was typical rather of his educated contemporaries in combining a broad-minded, a personal and "internal," understanding of religion with a total lack of critical sense about miracles, the Scriptures, and the efficacy of prayer.

With this work of clarification behind him, Febvre was ready for his third task—the delineation of the metaphysical and scientific universe of the sixteenth century. For Bloch and Febvre, the supreme sin of the historian was to fall into anachronism—and such, the latter found, had been the way in which writers like Lefranc had dealt with Rabelais and his

---

[85] *Le problème de l'incroyance*, p. 18.

contemporaries. The men of the sixteenth century, Febvre contended, could not possibly have been atheists in any twentieth-century meaning of the term: their existence was enclosed by the atmosphere and paraphernalia of religion; their notion of science was a compound of childlike curiosity and occult experimentation; they were innocent of the concept of a single truth or of radical choice between contradictory assertions. In brief, they lived in a century which "wanted to believe"—a century which "sought in everything . . . a reflection of the divine."[86]

Most readers found this third aspect of Febvre's work by far the most interesting, and they regretted, as Bloch did, that he had left so much of his "Rabelaisian scaffolding" around it.[87] But Febvre had never intended to proceed otherwise: in the form in which he offered it, his book exposed to professional historians and to the general public alike the method he had adopted and which by implication he was urging on others. Febvre's purpose had been doubly polemical: besides settling a question of substance, he had introduced a new genre of historical study. To this day, historians divide their products into "monographs" and "general works"; they make a similar distinction between social and intellectual history. Febvre's *Rabelais* bridged both these divisions. It was a work of original scholarship on a highly specific theme which had broadened out to encompass a historical question of major dimensions. It was also a study of intellectual monuments—literary and theological—which never lost sight of the social realities and the psychological atmosphere in which those writings had been conceived. After the publication of *Rabelais*, the "history of ideas" could never be quite the same again.

Within two years of each other, Febvre and Bloch had

[86] *Ibid.*, p. 500.
[87] Letter of Bloch to Febvre, February 13, 1943: "Témoignages," pp. 28-29. Contrast Febvre's statement: *Le problème de l'incroyance*, p. 10.

reached the summit of their achievement. With the appearance of the second volume of *Feudal Society* in 1940 and of *Rabelais* in 1942, the corpus of their larger studies was complete: their two decades of collaboration had produced the best that either had to offer. In the case of the older man, age and new responsibilities now intervened. The younger was cut off in his intellectual prime. After 1939 Bloch and Febvre were unable to continue their joint endeavors. Circumstances parted them: the former went off to the volunteer service that brought martyrdom in his country's cause; the latter lived on, finally gathering in the honors and acclaim that had accrued to the labors of both.

III. *The War Years and Bloch's Three Testaments*

Although he was fifty-three years old and the father of six minor children, Bloch chose to reactivate his reserve commission and to enroll for service on the outbreak of war. He was, he joked, the "oldest captain in the French army." Assigned to staff duties, he fretted at his routine tasks and felt that his talents could have been better employed as a liaison officer with the British. At the beginning of the winter of the "phony war" something more interesting came his way—the responsible but incongruous duty of managing a vast gasoline dump.

Thus Bloch was in a position to appreciate what had gone wrong with French staff procedure when the Germans struck in May. Caught up in the great retreat, and evacuated from Dunkirk to England, he was shipped back to the Brittany peninsula just in time to witness his nation's utter defeat. It is not hard to imagine the grief it caused him. Yet from the boredom and tragedy of his military experience, Bloch—ever the historian—was able to distill a series of reflections which he hoped might someday be of benefit to his countrymen. The little book *Strange Defeat* in which he outlined what he had learned was published only after his death; it was the first of three wartime testaments that he left behind him.[88]

After the liberation of France, when the book appeared, people were surprised that a mere historian—and a medievalist at that—should have understood so well the technicalities of troop deployment. *Strange Defeat* quickly became accepted as one of the first—perhaps the very first—work in which the collapse of 1940 was adequately explained. To those who knew Bloch's earlier writings, the reasons were apparent: his feeling for the interplay between geography and psychology illuminated his whole account. He understood terrain at least as well as most professional officers; he appreciated far better than they did the way in which mechanized warfare had changed the relationship of space to time. He judged his staff colleagues severely: their minds had been too rigid to learn the lessons that Blitzkrieg had taught. But his harshest strictures Bloch reserved for France's economic and governing elite—for its narrowness and egoism and its lack of feeling for "la patrie en danger." On the little people his verdict was milder: the average Frenchman had been caught psychologically unprepared, and his rulers had made the catastrophic error of not taking him into their confidence. Bloch's wartime letters confirm the impression that emerges from his book: although far from being a militant of the Left, his sympathies lay with the common people, and he found in them reserves of good sense and humanity that the upper classes had almost entirely lost.[89]

Yet the over-all effect of *Strange Defeat* is not as depressing as one might suppose. Like Bloch's more strictly historical writings, it has a tone of serenity and of quiet confidence in the future. Such was Bloch's attitude during the German occupation. Reunited with his family near his country place in the Massif Central, he tried to resume his university teaching, although as a Jew he knew the threat that hung

---

[88] *L'étrange défaite* (Paris, 1946), translated by Gerard Hopkins as *Strange Defeat* (London, 1949).
[89] Letter of Bloch to Febvre, May 3, 1940: "Témoignages," p. 19.

over him. In fact, Bloch was one of the few professors of
Jewish origin whom the Vichy government kept on the rolls.
But only by a subterfuge: he was transferred from Paris to his
old university of Strasbourg, which had been evacuated to
Clermont-Ferrand in the Unoccupied Zone. Here he remained for a year, then shifted south to Montpellier when
his wife's health required a milder climate. His versatility and
capacity for work were unimpaired: at Montpellier he gave a
course on the economic history of the United States, and he
was projecting a history of the Second Reich that would explain Germany's subsequent aberrations. In his Strasbourg
days, Bloch had profited from the university library's extensive German holdings to become thoroughly familiar with
Central European history; it was the Germans who prevented
him from completing his studies.

Bloch's older sons had crossed the Pyrenees to join the
Free French. Their father was soon to follow them into the
Resistance. In the autumn of 1942, when the Germans occupied the whole of France, he was obliged to give up his
teaching. The safe course would have been to go into hiding
and await the liberation. Bloch chose to move to Lyons—his
birthplace and the capital of the Resistance—and to sign up
a third time for active service. He joined the group *Franc-
Tireur*, in which he quickly rose to a position of leadership.
A Resistance colleague has described how a twenty-year-old
résistant arrived proudly at headquarters with his "new
recruit, a gentleman of fifty, wearing the legion of honor,
with a refined face below silver-gray hair and a penetrating
gaze behind his glasses, his briefcase in one hand, a cane in
the other." There was also "mischievous gaiety" in those
eyes, and Bloch thrived on the adventurous side of his new
profession. His co-workers appreciated the "taste for precision,
for punctuality, for logic which gave his calm courage . . . a
kind of absurd charm" that "enchanted" them. Bloch certainly took too many risks: he went through three different
noms de guerre as he circulated about the country trying to

maintain liaison among the disparate groups that had come
together as the Mouvements Unis de Résistance. On one of
his furtive trips to Paris he saw Febvre for the last time. His
older friend found him unchanged: "lucid, optimistic, active."
. . . "Be careful! We need you so much afterward," Febvre
warned him. Bloch replied: "Yes. I know what's in store for
me, if . . . Death? not only that . . . A horrible death
. . .", and he vanished down the staircase.

In the spring of 1944, just a few weeks before the landing
in Normandy, the Gestapo caught up with him. He was
tortured and refused to speak. In mid-June his tormentors
took him with twenty-six others to a field north of Lyons,
where they were all shot. Alongside Bloch a boy of sixteen
"was trembling: 'It's going to hurt. . . .' Marc Bloch took
him affectionately by the arm and told him: 'No, *petit*, it
won't hurt,' and was the first to cry 'Vive la France!' as he
fell."[40]

He left behind him a "spiritual testament" which he had
written in Clermont-Ferrand more than three years before.
In it he explained why he did not want read at his grave the
"Hebrew prayers, whose cadences . . . accompanied so many
of my ancestors and my father himself to their last rest." He
refused them because he valued above all a "total sincerity in
expression and spirit," and it would be dishonest to have recourse to the rites of a religion in which he did not believe.
But—like Bergson in similar circumstances—he found it "still
more odious that anyone might see in this act of probity
something resembling the cowardly behavior of a renegade.
. . . Face to face with death," he affirmed that he was born
a Jew. "Above all," however, he felt himself "very simply
French"; he was so attached to his country and so "nourished
by its spiritual heritage and history" that he was "incapable

[40] This account of Bloch in the Resistance is drawn from Febvre's
"Marc Bloch et Strasbourg," *Combats*, pp. 405–407, and Georges Alt-
man, "Notre 'Narbonne' de la Résistance," *Annales d'histoire sociale*,
VII (1945), 11–14.

. . . of conceiving another" in which he could "breathe easily."[41]

The third of Bloch's posthumously-published writings from the years of occupation and resistance was a book of precepts for historians. The author himself never settled on a definitive title for this unfinished mélange of technical methodology and general reflections, known to the English-speaking public as *The Historian's Craft*. It is hard to tell what its full content would have been if Bloch had lived to complete it; the only indication is a very brief outline which Febvre found among his papers. Yet unsatisfactory as the book is in its fragmentary state, it is the last thing he wrote on the subject and all we have to go on in making a final assessment of his thought.

The Historian's Craft codified a number of the procedures that Bloch had already applied in his major works—notably the method of extrapolating back from present-day observation developed in *Les caractères originaux*, and the detection of the psychological reality behind an apparent untruth as in the case of *Les rois thaumaturges*. On concrete matters such as these, Bloch's little volume was probing and unambiguous. It was also quite clear in its demands on the historian: "What a curious contradiction there is in the successive attitudes of so many historians: when it is a question of ascertaining whether or not some human act has really taken place, they cannot be sufficiently painstaking. If they proceed to the reasons for that act, they are content with the merest appearance, ordinarily founded upon one of those maxims of commonplace psychology which are neither more nor less true than their opposites."[42] Such, in capsule form, was the reproach that Bloch and Febvre had so long directed against their colleagues—the latters' hopeless amateurishness in the matter of historical explanation.

41 "Testament spirituel de Marc Bloch," *Annales d'histoire sociale*, VII (1945), i–ii.
42 *Historian's Craft*, p. 195.

Yet here also lay the difficulty with Bloch's handbook. It pointed out what was wrong with the practices of his predecessors and contemporaries, but it did not go very far in specifying how to correct them. Strong on procedure, *The Historian's Craft* offered only tantalizing hints about the philosophical problems confronting the work of historical explanation. The sections missing from the manuscript were precisely those which might have been most helpful on this score: they were to have dealt with cause and chance—including the matter of unconscious motive—"the problem of 'determinant' acts or facts," and "prevision, a mental necessity."[48] Had he lived to write these, Bloch might have settled some of the unresolved difficulties that burden his intellectual legacy. But possibly not: to judge from his earlier writings and the parts of *The Historian's Craft* that he did finish, Bloch preferred to leave his methodological advice fluid and flexible and shied away from a philosophical specification of what he meant.

Much in his little book recalled the neo-idealists. Bloch echoed Croce in protesting against the notion that "Clio's chastity" should be spared the "profanation of present controversy"; he agreed that the questions the historian asked himself were those posed by his own time. He also aligned himself with Dilthey and Weber in arguing that history (like any science) necessarily had recourse to "abstractions" and that one must dissect reality "in order to observe it better"; only then could the work of synthesis begin.[44] Precisely how this synthesis proceeded remained unclear: Bloch limited himself to figures of speech such as "delicate network" and "converging searchlights." Hence a further difficulty: Bloch's colored and metaphorical language makes it almost impossible to give an unambiguous account of his criteria of explanation.

Such an objection might have struck Bloch himself as purist and excessive. Although he had doubtless read the

[48] *Ibid.*, "Note on the manuscripts" by Febvre, p. xvi.
[44] *Ibid.*, pp. 37, 147, 150–151, 155.

standard works in the analytic philosophy of history, he
seldom referred to them. His strength, he knew, was his skill
as a "craftsman"; some of the greatest of those who presumed
to give philosophical direction to historians had no idea of
the métier. Yet not all: men like Croce and Collingwood
were both eminent philosophers and fully-accredited members of the historian's guild. It is a matter for everlasting
regret that Bloch, who was in so many respects the best
craftsman of all, should have had no time (or inclination?)
to spell out the philosophical basis of his practical precepts.

    Consequently it is difficult to locate him in reference to
contemporary schools of historical thought. I have elsewhere
speculated that Bloch was heading beyond the neo-idealists
toward a sophisticated brand of latter-day positivism in the
spirit of a skeptical and pluralistic natural science.[45] In the
completed portion of *The Historian's Craft* he played with
the idea of using the calculus of probabilities to determine
whether events were actually or only coincidentally con-
nected. At the beginning of the unwritten sections there was
to have been a discussion of "the generation of skeptics (and
scientists)." We can also call to witness the gravest lacuna of
all, the section on prevision and regularities, which promised
to be the most original part of the whole work. What Bloch
would have done with these we can only guess; his temperament suggests that he would have restricted them to a mere
outline of possibilities.

    Compared to Febvre, however, Bloch's notion of procedure
was a model of order. It is symptomatic of the difference between the two that Bloch tried at least to put his thoughts
into some coherent shape while Febvre simply scattered his
advice along the way in the form of polemical articles. To
The Historian's Craft the older man gave his "unreserved"
approval. Bloch himself was less sure: while he recognized
that a great deal of what he had written was their common
property, he predicted that his friend would "sometimes re-

[45] See my *History as Art and as Science* (New York, 1964), pp.
14–17.

buke" him.[46] That this never happened—that Febvre un-
swervingly maintained a cult of Bloch's work until his own
death—was only natural in view of the tragic fashion in which
the younger man's life had been cut off. It did not mean that
there were no significant matters at issue between them. It
suggested rather that Bloch understood better than Febvre
where their minds diverged.

From the start there had been an anomaly in their relationship that apparently never came into the open. The junior
partner was the greater historian of the two—or at least he
developed into such as he gradually gained mastery over his
novel techniques. Within France, Febvre might be the better
known; abroad Bloch has gained a larger reputation. (Four
of his books, for example, have been translated into English,
and only two by Febvre.) We may suspect that their relationship was held together by more in the way of diplomatic
deference on the part of the younger man than either was
willing to admit. Where Bloch's mind was careful and disciplined, Febvre's was explosive; the latter's categories of
thought were spongier, and his enthusiasms less discriminat-
ing. All this, which had lain concealed for two decades, became amply apparent during the years when Febvre carried
on alone, after Bloch's death and the liberation of his country.

IV. *The Postwar and the Febvre Pontificate*

In the natural order of events Bloch could have been expected to outlive Febvre. That the reverse happened was
fateful for the future of historical studies in France. For in
the postwar era Febvre assumed a position of chef d'école—a
quasi-pontificate—which was quite foreign to Bloch's temperament and working methods.

Too old for military service, Febvre passed the war years
in his regular scholarly pursuits, alternating as before be-

[46] "Vers une autre histoire," *Combats*, p. 426; dedication to *Historian's Craft*, pp. v–vi.

tween his apartment in Paris and his country home in the Jura. "Have patience, . . . last it out," he advised his friends, and so far as possible he adopted a business-as-usual attitude. He completed his *Rabelais* and the two further books related to it; he had long ago discovered that burying himself under a mountain of work was the most reliable antidote to depressing thoughts. Yet life in fact was desperately changed: even to reach his country retreat he had to cross the demarcation line between the Occupied and Unoccupied Zones clandestinely and on foot (in itself a sign of his undiminished vigor). Then there was the question of the *Annales*. As a Jew, Bloch could no longer serve on its editorial board, and he personally wanted to concede nothing to Vichy's requirements. Febvre counseled a minimum of accommodation: leave Bloch's name off the cover but change nothing of the content inside. To him the continuity of the *Annales* took precedence over everything else. A painful disagreement threatened—the first, apparently, to trouble the long collaboration of the two. In the end Bloch let Febvre have his way.[47]

When in the late summer of 1944, the American troops swept in to liberate the Franche-Comté, one of Febvre's sons had taken to the hills to help the Resistance and he himself had received the crushing news of Bloch's death. He returned to Paris, overwhelmed by the conviction of a vast labor to be performed and the sense that there were too few men of his generation left who were qualified to do it. A few months later he resumed his everlasting round of public commitments, including several new ones. From 1945 to 1950 Febvre served as a French delegate to UNESCO—a position which entailed numerous trips abroad—and in 1947 he had the enormous satisfaction of seeing established under his direction the "Sixth Section" of the Ecole Pratique des Hautes

[47] For this disagreement, see the correspondence in "Témoignages," pp. 22–24; further material on Febvre's attitudes and activities during the war years may be found in Braudel, "Présence de Lucien Febvre," pp. 2, 7–15.

Etudes, a center for intellectual cooperation among the social sciences, in which historians were to play the most influential role.

This new responsibility put the official seal on the position of leadership among historians with a concern for social science which Febvre had so long exerted in practice. His intellectual heir has maintained that he could not imagine Febvre as the authoritarian founder of a "school."[48] Perhaps such was not his conscious wish. But in fact Febvre's activities and writings in the postwar period all worked in that direction, reinforcing a primacy which he no longer shared with Bloch. His articles from these years have a more than customarily peremptory and hortatory tone; they sound like bugles marshaling the historical battalions for the "combats" that lie ahead. Besides the familiar attacks on the sins of the profession and the call for comparative history, these essays are both specific and visionary in projecting the great collective enterprises, the teamwork of the future; some of Febvre's postwar prose could have been written by an American foundation executive.[49]

After 1950, when he retired from the Collège de France, Febvre's life was quieter. Perhaps he even became less fearsome. Although his articles and reviews had always been savage, he had lived enclosed in family warmth and in the respect of disciples that eventually grew into affection. "Attentive, charming, passionate, . . . dazzling, scattering about him ideas and memories, happy to see everything, to discuss everything": so one of them has described him. Another has told how Febvre looked at his visitor brightly and straight in the eye—like a "prince of history"—as he sat behind his desk in his large library, with its serene view of the dome of the Val-de-Grâce.[50]

[48] Braudel, "Lucien Febvre et l'histoire," p. 20.
[49] See particularly the statements in "Vers une autre histoire," *Combats*, pp. 427, 434.
[50] Braudel, "Présence de Lucien Febvre," p. 5; Mandrou, "Lucien Febvre," p. 7.

Death overtook him, as he would have preferred, in the Franche-Comté, in September 1956. Although he had suffered a heart attack the previous winter, he had apparently made a complete recovery. He had returned with joy to his familiar tasks—above all to the *Annales*, which to the end remained the responsibility he cherished most. One final detail may sum up the rest: very early one morning the old historian, now nearly eighty, had been discovered chopping down a tree which was interfering with the growth of a new one he had planted.

Febvre's successor at the Collège de France, whose doctoral thesis on the sixteenth-century Mediterranean world he had acclaimed as a masterpiece, was Fernand Braudel. If Febvre's primacy had already marked a falling off from the discrimination of Bloch's method, the succession of Braudel to Febvre marked a further step away from clarity of thought and presentation. For the work which the new master had written and which the old master held up as a model to be followed was sprawling and invertebrate. Although fascinating in detail and alive with fresh observations on the relation of geography to history, it lacked a discernible focus. It had taken twenty years to complete; its bulk was enormous; into it its author had apparently tumbled all the miscellaneous lore he had acquired in the course of two decades of study about a region he "passionately loved."[51] The result was to reinforce a tendency toward the gigantic which was already the curse of French historical scholarship.

Braudel claimed to have absorbed the thought of Marc Bloch. But his book showed little of Bloch's talent for establishing a tight relationship among the various strands of his account. In Braudel's work the three major sections—

[51] *La Méditerranée et le monde méditerranéen à l'époque de Philippe II* (Paris, 1949), p. ix; see the critique of Bernard Bailyn: "Braudel's Geohistory—a Reconsideration," *Journal of Economic History*, XI (Summer 1951), 278–282.

dealing successively with geography, with society, and with "events"—never quite came together. And its tone was subject to disconcerting shifts, oscillating erratically between the statistical and the poetic. Such was to be the character of a number of subsequent studies by younger historians who looked to Febvre and Braudel as guides. Romantic flights of rich prose alternating with long stretches of merciless quantification—this was apparently the fashion in which the new generation had understood Febvre's method.

Part of the trouble lay in the predictable exaggeration by epigoni of the lessons they had learned too well. But the fault was also Febvre's own—and to a lesser extent that of Bloch besides. Febvre had not bothered to put his thoughts in order: the nearest thing to a systematic presentation he left behind him was the article he had written with Berr for the *Encyclopaedia of the Social Sciences* a quarter century earlier, and this, as we have seen, was cryptic and unsatisfactory on the crucial issues. Like his master Michelet, Febvre was intoxicated by the pulse of living. He also stayed sufficiently close to the tradition of Berr to be infatuated with science and scientific method: hence his emphasis on teamwork and on the converging action of the different social sciences. These two aspects of his writing remained distinct and sometimes in contradiction.

On the one hand there were the manifestations of Febvre's expansive temperament—the reiteration of the word "human" (which at his hands, as at Bloch's, gradually degenerated into a historical truism) and the constant resort to figurative, colorful language. At all costs, Febvre and Bloch wanted their prose to be "alive." And perhaps when they began their labors nothing less would have sufficed to shake the French historical profession out of its complacency. Yet the price was a heavy one: reading Febvre today is sometimes a downright embarrassing experience, and the imprecision of his language makes it even harder than with Bloch to discover exactly what he means. The true historian, Febvre claimed, must

throw himself into life totally, with the sense that in
plunging into it, bathing in it, suffusing himself with
human presence, he is increasing tenfold his powers of
investigating and of resurrecting the past—a past which
. . . gives him back in return the secret meaning of
human destiny.[52]

This flight of Bergsonian prose requires little comment; it
may suffice to observe that in Febvre's programmatic statements of the postwar years it grew increasingly difficult to
recognize the meticulous scholar whose *Rabelais* had become
a model of intellectual-history method for a whole generation
of younger historians.

Which is all to say that Febvre—like Bloch—was almost
invariably more impressive as a practitioner of his craft than
as a theorist of it. And this in turn is explicable by the reluctance of both to adopt any terminology that might seem
to limit the flow of history itself. Febvre disliked the term
"structure"; he preferred to speak of "rhythms," "pulsations," and "currents." But was there so much difference
between the two types of expression? Both were merely
metaphors—both no more than verbal devices for conveying
something of what the historian had finally understood of
the thoughts and actions he had studied. The flow metaphors might be aesthetically the more satisfying, but structural explanations would have brought the discipline of history closer to the vocabulary of the other social sciences.

The second aspect—the "scientific" guise of Febvre's
thought—was less authentic than the first. He himself strove
mightily to keep up with both the social science and the
natural science of his day. Almost his last angry word to
his professional colleagues—written on the occasion of Einstein's death—was a long rebuke for their failure to acquaint
themselves with contemporary scientific method.[53] But the
very tone in which he reproved them betrayed him as an

[52] "Face au vent" (first published in *Annales: économies—sociétés—
civilisations*, I [1946]), *Combats*, p. 43.
[53] "Sur Einstein et sur l'histoire: méditation de circonstance," *Annales*, X (July–September 1955), 305–312.

amateur. Febvre knew that most historians were grossly ignorant of natural science. He also knew that the way to make the study of history itself more scientific was by refining its techniques of interpretation—by improving its conceptual armory. But he never succeeded in demonstrating how this could be done.

We have seen that in his earlier writings his notion of sociology did not extend much beyond comparisons among social "types" and that his understanding of the psychology of the unconscious was inadequate for exploration in depth. By the time he published his study of sixteenth-century disbelief, his grasp had become surer. But what he had acquired in the meantime had not been any specific new method: there was no evidence in *Rabelais* that its author's theoretical equipment in psychology (or indeed that of the psychological profession in France as a whole) had improved during the decade and a half which had intervened since the appearance of his *Luther*. It was rather that Febvre's "feel" for the subject had been enhanced. And this, as any teacher of history knows, is an intangible that is extremely difficult to impart to others.

So Febvre the expansive heir of Michelet and Febvre the apostle of scientific historiography failed to fuse. Had they done so, he might have understood better than he in fact did the relation of his own value system to his "scientific" labors. We have noted that on this score the article for the *Encyclopaedia of the Social Sciences* merely touched the surface of the problem. The idea that in collaborative history the "involuntary biases" of the different writers would cancel each other out was both ingenious and comforting, but it was far from proved, and it said nothing about how the individual historian might come to terms with his own emotions and loyalties. Nor did Febvre subsequently offer a fuller explanation. His treatment of the perennial question of values made no advance over that of men senior to him— notably Max Weber and Benedetto Croce. On the contrary, it marked a step backward from them.

Croce and Weber had known, as Febvre did, that great

historical writing of necessity derived from some passionate commitment on the part of the historian himself. They had added—and this was the nub of the matter—that the historian could rise above mere partisanship only if he examined his own values with sufficient "objectivity" and discernment to recognize their place in a long succession of opposed or comparable commitments. This process of "self-relativization" Bloch and Febvre never quite accomplished. The life-choices they faced were not sufficiently ambiguous; they had too clear a conscience. Their patriotism carried the force of the self-evident: they were in the peculiarly fortunate position of being untroubled by doubt in two world wars as to the justice of their country's cause. Even the murkier aspects of these conflicts did not worry them unduly. They never seemed to notice that the gain for France in the acquisition of the University of Strasbourg was also the loss to German scholarship of the great institution at which Friedrich Meinecke had taught and Albert Schweitzer had studied. What attitude would Bloch and Febvre have taken toward the brutal struggle that raged in Algeria at the end of the 1950's? Would they have conformed to what their government expected of them or would they have aligned themselves with the dissenters of the Left? Fortunately for their peace of mind, Bloch was no longer alive when the Algerian War broke out, and Febvre died before its bitterest phase began—before an eruption of indignation on the part of his fellow-intellectuals not unlike that aroused by the Dreyfus Case, which had provided the ideological coming of age for both of them.

Despite their knowledge of foreign languages and their international renown, both Bloch and Febvre remained curiously provincial in their stubborn adherence to French norms. Even their lack of interest in the philosophical analysis of their working methods had about it a Gallic quality of the self-contained. This type of inquiry has not been particularly at home in the French-speaking world: with certain notable exceptions such as Raymond Aron and Henri-Irénée

Marrou, its main contemporary proponents have been Germans and Italians, Englishmen and Americans. Not until the mid-1950's, with the publication of a treatise by Marrou on the problem of historical knowledge,[54] did the French historical profession come fully abreast of the work of criticism that for more than a generation past had been in progress abroad.

We are left with a perplexing contrast. From one standpoint, Bloch and Febvre and the school they founded was intransigently French, turned inward and cut off from coworkers in other countries. From another and more permanently significant standpoint, theirs was the most original and fruitful of any such attempt at the renewal of historical writing in the second quarter of the twentieth century. For they had endowed social history—in the widest meaning of the term—with a new standing and a new consciousness of its possibilities. It was not merely that in quantitative terms their example had swept all before it. (By 1961 more than two fifths of the modern history theses being prepared in France were in the economic and social field.)[55] It was also that their successors as social historians, despite the literary flaws and the inordinate length of what they wrote, were setting the model for the rest of the world in combining imaginative sweep with close attention to detail.

Bloch and Febvre had undertaken to give—and in part had succeeded in giving—a new unity to the study of man, which the nineteenth century had fragmented. As against the heterogeneity of explanation in terms of ideal types, they sought a central core of meaning. History they redefined as "retrospective cultural anthropology,"[56] putting their emphasis on the expressions and usages, the styles of thought and

[54] *De la connaissance historique* (Paris, 1954).

[55] See Jean Glénisson, "L'historiographie française contemporaine: tendances et réalisations," Comité français des sciences historiques, *Vingt-cinq ans de recherche historique en France (1940–1965)* (Paris, 1965), I, xi, xxiv–xxv, lxiii.

[56] The term is mine, not theirs.

emotion, that distinguished a given society from its neighbors in space and time.

Through most of human history, they well knew, such life styles had been couched primarily in religious terms. Again and again Bloch and Febvre returned to religion as the base point of their researches. Marc Bloch, his friend recalled, had no real sympathy for religious emotion; he was obliged "to circle rather than truly to penetrate religious problems."[57] Febvre was right in suspecting that in this field—and perhaps in this field alone—he himself was the superior historian. Neither, however, had experienced religion at first hand. When they wrote of it, it was to evoke something from the vanished past—the aspect of life that most clearly marked off the Middle Ages or the sixteenth century from their own era. Yet at the very time they were writing, the faith whose historical significance they had so accurately assessed was experiencing an intellectual revival—and a revival whose leading exponents were Frenchmen of their generation. Bloch and Febvre's renewal of historical studies might have religion as its central focus, but it was not itself inspired by religious belief. To rephrase that faith in terms which would carry conviction to the twentieth century was a wholly distinct line of investigation, pursued by philosophers and imaginative writers whose work met that of the historians only in tragic circumstances when ultimate social commitments were laid bare.

[57] *Architects and Craftsmen in History*, p. 79.

CHAPTER

3

The Catholics
and the Human Condition

IN March 1929 the philosopher Gabriel Marcel joined the Catholic Church. It was the last of the great conversions which in the course of forty years had brought to Catholicism so distinguished a roster of France's literary and intellectual spokesmen. First had come the poet Claudel a decade and a half before the turn of the century, then Maritain twenty years later, Péguy on the eve of the First World War, and during and after the war a succession of essayists and imaginative writers. If Marcel's conversion closed the series, its emotional tone also differed from most of the others. It came without painful struggle, without the sense of forcing a stubborn will, without any sacrifice of intellectual independence or agnostic friendships. Its quiet effortlessness was consonant with Marcel's own harmonious personality. It was likewise a sign that by the end of the 1920's the enrollment of a leading thinker in the ranks of Catholicism no longer gave cause for public scandal of jubilation; the new position of religious faith among France's intellectual elite had become accepted as a normal feature of literary life in the interwar years.[1]

[1] For a survey of the Catholic members of this elite, see Gonzague Truc, *Histoire de la littérature catholique contemporaine* (Tournai, 1961).

Yet it was normal in France alone. Elsewhere in the
Western world, the situation of Catholicism—or of Christianity in general—was not much different from what it had
been in the late nineteenth century; it was marginal to the
main course of intellectual endeavor. In a country like Italy,
which resembled France in being nominally Catholic, nearly
all the dominant thinkers remained outside the Church. In
countries of mixed religion such as Germany and the United
States, the Protestants held a clear lead over their Catholic
fellow citizens. Indeed, the revival of Protestant theology in
Germany was the only movement of the 1920's comparable
to what was taking place within French Catholicism. But its
range was narrower: the neo-orthodoxy of Karl Barth was
more austere than French neo-Thomism and had fewer
aesthetic connections and affiliations. Only in France did
Catholic thinkers—in large proportion converts to the faith—
succeed in establishing their view of the universe at the center
of intellectual and literary discourse.

Why did this happen in France alone? Or perhaps better,
why did a revival of Catholic thought appear first among the
French? In France, as elsewhere on the European continent,
the last generation of the nineteenth century had been
dominated by the defiantly irreligious; the first generation of
the twentieth—the generation that came to intellectual
maturity in the 1890's—had reacted against the bleak skepticism of their fathers by a rediscovery of religious values. But
this return to religious concerns had been detached and impersonal. While Durkheim and Bergson and their American
counterpart William James had demonstrated the indispensability of faith for ideal aspiration and social solidarity,
they had refrained (at least until the very end of Bergson's
life) from proclaiming a religious commitment of their own.
They had been fascinated by the works of belief, but they
had not become the advocates of any particular belief themselves. That was to be the calling of men a generation
younger, born in the 1880's, in whom their elders' abstract
will to believe had been translated into a longing for the in-

finite that gradually suffused their whole being and led them to find in the Catholic Church the inevitable and unchallengeable vessel of transcendance in the secular world.

The Church that welcomed them was far from typical of twentieth-century Catholicism. We may find in the very special situation of the Catholic Church in France—its public humiliation and weakness, its hidden wellsprings of spiritual energy, its desperate factional quarrels and spectacular mutual condemnations—the signs of a vitality that offers a preliminary answer to the question why so many men of intellectual and aesthetic distinction sought shelter within its fold.

1. *The Decade of Choice*

The events of the decade from 1926 to 1936 faced French Catholics with a set of unavoidable choices. The ten years that stretched from the Papal condemnation of the Action Française to the outbreak of the Spanish Civil War made it impossible for Catholics to remain neutral observers of the social and ideological struggle. These were the years when there began what Marcel called a process of "laying utterly bare . . . our human condition."[2] Thinkers who through training or temperament had adopted a stance of detachment were forced to take sides; others who had already committed themselves were obliged to revise or repudiate their earlier allegiances.

From our post-Johannine vantage point—from our perspective on the far side of Pope John's pontificate and the Second Vatican Council—it requires a mighty effort of imagination to appreciate the shock that ran through French Catholicism when Pius XI put on the Index the works of Charles Maurras and the newspaper that was his mouthpiece. To us the condemnation seems only natural; our question

[2] *Les hommes contre l'humain* (Paris, 1951), translated by G. S. Fraser as *Men against Humanity* (London, 1952), p. 73.

would rather be why it was not done earlier. For Maurras had made no secret of his own disbelief and positivist philosophy; he was quite frank in stating that the Action Française favored the Catholic Church for instrumental reasons—as spiritual support for political reaction. But most of the French Catholic elite had been blind to such distinctions. Obsessed with the sins of the godless Republic, they had given thanks to heaven for ideological support from however suspect a source. The Action Française had grown up in the wake of the Dreyfus Case and the separation of church and state that had been its sequel. In *this* perspective, Maurras and his co-workers appeared as avenging angels, come to rescue French Catholicism from intellectual scorn and material spoliation. To the great majority of the bien-pensants, it seemed incredible that the Holy Father himself should have repudiated the gallant defender of the Church in France. For them the association of Catholicism with royalism and reaction was simply assumed as the normal order of things human and divine.[8]

Before 1926, nearly all the chief figures in the Catholic intellectual revival—with rare exceptions such as Claudel and the novelist François Mauriac—had been either members of the Action Française or within its ideological orbit. After the Papal condemnation, such an association could no longer be automatic. Each individual was obliged to examine his conscience and to make his personal decision. After 1926, the French Catholic was on his own in a fashion almost without precedent. Two decades earlier the act of separation had cut him off from the material reassurance of state support; now he was required to break a further tie—either with Rome or with the secular organization that had long appeared his strongest bulwark. Most conservative Catholics, quite predict-

[8] For general accounts of this crisis, see Adrien Dansette, *Histoire religieuse de la France contemporaine* (Paris, 1948), translated by John Dingle as *Religious History of Modern France* (New York, 1961), II, 378–413, and Eugen Weber, *Action Française: Royalism and Reaction in Twentieth-Century France* (Stanford, Calif., 1962), pp. 230–255.

ably, tried to avoid the choice: they made formal submission to the Papal ban while sabotaging it in practice. Such was the path of a number of the literary mediocrities who populated the French Academy. The more rigorous thinkers scorned so slippery an evasion. Very few defied Rome openly: it took the exceptional ruggedness of a Georges Bernanos to go for years without the sacraments as witness to his political allegiance. It happened much more frequently—as in the case of Jacques Maritain—that the condemnation reinforced doubts which had earlier been held just under the surface of consciousness and pointed the way to a radical rethinking of positions which had had behind them little besides mental inertia and the approval of literary peers.

The French Catholic community was far from recovered from the controversy over the Action Française when the eruption of civil war in Spain faced it with a new and contradictory dilemma. This time the Pope and the bien-pensants were on the same side; in France, as nearly everywhere else in the Catholic world, the overwhelming preponderance of Catholic opinion favored Franco and the Nationalist forces. Once more the adherents of the Action Française found that they and the Vatican had the same enemies. The renewed alignment of the Pope and the French reactionaries in their attitude toward Spain could not fail to encourage friendlier feelings in both parties. The turn to the right in Papal policy which the Spanish War entailed almost inevitably prompted second thoughts on the condemnation of 1926. When Eugenio Pacelli was elevated to the Papal throne as Pius XII at the beginning of 1939, one of his first acts was to accept the submission of Maurras and to lift his predecessor's ban on the Action Française.

By the outbreak of the Second World War, then, it might seem that French Catholicism's position in the secular world had come full circle—that its authoritarian wing was once more dominant. But in fact a return to the *status quo ante* was out of the question. Too much had happened in the meantime: too many consciences had been torn and shaken during the decade of ideological uncertainty. The majority of French Catholics might still acclaim Franco as the strong right arm of the Church—but in France, almost alone in the Catholic world, a scrupulous and well-informed minority refused to accept the legend of the Spanish Nationalist insurrection as a holy crusade. Some of these, like Maritain, were men whose eyes had already been opened by the events of 1926. More surprising was the case of Bernanos, who without denying his reactionary sympathies could not refrain from telling the truth about Nationalist atrocities. By 1936, a certain independence of mind had become characteristic of French Catholic intellectuals. And increasingly this independence expressed itself in social consciousness and in a political evolution toward the Left. The years of disarray in the ranks of the Action Française had also been years of economic depression and fascist advance. In the first half of the 1930's the Catholic trade unions and workers' youth organizations had met these new dangers in a mood of militancy and self-confidence. At the same time and with the same sense of social peril, leading intellectuals were more and more inclined to throw their support to the Catholic Left. The end of the decade found French Catholicism at least as divided as before: on balance, however, the conservatives had lost ground; the forces of social and intellectual renovation now felt that they had the future on their side.

After the Second World War, the French Church—both laymen and clergy—emerged as the most "left" and reformist among the major national branches of Catholicism. This situation was already implicit in the evolution of the 1930's. Still more, it had been latent since the early years of the century. After the separation of 1905, the most promising course for French Catholics was to find virtue in the state of penury to which their Church had been reduced—to cut their remaining links with the established powers and set out to rechristianize the poorer classes. Such had been the contention of Marc Sangnier and the other founders of the French

Catholic Left. But the circumstances of the time had made this impossible: Sangnier's movement, the Sillon, incurred Papal disapproval for a mixture of reasons that the Vatican never disentangled: to the valid charge of organizational indiscipline it had added the less justifiable accusation that the Sillon was tainted with doctrinal "Modernism."[4] In 1910, Saint Pius X had formally condemned it. The parallel action against Maurras—which had been prepared as early as 1914— was allowed to lie buried in the Vatican archives.

Not until the Liberation of 1944 did Sangnier and the younger men who had followed his lead receive the ecclesiastical sympathy he had been denied a generation earlier. French Catholicism of the post-Liberation period was very different in tone from the faith of those who had supported the Action Française. It had shed its conformism and authoritarianism: it had become "both more personal and more social."[5] In its openness of mind, in its willingness to experiment, the Church in France stood as the model for progressives and reformers throughout the Catholic world. That it had become so was in great part the work of obscure men— of Christian trade-union leaders and parish priests who had labored among the poor. It was also the result of a mighty effort of intellectual restatement. One aspect of this renewal had been expressed in imaginative literature, as in the novels of Bernanos and Mauriac. Another aspect was the work of historical scholars such as Daniel-Rops and Etienne Gilson. But the voices of French Catholicism which carried farthest were those of its philosophers—more particularly the exemplary and sharply contrasting figures of Jacques Maritain and Gabriel Marcel.

[4] Charles Breunig, "The Condemnation of the *Sillon:* an Episode in the History of Christian-Democracy in France," *Church History,* XXVI (September 1957), 8–10.
[5] Dansette, *Religious History,* II, 375; see also by the same author, *Destin du catholicisme français 1926–1956* (Paris, 1957), and Livre VII (by René Rémond) in Andre Latreille et. al., *Histoire du catholicisme en France,* III: *La période contemporaine* (Paris, 1962).

ii. *Jacques Maritain in the Ideological Arena*

"What am I?" Maritain wrote to Jean Cocteau. "A convert.
A man God has turned inside out like a glove."[6] Of all the
great conversions of the twentieth century's opening years,
Maritain's was to become the most celebrated. It concentrated in a single personal experience the full range of
characteristic influences on a sensitive man of his generation
—an impeccably republican and freethinking upbringing, a
period of growing despair with the mentality of bleak
"scientism" that ruled the Sorbonne, a marriage based on
deep sympathy rather than social considerations or closeness
of milieu, the friendship of Péguy and the tonic of Bergson's
lectures, finally the shock of meeting in the person of Léon
Bloy a secular saint manqué who took his Catholicism with
total seriousness.

By 1906, when he was baptized into the Church, the
twenty-three-year-old Maritain had already behind him the
most severe emotional trials of his life. Each element in his
adolescence and youth seemed calculated to bring to maximum lucidity his anguished search for spiritual shelter. His
mother—separated from his father and almost solely responsible for his education—was a strong-willed woman, the
daughter of the elder republican statesman Jules Favre,
formally a Protestant but in practice an adept of the
strenuous Kantian ethic of the late nineteenth century which
found no need for divine sanction. His closest friend was
Ernest Psichari, whose similarly freethinking antecedents
were suggested by the fact that his grandfather was Ernest
Renan. Together the two had discovered Péguy, who had
taken them to hear Bergson. And along the way the young
Maritain had also found his life companion—a fellow-student,
Raïssa Oumansoff, whose Russian Jewish parents had fled

[6] *Réponse à Jean Cocteau* (Paris, 1926), translated by John Cole-
man as *Art and Faith* (New York, 1948).

from Tsarist persecution when she was ten years old and who like her future husband was desolated by the positivist tone of the teaching imparted to her.

In the case of Jacques Maritain, this scientism impinged in a form that was depressing to the point of caricature. His chosen field was biology, and his mentor, Félix Le Dantec, seriously proposed to fabricate human life by synthesis in his own laboratory. As against such an influence, the teachings of Bergson could not have been more appropriate: for young men of Maritain's generation, they came just at the point they were needed most. But unlike the run of his contemporaries, Maritain did not remain content with the Bergsonian philosophy: for him it served as no more than an avenue of approach to an unsuspected world of the spirit. For his initiation into the Catholic faith he sought out the neglected, impoverished, and totally authentic Bloy. For the intellectual formulation of his new commitment he went directly to St. Thomas Aquinas.

Curiously enough, the man who was to become the most prominent exponent of contemporary Thomism originally believed that his conversion to Catholicism entailed renouncing philosophical speculation. He went off to Germany to continue his biological studies, and it was not until his return to France and nearly three years after his conversion that he began a serious reading of St. Thomas. Once launched in this direction, however, Maritain's progress was both rapid and sure-footed: he had discovered in Thomism a method so congenial to his nature that it sufficed him for more than half a century of intellectual endeavor. By 1910 he had published his first essay on Aquinas; two years later he began to teach Thomism at the Collège Stanislas in Paris. And after two further years he was called to the Institut Catholique, the greatest center of French Catholic learning. By the outbreak of the First World War, Maritain—just over thirty—was an established influence in the literary life of his country. Still more, he had clearly marked out his own differences with Bergson and unequivocally broken with the philosophy of the élan vital. His first book, published in 1913, was a thoroughgoing critique of his earlier allegiance; in his *Bergsonian Philosophy* Maritain rejected intuition as a way to metaphysical understanding, proposing in its stead the severe intellectualism that was to become the hallmark of his thought.[7]

The first war marked less of a hiatus in Maritain's career than one might suppose. Himself rejected for military service on physical grounds, he lost his friends Péguy and Psichari in the first months of combat. But the war as such figured only marginally in his published writing. At this stage in his life his commitment to Thomist study was so intense that it left little mental energy for the affairs of the secular world. And he maintained the same critical detachment into the immediate postwar years. By the mid-1920's, a permanent impression of Maritain seemed fixed in the public mind: his writing was austere, difficult, and mercilessly abstract; his personal polemic could be devastating, as his break with Bergson had shown; his own predilection was against nearly all the manifestations of the modern world—in brief, reactionary. In 1922 he had published a little book, *Antimoderne*, whose title gave sufficient evidence of its contents, and in 1925 *Three Reformers*, whose targets, predictably enough, were Luther, Descartes, and Rousseau.

Had the great explosion over the Action Française not intervened, Maritain might never have attained to the serenity and humanity that were characteristic of his later judgments. Nor would he have figured in a prominent place in the history of contemporary French social thought. Maritain himself was fully aware of the significance of this turning point. Several years later he noted in his diary:

[7] For the chronology of Maritain's early years, besides the autobiographical writings of Raïssa Maritain, see Henry Bars, *Maritain en notre temps* (Paris, 1959), pp. 367–373; Charles A. Fecher, *The Philosophy of Jacques Maritain* (Westminster, Md., 1953), pp. 3–35; and Donald and Idella Gallagher, *The Achievement of Jacques and Raïssa Maritain: A Bibliography 1906–1961* (Garden City, N.Y., 1962), pp. 37–38.

Today more than ever, I bless the liberating intervention
of the Church which . . . exposed the errors of the
Action Française, following which I finally examined
Maurras' doctrines and saw what they were worth. There
began for me then a period of reflection devoted to
moral and political philosophy in which I tried to work
out the character of authentically Christian politics and
to establish, in the light of a philosophy of history and
of culture, the true significance of democratic inspiration
and the nature of the new humanism for which we are
waiting.[8]

Before 1926, Maritain had never formally adhered to the
Action Française. But the influence of the priest who was his
spiritual director and his own polemic against the modern
world had led him to extend to it his sympathy and to write
on occasion for its journals. Among the wider public many
assumed him to be *the* philosopher of the movement. His
"apostasy"—as Maurras's adherents called it—surprised both
ideological wings of French Catholicism; to the democratic
and social Catholics it brought welcome reinforcement in the
struggles that lay ahead.

The condemnation of the Action Française impelled
Maritain into the public arena. Here he was to remain for
the next quarter century, gradually establishing himself as the
most widely listened-to spokesman for Catholic social principles, first in France and subsequently in the United States.
By the end of the 1920's his home in Meudon near Paris had
become the gathering place for an extensive circle of
Christian artists and writers, which included the painter
Georges Rouault and the exiled Russian philosopher Nicholas
Berdyaev. The range of these associations seems to have
broadened Maritain's sympathies: his prose became less arid,
and his intellectual exchanges more forgiving; in 1937 he was
reconciled to Bergson, now old and sick and moving toward
Catholicism.

[8] Quoted in *The Social and Political Philosophy of Jacques Maritain*,
edited by Joseph W. Evans and Leo R. Ward, Image edition (Garden
City, N.Y., 1965), p. 9.

By 1934, Maritain was ready to formulate his new view of
the social universe. *True Humanism*, based on lectures he
delivered in that year in Spain and published as the Spanish
Civil War was breaking out, became the cornerstone of
everything further he was to write on the subject. All his
subsequent volumes of polemic and public philosophy were
footnotes to or expansions on the themes that *True Humanism* had announced.

The course of recent history, Maritain now recognized,
could not be undone: democracy and its stepchild, socialism,
had come to stay. What *True Humanism* set out to do was
to suggest how the heroic and saintly values of the Middle
Ages could be translated into terms applicable to the contemporary world. Basing himself, as always, on the method
of Aquinas, and proceeding in the architectonic order of his
master, Maritain traced the historical origins of the kind of
humanism he proposed and projected into the future his
vision of a Christian society. One would be greatly mistaken,
he argued, to see in the popular political faiths of the last two
centuries no more than the work of atheist corrosion. The
historical roles had been reversed: the purveyors of apparent
evil had in fact become the heralds of beneficent change.
Such a one was Marx—whose "cynicism," like that of Freud,
had unveiled a number of important truths. More precisely,
Marx had exposed the materialism and heartlessness of
capitalist values—its treatment of human beings as tools
rather than persons—and had awakened the working class to
a consciousness of its dignity and humiliation. For a Christian, the answer to Marxism was clear. It was to make a
reality of the teaching in the gospels.[9] The encyclicals
Rerum Novarum and *Quadragesimo Anno*—the latter having appeared just three years before Maritain's own lectures—
had already pointed the way.

Within this ideological framework, Maritain only lightly
sketched the outlines of the future democratic society he had

[9] *Humanisme intégral* (Paris, 1936), translated by M. R. Adamson
as *True Humanism*, 4th ed. (London, 1946), pp. 42, 86, 108, 223–225.

in mind. Its emphasis would be on fraternity and understanding among the classes rather than on a fictitious equality.
Its institutions would be pluralist and permissive: while
Christian values would give the lead, the Catholic element
would not attempt to impose its will on fellow citizens of
other faiths or no faith at all. This was the view that Maritain developed more fully in the works he subsequently published in the United States, *Christianity and Democracy*, of
1942, and *Man and the State*, which appeared in 1951 and
closed the ideological phase of his career.

The first of these suggested why its author had so long
hesitated to use the word "democracy" at all. As his polemic
against Rousseau had implied, Maritain had earlier considered the term almost irremediably corrupted by senti-
mentality, intellectual confusion, and a general failure to live
up to its professions. "The tragedy of the modern democracies," he now explained, was that they had "not yet succeeded in realizing democracy": its political accomplishments
had no sufficient counterpart in the social realm; modern
society had proved itself impotent "in the face of poverty
and the dehumanization of work."[10] Such had been the
melancholy balance sheet of more than a century of ideological struggle in Western and Central Europe at the time that
the great democracies had succumbed to fascist domination.

Across the Atlantic Maritain found greater reason for
confidence in democratic values. "The very name democracy," he discovered, had "a different ring in America and
in Europe." In the United States, "despite the influence
wielded by the great economic interests," it had "penetrated
more profoundly into existence, and . . . never lost sight of
its Christian origin."[11] Logically enough, it was in an American setting and in lectures delivered in the English language
that Maritain succeeded in completing the definition of the

[10] *Christianisme et démocratie* (New York, 1943), translated by
Doris C. Anson as *Christianity and Democracy* (New York, 1944), pp.
25, 27.
[11] *Ibid.*, p. 31.

democratic society he had projected in his earlier writings. In
Man and the State he finally reconciled his previous insistence on authority with his subsequent belief in popular
government. A democratic ruler, he surmised, in trying to
rise above the passions of the moment, might well incur "the
disfavor of the people"—yet such a leader could still be act-
ing "in communion with the people, in the truest sense of
this expression." And if he were "a great ruler," he might
"perhaps convert that disfavor into a renewed and more profound trust." Here, as throughout Maritain's political and
social writings, the emphasis was on the mutual responsibility
between rulers and ruled, and of each individual to his fellow
citizens. And—as at the very start of his ideological inquiry—
the key term was "pluralism," to which he now added the
"personalist" note that a younger Catholic thinker, Emmanuel Mounier, had in the meantime brought into general
currency.[12]

When these final lectures were delivered, Maritain had become a stranger in his own country. The high tide of his influence in France had been suddenly and brutally interrupted
by an involuntary exile that was gradually to extend into two
decades of absence from home and a growing alienation from
the French intellectual scene.

On the eve of the Second World War, Maritain's position
in France seemed assured: to his earlier role as the greatest
contemporary interpreter of St. Thomas, he had added that
of a militant spokesman for social Catholicism. Abroad, he
was becoming almost equally famous. He had lectured
throughout Europe and in Canada and South America as
well. He had made three lecture trips to the United States.
On a fourth such journey events overtook him: the fall of
France left him stranded in the country that was to become
his second home.

Here he adjusted rapidly to his new surroundings. He

[12] *Man and the State* (Chicago, 1951), pp. 109, 137. In this case
the English version is the original.

taught at Columbia and at Princeton. Together with Raïssa he made his apartment in Greenwich Village an intellectual and social haven for others similarly exiled from France. Toward his own country his attitude was unequivocal: he had refused to back Franco in 1936; he extended the same refusal to Pétain in 1940. Maritain's wartime writings were a series of appeals to his countrymen to stand fast for the values of liberty and humanity; they were briefer, simpler, more direct than what came before and after. Although he never formally rallied to De Gaulle, Maritain's Free French sympathies were amply apparent. It was only natural that after the Liberation the General should have called on him for assistance in the task of rebuilding the moral confidence of his countrymen. De Gaulle asked Maritain to go to Rome as ambassador to the Vatican, and the philosopher—now sixty-two—felt obliged to accept.

This second exile (and this time self-imposed) lasted until 1948. There followed a third and more puzzling period of life abroad. On resigning his embassy—having done what public duty seemed to demand—Maritain did not return to France to resume his old life as a teacher and writer which had been interrupted for nearly a decade. He went instead to the United States, to take up for five years a professorship at Princeton and then to live in retirement in New York. Not until the death of his wife at the end of 1960 did he resolve to go back to France. And when he did so, it was as an old man, with "a great thirst for silence," come home not for a public role but to prepare himself for death.[18]

By 1961, Maritain's ideological phase was far behind him. He now spoke of his political and social writings as though they were past history. He had no wish to return to the theater of intellectual encounter. France's old intelligentsia pleased him "less than ever"; the young intelligentsia of the new society, which was closer to the world of reality and of manual labor, did not need him as a guide. In these young

[18] Preface to Henry Bars, *La politique selon Jacques Maritain* (Paris, 1961), p. 13.

people, whose way of thinking struck him as "healthier and better ventilated" than that of their immediate forebears, Maritain vested his hopes for the future of Thomism in France.[14] As for himself, he had come full circle: he had returned to the longing for quiet contemplation that had first led him into the Church more than half a century ago.

No doubt we can find in Maritain's disgust with the intellectuals who were holding the front of the stage—the "mandarinate" of the immediate postwar years—a clue to his reluctance to go home in 1948. A France in which Jean-Paul Sartre was the philosophical star could scarcely be to Maritain's liking. Under the influence of writers close to Sartre, Marxism had become the standard pattern of thought for the segment of the French intelligentsia that considered itself ideologically advanced: to Maritain Marxism was an atheist counterfeit of the eternal criteria for a just society. Similarly Sartre and his school had popularized (while misunderstanding them) the works of Freud on French soil: Maritain saw in psychoanalytic theory no more than a fragment of the truth, "a punishment inflicted upon the pride of that conceited, pharisaic personality, which rationalism had built up as an end supreme in itself."[15] By 1948, French Catholics had already absorbed what Maritain had to teach them. The others were not prepared to listen.

In America the situation was reversed. Here the intellectual revival among Catholics had just begun. And there were few of the native-born who could hold their own in an exchange with the irreligious. The Church in the United States desperately needed a spokesman like Maritain. Although the American hierarchy pretended most of the time that he did not exist, the growing reform element among the clergy and laity were eager for his message. Just at the time that Maritain was being neglected in France, he was becoming in-

[14] *Ibid.*, pp. 10–11, 14.
[15] *Scholasticism and Politics*, Image edition (Garden City, N.Y., 1960), p. 158. These lectures were originally delivered in English in the United States in 1938.

tensely relevant in the United States. The wisdom of his choice of where to spend the last decade of his active life became apparent only after his return to his own country. In the early 1960's the response of American Catholics to Pope John and the Vatican Council vindicated Maritain's efforts in his final years of teaching.

III. The Spiritual Journey of Gabriel Marcel

Born in 1889 and seven years younger than Maritain, Gabriel Marcel from the start seemed to live in a different mental universe. Where Maritain prized clear formulations, Marcel saw in words and in reasoning no more than the external trappings of the mysteries of being. While Maritain very early in life discovered his philosophical master, Marcel groped his way for two decades among contradictory influences and inspirations. The fact that both found a spiritual home in Catholicism was evidence in itself of the permissive range within the French Church. Marcel was anything but a Thomist. Most frequently he is referred to as an existentialist, but the label is not particularly helpful in assessing his social thought. Although he was the first French writer to use the term—as early as 1925—he was not simply the disciple of Karl Jaspers, the man who transplanted a German doctrine to French soil, that he has sometimes been called. By the time he read Jaspers, Marcel had already arrived at his own highly personal philosophy of existence.[16] By that time, by the opening of the 1930's, his philosophical and religious course had finally been set.

For Marcel the central metaphors of his endeavor were "search" or "journey"—or better still, the response to a "call." Born, like Maritain, of a prominent and relatively prosperous family, Marcel experienced even earlier than he had a sense of desolation at the mental world within which he was con-

---

[16] Seymour Cain, *Gabriel Marcel* (London, 1963), pp. 29–30; Paul Ricoeur, *Gabriel Marcel et Karl Jaspers* (Paris, 1947), pp. 435–436.

fined. His childhood was inordinately protected; his family
took enormous care over his schooling, and the little Gabriel
had no recourse but to be the model student they expected
of him. His father, who held the rank of Councilor of State
and was later administrator of France's museums, was a man
of disciplined mind and impressive cultural equipment. "Im-
bued with the ideas of Taine, Spencer and Renan, his position was that of the late nineteenth-century agnostics; acutely
and gratefully aware of all that . . . art owes to Catholicism,
he regarded Catholic thought itself as obsolete and tainted
with absurd superstitions." The elder Marcel was a widower.
His deceased wife's sister, who brought the boy up, although
Jewish by origin, had converted to an ultra-liberal form of
Protestantism. In his conscious mind, the boy Gabriel loved
and respected his father and his aunt. Deeper down, he felt
that he lived in a "desert universe," and even as a child he
was haunted by unexpressed thoughts about death.[17]

His "whole childhood" and, he suspected, his "whole life"
had been overshadowed by his mother's death when he was
four years old. This figure, whom he scarcely remembered,
"remained . . . mysteriously . . . present" to him. In the
boy's secret cult of his mother's memory lay the origin of his
later emphasis on fidelity—on a loyalty extending beyond the
grave. It was also responsible for his sense of a "hidden
polarity between the seen and the unseen" and for his interest
in meta-psychic experiments and in extra-sensory perception.[18]

At the age of eight Marcel went to Stockholm, where his
father had been appointed French minister. Although his
stay in Sweden was only brief, it revealed to him that other
ways of life were possible besides the austere intellectualism
of his home, and it opened vistas on the adventurous and the
exotic. From this point on, Marcel was to have a passion for
travel; his longing to discover and to explore was of a

---

[17] Gabriel Marcel, "Regard en arrière," *Existentialisme chrétien:
Gabriel Marcel*, edited by Étienne Gilson (Paris, 1947), translated as
"An Essay in Autobiography" by Manya Harari, *The Philosophy of
Existence* (London, 1948), pp. 81–82.
[18] *Ibid.*, pp. 83–84.

Proustian intensity. And when he finally came to read Proust himself, it was with the sharp emotion of discovering an abiding affinity between the novelist's search for a lost past and his own quest for a world beyond that of everyday things to which the memory of his mother beckoned him.

Perhaps it was inevitable that such a boy should become a philosopher—but of a very special and unsystematic variety. He might also have been a musician or an imaginative writer. Music was one expression of the infinite that Marcel cultivated as a gifted amateur; the drama was another. In the dialogue of the stage he found the ideal vehicle for the exchange between the "I" and the "thou" which was central to his view of human relations. As a child playing in the Parc Monceau or in the gardens along the Champs-Elysées, Marcel, lonely and constrained, had invented imaginary characters to people his solitude. "The richness of his thought on the relations between himself and another" may have been "born of this suffering at an isolation too heavy for a child's heart to bear."[19] As a man in his mid-twenties, chance handed Marcel an opportunity to touch the lives of others under tragic circumstances. On the outbreak of the war, too frail for combat service, Marcel found appropriate employment as head of the information service organized by the Red Cross. Here his job was to deal with the constant requests for news of soldiers listed as missing in action. Every day he "received personal visits from the unfortunate relatives who implored" him to find out what he could; "so that in the end every index card" became "a heart-rending personal appeal."[20]

The war was the first great shock to Marcel's life. It broke up the security of the grand bourgeois universe within which he had earlier been both protected and confined. It was responsible for a new tone of anguish in the *Metaphysical Journal* to which he was confiding his search for ultimate

[19] M.-M. Davy, *Un philosophe itinérant: Gabriel Marcel* (Paris, 1959), p. 20.
[20] "Essay in Autobiography," p. 90.

reality. At the same time he was grateful for the state of illusion in which he had earlier lived, since it had enabled him to get over the most difficult part of his apprenticeship as a philosopher.

By 1910—at the almost unbelievably early age of twenty—Marcel had passed the agrégation in philosophy, but he never went on to the doctorate or to become a university professor. Instead he taught from time to time at various lycées, as inclination or necessity dictated. Just after the war he married into a leading Protestant family. Although his wife was a woman of talent to whom he was totally devoted, the idea of conversion to her faith never occurred to him. The contrary happened: three years before her death in 1947, she followed him into the Catholic Church. Their life together displayed the harmony that Marcel brought to all his concerns. A Parisian by birth, but far from convinced of the virtues of a great city, he finally found the quarter that suited him, between the Luxembourg and the Sorbonne. He also bought a small château near the Dordogne, which served as his refuge during the Vichy era. A luminous conversationalist, widely read and on terms of easy familiarity with the arts, going almost nightly to the theater, such was this worldly philosopher whose technical specialty was ontology and whose aspiration was for the infinite.[21]

His philosophical antecendents similarly put him into no clear category. First he had turned his attention to the Romantics—especially to Coleridge and Schelling—then to Americans like Josiah Royce and William James and William Ernest Hocking. Quite predictably he followed Bergson's lectures "with passionate interest," and he remained faithful throughout his life to the inspiration Bergson had given him. But his debt to American philosophy was primary. It enabled him to shake himself clear of German abstractions and more particularly of the "idealism based on the impersonal or the

[21] Davy, *Un philosophe itinérant*, pp. 12–14, 20–24, 41, 50.

immanent" which became his bête noire.[22] In the Americans he discovered that pragmatism and a feeling for transcendence—which conventional academic philosophy kept apart —could live comfortably together. He was searching for a kind of understanding which would be both transcendent and tangible; and such a conjunction, he gradually realized, could come only through an intense focus on the interpersonal. This was what he meant when he gave one of his essays the extraordinary title "Position of and Concrete Approaches to the Ontological Mystery."

Marcel preferred to think of himself as a Christian Socratic. He liked to make explorations rather than to propound final answers. His *Metaphysical Journal* did not appear in print until he was in his late thirties. He waited another eight years before publishing his second major philosophical work, *Being and Having*, in 1935. Meantime he had become a Catholic. Yet in a sense he had been a believer all along. His concern for fidelity, for trust, for hope, for witness and promise and natural piety had led him effortlessly toward the Church. One day he received a friendly letter from François Mauriac who asked him quite simply: "Why aren't you one of us?"—to which he reacted, equally simply, with the realization that it was among the Catholics that he belonged.[23] Once more, as so often in his life, he responded to a call. His conversion changed his definition of his métier scarcely at all. He became in no sense a polemicist or an official apologist for the Church. He had always resisted and continued to detest the theatrical attitude toward religion— the giddy sense of a desperate wager—characteristic of Pascal or of so many contemporary converts. Marcel remained a

[22] Gabriel Marcel, *Homo Viator: Prolégomènes à une métaphysique de l'espérance* (Paris, 1945), translated by Emma Craufurd as *Homo Viator: Introduction to a Metaphysic of Hope* (London, 1951), p. 137; on Marcel's debt to American thought, see the lectures he gave at Harvard in 1961: *The Existential Background of Human Dignity* (Cambridge, Mass., 1963), pp. 1–3.

[23] Davy, *Un philosophe itinérant*, pp. 42–43, 48.

philosopher writing primarily for the irreligious and deeply
embedded in the secular world.

If Marcel arrived only slowly at his articulate philosophy,
he came more slowly still to the formulation of his social
thought. In this realm, according to his own account, the
key date was the year 1936. But the events of what in retrospect was to appear the decisive spring and summer in the
advent of the Second World War impinged on him with less
explosive force than in the case of Maritain or Bernanos.
They entailed no radical revision of his earlier convictions.
He did not feel it necessary to take sides in the Spanish Civil
War; on the contrary, he believed it wrong for a Frenchman
(as an outsider) to do so. The events of 1936 confirmed,
rather, the sense that had been growing on him of a "broken
world"—which was the title of a play he had written three
years earlier. Such a world was like a watch that had ceased
to tell time, or a heart that had stopped beating. Externally
things went on as before; within, the human soul was
empty.[24]
In 1936, what impressed Marcel most of all was not the
Spanish Civil War or the Popular Front government of
Léon Blum—which he dismissed as a "failure"—but the
pervasive "spirit of surrender . . . concealed . . . by an
anti-Fascist rhetoric in which no clear intelligence could place
any trust."[25] The defeat of 1940 turned these forebodings
into bitter reality. Like the good Frenchman he was—and for
all his foreign travel Marcel was strictly faithful to his national heritage—he suffered profoundly from the distress and
humiliation of his country. Yet in another sense the experience of German occupation gave Marcel's philosophy a
topical relevance that it had never had before. In this context, themes that might once have seemed the disembodied
musings of a gentle spirit took on an anguished urgency. It
is significant that the first of Marcel's books to deal even

[24] Cain, *Marcel*, pp. 60–61.
[25] *Existential Background of Human Dignity*, pp. 114–115.

tangentially with current problems was a collection of his essays and lectures dating from the years of occupation. Its title, *Homo Viator*—"man the voyager"—sounded a note that was to recur throughout his later thought; its contents stressed the themes of exile, of separation, of captivity, and of hope—above all, of hope—which his audience or his readers did not need to be told how to interpret.[26]

The publication of only one of these wartime essays was actually forbidden by the Vichy censor. In this case the reason was quite apparent: in distinguishing between the concepts of "obedience" and "fidelity," Marcel had come too close to a direct attack on the cult of "systematic docility" that Pétain's government was fostering. Most of the time he restricted his critique to less transparent abstractions. Yet even in discussing a theme ostensibly as inoffensive as "a phenomenology and a metaphysic of hope," Marcel deftly slipped in a series of unmistakable references to his countrymen's current perplexities. A quasi-theological demarcation of the confines of hope and despair imperceptibly passed over into quiet defiance of the Vichy orthodoxy of passive acceptance. "Must not the true believer," Marcel innocently inquired, "be ready to accept the death and ruin of his dear ones, the temporal destruction of his country, as possibilities against which it is forbidden to rebel? . . . If these things come about, must he not be ready to adore the divine will in them?" Having put the matter in terms of a situation at the limits of human endurance, Marcel could readily reject the bien-pensant affirmative answer and proceed to a condemnation of the "softening processes" that made such a chain of reasoning possible. And two paragraphs later he was ready to go over to the counterattack:

> Here I take the example . . . of the patriot who refuses to despair of the liberation of his native land. . . . Even if he recognises that there is no chance that he will himself witness the hoped-for liberation, . . . he refuses

26 Cain, *Marcel*, p. 75.

with all his being to admit that the darkness which has fallen upon his country can be enduring. . . . Still more: it is not enough to say that he cannot believe in the death of his country, the truth is much more that he does not even consider he has *the right* to believe in it, and that it would seem to him that he was committing a real act of treason in admitting this possibility.[27]

When he reissued these essays almost two decades later, Marcel found that the passage of time and the "radical transformation of the historical context" had not brought much change in his "general perspectives." Yet his tone had become more somber. He now believed that the results of the second war had been even worse than he had feared.[28] Most pointedly, he saw contemporary life as "dehumanized" on a frightening scale.

His anxieties about his own era Marcel had conveyed in another series of informal essays entitled *Men against Humanity*, which he had published in 1951. Now at last applied to contemporary society, Marcel's ideas conformed no better to conventional demarcations than they had while they remained on the level of philosophical speculation. His temperamental reactions were conservative: he was unimpressed with the ideology of the Resistance and appalled at the injustices committed in the purge of suspected collaborationists; he doubted whether wars of colonial repression were as iniquitous as most intellectuals thought; he distrusted the dominance of a technology that he believed could *"end only in despair."*[29] At the same time he coupled these counsels of prudence with other ideological stands ordinarily associated with the French Left: he spoke out uneqivocally against all forms of racial or religious intolerance, and he found *"anything"*—even "capitulation"—preferable to the universal havoc of thermonuclear war.[30]

[27] *Homo Viator* (English translation), pp. 47–48, 125.
[28] Preface to new edition of *Homo Viator* (Paris, 1962), pp. i–ii.
[29] *Men against Humanity*, pp. 23–25, 71, 80–83, 113, 184–185.
[30] Preface to new edition of *Homo Viator*, p. i.

Such apparent inconsistencies troubled Marcel not at all. He was unconcerned about whether a particular attitude he adopted might give temporary comfort to one or another of the contestants in his country's ideological battles. What did concern him was to keep from being the "vassal" of any organized political allegiance—and by the same token to resist "the spirit of abstraction" which he found responsible for the violence in the contemporary world. Against the spirit of abstraction, Marcel pitted the force of love. His plea was for a restoration of simple human values—for the introduction of a social and political order which would rescue "the greatest number of beings possible" from a state of mass "abasement or alienation."[81]

Whether one called such a goal conservative or leftist was quite immaterial to him. Marcel rejected the terms as the source of "frightful confusion,"[82] although in practice he usually came down on the conservative side. His social philosophy, however fragmentary and amateurish, was of a piece with his speculative writings. It sprang from grief at human distress and a longing to give meaning and depth to concrete personal relationships. In this sense it had the eternal validity to which Marcel aspired. It was also conditioned and limited by the era of its composition. Like George Orwell's 1984, for which Marcel expressed his unqualified admiration, it conveyed an atmosphere of impending catastrophe—a tone better suited to the tormented Europe of the 1940's than to the complacent Continent of two decades later.[83] The anguished, almost hysterical character of Marcel's social writings had begun to date while their author was still alive. This is one of the major problems that confronts us in

[81] *Men against Humanity*, pp. 8, 94, 117.

[82] *Homo Viator*, French edition of 1962, p. 364 (this passage is not in the translated edition).

[83] *Men against Humanity*, pp. 140, 173. Marcel returned to similar themes in *Le déclin de la sagesse* (Paris, 1954), translated by Manya Harari as *The Decline of Wisdom* (London, 1954). On Marcel's condemnation of "fanaticism," see Roger Troisfontaines, *De l'existence à l'être: la philosophie de Gabriel Marcel* (Namur, 1953), II, 131–136.

trying to assess the enduring viability of the independent
Catholic style of thought for which he stood.

IV. *"Philosophers Who Were Catholics"*

"Gabriel Marcel . . . has his Left where Maritain has his
Right and vice-versa." Thus one of the latter's most subtle
and sympathetic expositors has epitomized the difference between the two.[34] Marcel was the more permissive on matters
of faith, Maritain the more "advanced" in his social philosophy. Readers who were exhilarated by the flexibility and
openness of Marcel's speculative writings might find certain
of his political attitudes reactionary. Those who admired
Maritain's ideological stands were frequently repelled by
his uncompromising adherence to the Thomist method. At
one time or other both combated the works of the modern
world, but from the 1930's on, Maritain became more at
home in it, while Marcel grew less reconciled to mass industrial society.

One winter they saw a great deal of each other at the
Versailles home of a fellow convert, Charles du Bos. But
the experience failed to bring them intellectually closer together. Maritain, after trying in vain to persuade Marcel of
the merits of Thomism, simply refrained from mentioning
him in his own writings. Marcel referred periodically to
Maritain, and usually in disparaging terms. On one occasion
he went so far as to call him a "fanatic."[35] Apparently the
temperamental difference between the two was too great to be
bridged. One had been a philosophical prodigy, who at the
age of thirty had done battle with the great Bergson himself: the other had spent nearly two decades struggling toward the light. One was rigorous in his use of language and
unsparing toward his readers: the other wrote in a relaxed,

---

[34] Bars, *Maritain en notre temps*, p. 100.
[35] *Existential Background of Human Dignity*, pp. 80–81; *Les hommes
contre l'humain*, p. 112 (this passage is omitted from the English
translation).

conversational style. One cultivated a severe intellectualism: the other distrusted the usual paths of the intellect and searched out epiphanies and vistas on the infinite. One was the leading spokesman of the most prestigious variety of Catholic thought: the other held his religious faith half veiled within a texture of discourse to which a nonbeliever might well subscribe.

The listing of contrasts between Maritain and Marcel could be extended further. Enough has already been said to suggest why they remained so far apart. Yet if we shift our focus from their philosophical differences and direct it toward human sympathies and life styles, a new series of parallels—and this time suggesting a latent understanding—begins to emerge. Both Maritain and Marcel came of mixed religious backgrounds; in both cases a liberal Protestant influence entered through the woman responsible for the boy's upbringing; in both cases there was also a Jewish aspect which each took pains to emphasize—Marcel, the antecedents of his mother, Maritain, the parentage of his wife. In this matter of origins, it is notable that each came to Catholicism quite innocent of any previous family association with the Church: each made a radically free choice. Both had been brought up by a strong-willed and intelligent woman; both selected a remarkable wife; both marriages were unusually close.

Perhaps one can do no more with such parallels than to align them in bare outline. A number of emotional affinities readily spring to mind. The high valuation both Maritain and Marcel put on warm personal relations is one. The kindness with which they reached out to near-strangers is another. Rather surprisingly, in view of Maritain's intellectualism and Marcel's absorption with human anguish and the dread of death, both were notable for their cheerfulness of manner. One is tempted to refer to them as merry philosophers. Although they cherished their own country, they were quite at home abroad. Each was an enthusiastic traveler, and each had ties to the United States that were far closer and more

understanding than was usual with Frenchmen of their
generation.

Even from the more strictly philosophical standpoint,
Maritain and Marcel had in common a distaste for both
idealism and positivism in their familiar late nineteenth-
century forms. Both were equally opposed to the tradition of
Descartes. Indeed, they can be thought of as offering the
first examples of French thinkers of our time to work quite
outside the tradition of Cartesian classicism. Bergson had
earlier tried to found a non-Cartesian school of philosophy—
but his prose had remained in the French classic mold.
Bergson wrote graceful and skillfully organized books. Maritain and Marcel published collections of essays. In the case
of the latter, the informal cast of his thought was thoroughly
consonant with the essay form. In Maritain's case, the
jumbled heterogeneity of his writings is more surprising: his
individual books overlap and repeat each other endlessly.
If a man whose mental processes were as disciplined as
Maritain's could take so little care with the ordering of his
literary production, there arises a basic question as to the
nature and applicability of such thought in our own time.

Neither Marcel nor Maritain considered himself a *Catholic*
philosopher—that is, in the sense of an official expositor of
the teachings of the Church. Even the latter, although he
stood for a way of thought to which Leo XIII had given
Papal endorsement, remained primarily in a secular context.
After all, when he settled in the United States, it was at
Princeton rather than a Catholic university that he chose
to teach. Both, then, could more properly be described as
"philosophers who were Catholics." And as such, their life
situation was of necessity ambiguous. They lived enmeshed
in a society to whose central values they were radically opposed. They wrote in large part for an audience which
could neither share nor even understand their religious beliefs. Maritain offered an intellectual method which the
majority of his readers refused to embrace; Marcel's method—
if such it can be called—was too personal and elusive to be

transmitted to others. Hence of necessity they wrote in frag-
ments. They offered evocations and possibilities rather than
a full exposition of an alternative way of life and of thought.
In the 1930's and 1940's they had shown their countrymen
a way out of an intellectual and moral impasse. At that
point only a few had been prepared to follow them. A quarter
century later, when they were old and tired, their words
found an echo in Rome itself. But this was in a very different
historical context and on the level of applied social philosophy rather than of abstract thought.

As a formal philosopher, Maritain had been acutely aware
of the incomplete and tentative nature of his own writings.
He had known that he would never write a summa; that task
had been performed once and for all by his master Aquinas.
Nor did he believe he lived in an era whose philosophy bore
the stamp of classical confidence. If one was looking for *that,*
one might as well go back to Descartes—and this was the
last thing Maritain would have urged on his readers. Superficially regarded, Maritain's lifelong hostility to the Cartesian
tradition sounds odd; the two seem to have in common a
schematic order and a penchant for lapidary formulations.
But in Maritain's case the intellectualism was no more than
the scaffolding of his thought; in Descartes it was the thought
itself. What the former could never forgive Cartesianism was
its radical separation of mind and body—of the process of
thinking from the world of external reality. And he conceived his own role less as that of a systematizer or mod-
ernizer of Thomism than as that of a liberator of philosophy
from the deadening influence of Cartesian categories. He
thought of himself as a realist whose work was necessarily
changing and growing under the pressure of historical actuality—a man ceaselessly rethinking the eternal verities in
terms of a consciousness of time and its fluctuations that
was thoroughly contemporary.[86]

All the above is almost equally applicable to Marcel. In
this final guise of philosophers embedded in the history of

[86] Bars, *Maritain en notre temps,* pp. 20–22.

their own time and yearning to unite metaphysical certainty
with a down-to-earth awareness of actual human relationships, Maritain and Marcel pushed one stage further the
revolution in French thought that Bergson had projected;
they gave twentieth-century anti-Cartesianism a new concreteness, and they did not hesitate to apply it to specific
historical situations. In *this* perspective, the fragmentary
character of their thought had its unsuspected advantages:
it meant that these philosophers "who were Catholics" could
not be dismissed as mere dogmatists; it left their readers free
to make a choice among the different aspects of their work.
In their contrasting personal styles, Maritain and Marcel had
set out in search of an intellectual method: what they had
found had been a series of ethical formulations which spoke
to the condition of a wide variety of men.

By the end of the 1950's these moral injunctions were
again becoming of topical relevance. Although their methodol-
ogies had begun to look quaint, Maritain and Marcel's words
of paternal counsel were being taken up not only in Rome
but still more widely among those Catholics and non-Catholics, both in France and abroad, who had become quite suddenly conscious of the ethical goals they held in common.

v. *Toward the Council*

Most of the time circumstances and temperament had kept
Maritain and Marcel apart. On at least one occasion, however, they had been aligned together. In 1934—the year of
the February riots in front of the Chamber of Deputies, the
year that began France's half decade of intense ideological
strife—they had joined fifty other Catholic intellectuals in
signing a manifesto entitled *Pour le bien commun*, "for the
common good." An appeal to the conscience of Christians,
this document laid down their responsibilities in face of the
unprecedented circumstances of the moment. The political
order it defined was pluralist, the social order one inspired

by the encyclicals of Leo XIII and Pius XI. On basic principles such as these, Maritain and Marcel saw alike. They were also in agreement in giving to the word "liberty" the broadest interpretation consonant with the Catholic faith— an understanding of the concept of religious freedom which was to receive official endorsement at the Second Vatican Council in 1965.

Their approach to the common needs and aspirations of humanity was similarly reflected in the decisions of the Council. In 1962—the year in which that body convened— Marcel had drawn attention to the progress of the ecumenical movement as one of the very few aspects of the contemporary world in which he could rejoice.[87] The previous year Maritain had condemned once again anti-Semitism in all its forms. Earlier in his career Maritain had repeatedly discussed the historical sufferings of the Jewish people: ever mindful of his wife's religious origins, he had urged on his fellow Christians an attitude of cordial and sympathetic understanding. The "racial" persecutions of the Nazi era converted this gentle sympathy into passionate indignation. In the years immediately preceding the Second World War and during the war itself, Maritain again and again expressed his moral solidarity with the Jews. Yet he still felt that he had not done enough. On returning to France in 1961, he stressed the need of a "serious examination of conscience" among Catholics on the entire subject of anti-Semitism, and he noted with approval the preparatory steps that Pope John XXIII had already taken in purging the Church's liturgy and teaching of anti-Semitic residues. "Of Israel," Maritain concluded, "we shall never speak with sufficient thoughtfulness and tenderness. . . . There is a certain exquisite refinement of sensibility and spiritual delicacy which is found only among the chosen people. . . . In comparison with the Jews, we shall always remain half-civilized barbarians."[88]

[87] Preface to new edition of *Homo Viator*, p. ii.
[88] Preface to Bars, *La politique selon Jacques Maritain*, pp. 8–9. In 1965 Maritain published his collected writings on the Jews (dating back to 1926) under the title *Le mystère d'Israël et autres essais*.

At the Council, echoes of the writings of Maritain and
Marcel—on freedom, on ecumenicism, on the Jews—were
omnipresent, even when the names of the French philosophers were not specifically cited. And from his contemplative
retreat in southern France, Maritain rejoiced at what had
occurred. He gave thanks to heaven that the "idea of freedom
—of that freedom to which man aspires with what is most
profound in his being, and which is one of the privileges of
the spirit—" had been "recognized and put in a place of honor
among the great directing ideas of Christian wisdom," and
that along with it the dignity of the human person had been
similarly consecrated. He was grateful for the vigorous fashion in which the Church now enjoined an attitude of
brotherhood toward non-Catholic Christians, toward those
of other religions, and even toward atheists. From the
theological standpoint, he regretted that alongside the work
of the Council there had sprung up a new version of doctrinal Modernism—a latitudinarian interpretation of dogma
which made the innovations of the early part of the century
look mild indeed. Yet his dominant impression was that the
Church had at last transcended the Counter-Reformation—
that its Age of the Baroque had come to an end.[89]

There was another Frenchman, younger than Maritain
and Marcel, whose memory was also in people's minds as the
progressive wing among the assembled Church fathers began
to gather confidence in its strength—Emmanuel Mounier,
the founder of "personalism" and of the review *Esprit*. Born
in 1905—the same year as Jean-Paul Sartre—Mounier was
even less than he an academic philosopher. Bergson's generation of philosophers had consisted almost exclusively of universitaires; in the next generation Maritain and Marcel had
taught philosophy even though they had passed the greater
part of their mature lives outside the French educational
system; with Mounier—who was of an age to be Bergson's
grandchild—there was no question of philosophy as an academic discipline. His purpose, rather, was to bring philo-

[89] *Le paysan de la Garonne* (Paris, 1966), pp. 9–11, 13, 16.

sophical inquiry to bear on the urgent social questions of
his own time. And it was with this aim that in 1932, at the
age of twenty-seven, he founded *Esprit*, which until his premature death in 1950 served as the most persuasive voice of
the French Catholic Left.

Quite consciously taking up the legacy of Péguy, Mounier
wrote like his master abundantly and without system. And
like Péguy, he ranks more as a public "educator," or as the
conscience of his generation, than as a figure in the formal
history of philosophy; similarly, his own writing was virtually
indistinguishable from the review he directed, and he inspired
a heartfelt loyalty among those who worked with him. This
close sense of an équipe of like-minded spirits was implicit in
his philosphy: he thought of personalism as a reawakening
of the human personality through participation in a living
community.

Although Mounier began with the individual personality
as the base point of his reflections, it was always at the social
group beyond the individual that he aimed. Like Marcel, he
was appalled by the dehumanization of industrial society; in
common with Maritain, he strove to make a reality of the
teaching in the Gospels. The way he chose to do so was more
revolutionary by far: Mounier never wavered in his hostility
to the capitalist order, and he was unsparing in his criticism
of parliamentary democracy and bourgeois values.

In the 1930's, such an attitude, however offensive to the
bien-pensants, gave rise to no serious problems of conscience.
After the war—and after a spell in Vichy's prisons—when
Mounier revived *Esprit*, he faced a radically altered ideological landscape; the strength of organized Communism presented him with a desperate dilemma. On the one hand, he
believed it essential to maintain contact with the French
working classes; at the same time he knew that the Communist party had become the only political body whose efficacy they recognized. Hence Mounier refused to adopt a
conventional anti-Communist stand; he also disdained to remain silent when Communist outrages in Eastern Europe

forced themselves on his attention. At almost any cost he
wanted to keep up a dialogue with the spokesmen of French
Communism—but not at the price of sacrificing his central
principle of respect for the human personality. In Mounier's
last years—and with the Cold War at its height—*Esprit*
was very nearly alone among publicly committed French
intellectual groupings in avoiding enrollment in the ideological camp of the embattled West while simultaneously
eschewing the line of the communisants.[40]

A similar dilemma faced the most militant wing of the
socially-conscious clergy. In 1944 Cardinal Suhard, Archbishop of Paris, had authorized the formation of a Mission of
Paris to evangelize the dechristianized workers of the capital
and its industrial suburbs. At first the young priests who
volunteered for service among the poor concentrated their
attention on pastoral activity and the establishment of community centers for mutual help. Such activities, they soon
found, while bringing comfort and support to derelicts of the
"sub-proletariat" and to women and children, failed to reach
the mass of the workers. To gain the confidence of working-
men themselves, the priests saw no alternative to going into
the factories and taking up manual labor; only by adopting
the way of life of French workers could they persuade men
who had grown up to regard the clergy as class enemies of
the genuineness of their commitment to social change. In
1946, a handful of priests were authorized to work in the factories of the Paris area; five years later their number
(throughout France) had risen to ninety.

Then the difficulties began. In the meantime Cardinal
Suhard had died, and his successor, Cardinal Feltin, although he continued the worker-priest experiment, was more
cautious and skeptical than his predecessor; the same was

---

[40] On the intellectual and moral legacy of Mounier, see the special
issue of *Esprit*, XVIII (December 1950), more particularly the articles
by Jean-Marie Domenach, François Goguel, and Paul Ricoeur. For an
over-all assessment of Mounier as a political thinker, see Roy Pierce,
Contemporary French Political Thought (London and New York,
1966), Chapter 3.

true of the other members of the French episcopate who were beginning to have worker-priests under their jurisdiction. And increasingly there was ground for doubt: working a full day at heavy manual labor, the priests were finding it difficult to keep up their normal religious observances; they were also undergoing a change of mentality themselves, as their working-class friendships and style of life bred in them a strong sense of solidarity with their new associates; unschooled in modern social theory of any sort, a number of them embraced a crude and sentimental variety of Marxism. The hierarchy could tolerate members of their clergy co-operating with Communist militants in Communist-dominated trade unions; they drew the line at worker-priest participation in Communist-led political demonstrations.

This was what happened in 1952 when two of them were arrested by the police. Shortly thereafter—and quite predictably—the Vatican intervened. In the previous years complaints about the worker-priests from conservative French Catholics had been pouring into Rome, which in 1951 had forbidden their further recruitment. Two years later, the Vatican decided that the worker-priest experiment had gotten out of hand and that the French episcopate had proved unable to control it. In July a new nuncio arrived in Paris bringing instructions to suspend the training and activities of the worker-priests. A public outcry ensued: both progressive Catholics, who had followed the experiment with growing sympathy, and the hierarchy itself attributed the hostility of the Curia to the shortsightedness of Italians unfamiliar with the real situation of Catholicism in France. In November, three out of the six French cardinals, including Feltin of Paris, went to Rome to plead with Pius XII. They received only meager satisfaction: the Pope agreed to permit the resumption of the experiment on a reduced scale, but on what the French regarded as the key question—whether the priests would be allowed to be in the factories for the full working day—Pius XII and his advisers were adamant; they limited manual labor to three hours, which in the view of the French was insufficient to give the priests a truly working-class character.[41]

The altercation between Rome and France sputtered along for another half decade until in 1959 the activities of the worker-priests were halted entirely. The irony of the whole succession of events was that the Pope under whose auspices the final ban was issued—John XXIII—was the same Angelo Roncalli who as nuncio in France from 1944 to 1953 had shown an open-minded appreciation of what the worker-priests were trying to accomplish, and whose brief pontificate was to steer Catholicism as a whole toward the positions that the reformers within the French Church had long been advocating. The future Pope John had received a belated political education in France: during the immediate postwar years, when he was serving in Paris in the corresponding capacity to that of Maritain in Rome, he had witnessed the revival of democratic political life in a context that was militantly leftist; his experience of cooperation between Catholic leaders and Socialists in France in the late 1940's prepared him for the understanding attitude he adopted as Pope toward the "opening to the Left" in Italian politics a decade and a half later.[42]

Despite their disappointment in the case of the worker-priests, the progressive wing of French Catholics had good reason to take comfort from the pontificate of John. His great encyclicals—*Mater et Magister* of 1961, *Pacem in Terris* of 1963—and the Council he summoned in the months between the two vindicated nearly everything the French had stood for over the past generation. And by the same token the message of Pope John and the Council began to resolve the

[41] On the worker-priests, contrast the judicious and moderately critical tone of Dansette's *Destin du catholicisme français*, Chapters 3–6, with the whole-hearted endorsement (including a few misstatements of fact) in the influential novel by Gilbert Cesbron, *Les saints vont en enfer* (Paris, 1952), translated by John Russell as *Saints in Hell* (London, 1953).

[42] E. E. Y. Hales, *Pope John and His Revolution* (Garden City, N.Y., 1965), pp. 175–176.

dilemma with which Mounier had been contending at the time of his death and which had brought the worker-priests to disaster.[48] By the 1960's the Cold War in Europe had spent its force; the Communists were shedding their dogmatism; the old ideological hatreds were losing their virulence. In the new France that was emerging it was possible at last for Catholics and unbelievers, Marxists and liberal democrats, to take up once more—and under vastly more favorable circumstances than in the past—their eternal dialogue on the human condition.

[48] See Marcel David, "Catholicisme et action syndicale ouvière," *Forces religieuses et attitudes politiques dans la France contemporaine* (Cahiers de la Fondation Nationale des Sciences Politiques, No. 130), edited by René Rémond (Paris, 1965), pp. 177–201, and Jean-Marie Domenach and Robert de Montvalon, *The Catholic Avant-Garde* (New York, 1967). In 1966 Pope Paul VI permitted the resumption—under close supervision—of the worker-priest experiment.

CHAPTER

4

The Quest
for Heroism

"THERE is nothing man desires more than a heroic life:
there is nothing less common to men than heroism.
. . . Is a heroic humanism possible?"[1] Such were the reflections that a reading of André Malraux had prompted in
Jacques Maritain. In the new tones that were coming to
dominate the novel of the 1930's, Maritain had caught an
echo of his own concerns. A heightened sense of tragedy, a
longing for heroic endeavor, were bringing the spiritual world
of imaginative writers closer to that of the Catholics, even
in the case of novelists who prided themselves on their uncompromising denial of God. Over the new literature there
also brooded an obsession with death: to die with dignity
and in full consciousness of the end—again and again we
find a theme that suggests a latent, more tortured understanding of what Gabriel Marcel was seeking in his extended
meditation on human mortality.

The new seriousness of tone in the novel of the 1930's
was only to be expected in view of the gravity of the times.
The interlocking series of crises—economic, diplomatic,
ideological—that gripped France and the Western world

[1] *Humanisme intégral* (Paris, 1936), translated by M. R. Adamson
as *True Humanism*, 4th ed. (London, 1946), pp. xi, xiv.

could not fail to have a sobering effect. In Britain or the
United States the reaction of writers was much the same.
But in France it came with particular vehemence: in France
alone the assertion and counterassertion of opposed heroic
values took on the dimensions of an intellectual civil war.
There was also in France a sharper awareness of both history
and religion: the French writer characteristically felt obliged
to explain his own and his countrymen's place in the tumults
that De Gaulle would speak of as the "surf" of history; he
was similarly impelled to draw up his reckoning with the
religion of his ancestors—which all about him was giving
signs of a renewed vitality—and he found himself unable to
pass it by, as was common practice in Protestant lands or in
countries where a semblance of conformity gave the tone to
Catholic life. In France, history and religion were living
realities: no novelist who hoped to interest the educated
reading public could afford to neglect them.

As early as 1931 Roger Martin du Gard had written: "The
future appears laden with catastrophic events. Our fiftieth
birthday will doubtless give us a chance to see the beginning
of a vast social upheaval in Europe. What then will remain
of our . . . books? How shall we adapt ourselves, with our
cumbersome baggage, to this new order . . . ?"[2] Martin du
Gard had always been distinguished among the established
writers for his ethical scruple and sensitivity to history; he
was also slightly younger than his literary peers. Hence he
could discern rather better than they the questioning of accepted humanist—or classical—attitudes that the new temper
implied. The literary generation of which Martin du Gard
was a junior member had been inordinately confident of its
aesthetic standards (which was still another reason for the
intensity of the challenge to it). Writers such as Gide and
Valéry, however shaken by personal self-doubt, had no hesitation when it came to the values and procedures of their
chosen craft.

[2] Quoted in Réjean Robidoux, *Roger Martin du Gard et la religion*
(Paris, 1964), p. 276.

Both were humanists—as Proust had been and Claudel and all the rest. That is, they believed in the continuity of something called human nature and in the human mind or spirit as transcending and ruling the realm of corporeal matter. Such was the assumption—frequently unstated—which had linked the most diverse writers in the French classical tradition. Catholics and nonbelievers, revolutionaries and conservatives had alike trusted in the human spirit and expressed a measured confidence in the voice of reason. Frequently skeptical or disabused, they had seldom been totally despairing. They had nearly aways succeeded in detecting some inner logic in human events, and they had only rarely doubted that their fellowmen were masters of their history. After the turn of the decade, all this began to change. Where their elders had found order in the social universe, the younger writers saw incoherence—a world dominated by brute force and the illogic of a tragedy too vast for the human mind to comprehend. "Wallowing in fatality," they considered "history as irremediably absurd, delivered over not to a secret law of progress, still less to the designs of providence, but to pure contingency and chance." Hence a "fundamental pessimism," an "anguish of the individual consciousness" bound to a collective adventure without meaning or final goal"[8]— hence a literature of anxiety which bridged the gap between the Catholic intellectual renewal and the existentialist writing that lay ahead.

The note of anguish had already marked the Catholic version of existentialism which Marcel had propounded. It would appear again in the atheist existentialism of Sartre. It was manifest in the atmosphere of tension and urgency that permeated the literature of the 1930's. For what all these expressions had in common was a consciousness of moral forlornness and a desperate search for the symbolic formulas that might hold it at bay.

The revival of interest in Péguy was one sign of the new

[8] Pierre-Henri Simon, *L'homme en procès: Malraux–Sartre–Camus–Saint-Exupéry*, 3rd ed. (Neuchâtel, 1950), pp. 7–11.

temper. It was also manifest in such sharply contrasting forms as the preaching of rural anarchism in the novels of Jean Giono or the recurring theme of despair in the plays of Armand Salacrou. Sometimes it took the guise of revolutionary protest. More often it found expression in an ethic of the stern performance of duty. In this perspective, the older generation, unimpeachable as literary craftsmen, were found morally wanting: after 1930, an intense contemplation of one's own ego seemed irredeemably frivolous. Face to face with desperation, the younger writers chose heroism.

Of the new themes of the 1930's and 1940's, the quest for heroism was the most pervasive. It gave unity to a variety of strivings that to the casual observer might seem to have little in common. The heroic ideal was nothing new in French literature (there was always Corneille) or in the Western tradition as a whole; what was unusual in the years of depression and war was its simultaneous revival in all quarters of the ideological landscape. At the time, certain of the figures who loomed largest were adherents of the philo-fascist Right: in the works of Henri de Montherlant or Pierre Drieu La Rochelle the young enthusiasts of the extra-parliamentary leagues could find endorsement for their aristocratic longings and disdain for the morality of the run of mankind. Drieu La Rochelle was a casualty of the Second World War: it was only gradually that his reputation began to recover from his record of collaboration and despairing suicide. Montherlant survived the conflict and even enhanced his position with his postwar dramas in verse. Yet even in Montherlant there was a cynical undertone, a fastidious nihilism, which disqualified him as a model for the young. After the Liberation, those who emerged as the incarnations of the heroic ideal were men who had participated in or expressed their solidarity with the Resistance—Bernanos from the older generation, Malraux and Saint-Exupéry among those in their middle years—these and Martin du Gard, the diffident precursor of the roman engagé.

There was another of Martin du Gard's contemporaries who had aspired to write the great symptomatic novel of the century's second quarter. Jules Romains's *Men of Good Will* was certainly the most ambitious work of fiction of the whole era; published in twenty-seven volumes between 1932 and 1946, it aimed to present an all-inclusive panorama of French society. Yet already its opening volumes seemed curiously dated. Whatever its literary defects—and they were many— the attitude of universal benevolence that its title implied no longer suited the tormented epoch in which it appeared. Romains had tried to write of much besides heroism; but the showpiece of the entire work, the volumes on which the public pounced most eagerly, were the two of *Verdun*, published in 1938. Although widely acclaimed as the finest French novel of the late war, *Verdun* failed to convey the ghastly shock of combat: its atmosphere was of heartbroken reminiscence rather than living actuality; the heroism it depicted was of stoic suffering and not of anguished endeavor. Significantly enough, Romains never really recounted the Battle of Verdun: he wrote of preparations and excursions, of peripheral conflicts and life on the home front; the center of the tragedy eluded him.

If there was any other candidate for the great novel of the era, it was unquestionably Martin du Gard's *The Thibaults*. Yet—as we shall very shortly observe—this work, in its efforts to come to terms with the circumstances in which it was composed, suffered what its author himself regarded as irreparable damage. For there was something about the 1930's that escaped the novelists' grasp: no one matched the achievement of Marcel Proust; all blundered in one fashion or another into a blind alley from which they could find no exit. Their historical environment changed too fast; the link between their work and the events around them slipped through their fingers. All of those we shall be considering—Martin du Gard, Bernanos, Saint-Exupéry, Malraux—eventually ceased to write novels. With all of them there came a point where they could only fall silent—or live their own imaginative creations. The more attractive alternative was action—the path shown them by the leader they all respected or served,

General de Gaulle, who in the quiet of retirement was himself to become the classic memorialist of the heroic years.

1. *Roger Martin du Gard and the Unattainable Epic*

I've had three black moments in my career. . . . The first changed the whole course of my youth; the second bowled me over in my middle years; the third . . . will play the devil with my old age. . . .

The first was when the pious, provincial-minded youngster I was then found out one night, after reading the four Gospels in succession, that they were a tissue of inconsistencies. The second was when I realized that a certain poisonous fellow named Esterhazy had done a piece of dirty work known as the Dreyfus *bordereau,* and that instead of punishing the culprit the French authorities were torturing a wretched man whose only crime was to have been born a Jew. . . .

The third . . . came a week ago when the papers published the text of the ultimatum, and I saw the billiard-stroke that was being prepared for . . . at the expense of millions of lives. . . .[4]

Thus one of Roger Martin du Gard's exemplary characters vents his bitterness on the outbreak of the First World War. The enumeration of successive "black moments" sharply delineates the author's own abiding concerns—his loss of religion, as epitomized by the Modernist crisis in the Catholic Church; the thirst for justice which the Dreyfus Case had awakened among his countrymen; a hatred of war, the residue of more than four years of front-line service that in recollection seemed a meaningless void. With Martin du Gard the religious question came first in time and in personal depth; a feeling for history grew on him as one baffling

[4] Roger Martin du Gard, *Les Thibaults: L'été 1914* (Paris, 1936), translated by Stuart Gilbert as *Summer 1914* (New York, 1941), p. 592.

decade followed another; his devotion to a specific ideology
was nearly always hesitant and reserved. It is in terms of these
three types of involvement—at bottom all moral in nature—
that we can best assess his place as critic and exponent of
French public values in the years of desperation.

Roger Martin du Gard was in more than one sense a transition figure. A young recruit to the band of lively talents
which just before the First World War had gathered around
the *Nouvelle revue française,* a longtime friend and counselor
of André Gide, he could be considered both a member of
the last classic generation and a herald of the literature of
engagement to come. If his themes announced the future,
his notion of the novelist's function was old-fashioned even
among his contemporaries. Tolstoy was his master—rather
than the more "twentieth-century" Dostoyevsky—and he
twice tried to write an "epic" on the scale of *War and Peace.*
There was something backward-looking also in the way he
held on to a faith in scientific positivism at a time when
imaginative Europeans were breaking away from this legacy
of the nineteenth century's waning years. Martin du Gard
distrusted the unbridled imagination and severely disciplined
his own. His literary canon was what Georg Lukács calls
"critical realism": while admiring and following the great
realists of the previous century, he refused to accept his own
society as a given and wrote of it in a "socialist perspective."[5]

Born in 1881—one year before Maritain, and five before
Marc Bloch—Roger Martin du Gard had made the kind of
total commitment to literary craftsmanship that these had
given to religious philosophy and the study of history. There
was in his family no trace of literary tradition: they were men
of the law for generations back—a most respectable and conservative subgroup among the French bourgeoisie. And it
was not until he had proved that he was sérieux through
training as a professional medievalist at the Ecole des Chartes

---

[5] *Wider den missverstandenen Realismus* (Hamburg, 1958), translated by John and Necke Mander as *The Meaning of Contemporary
Realism* (London, 1963), pp. 58–60.

that the young Roger broke to his parents the news that he
intended to be a novelist. His experience with historical
documents reinforced Martin du Gard's scientific definition
of his craft. It also made him ultra-scrupulous in the long
years of research with which he preceded the writing of his
novels. And it was perhaps responsible for a certain heaviness
of manner that he could never totally shed.

In 1913, Martin du Gard had made his reputation with
Jean Barois. A book whose central and most compelling
episode was the Dreyfus Case, *Jean Barois* was in fact more
intensely concerned with the conflict of science and religion;
it was, as Albert Camus put it, "the only great novel of the
'scientistic' age."[6] Already its author was looking both forward and back: in a mood of nostalgia for the era of scientific certainty which was drawing to a close, he had produced
the first of the major ideological novels of the twentieth
century.

During the bleak war years—when he served as a non-
commissioned officer with a motorized group supplying the
front—Martin du Gard also cherished the recollection of the
"unforgettable" winter of 1914, the last months of the belle
époque, when he himself, ordinarily shy and retiring, had suddenly become at home in the literary and theatrical world
of Paris. Life for him, as for so many of his generation, would
never be the same again. After a brief postwar venture with
work for the theater, to which he would return at intervals
to refresh himself from his more extended labors, he withdrew to the country. The rest of his life he was to pass in
semi-retirement, mostly in the south of France, far from the
literary cliques of the capital and faithful to the point of self-
torture to his exacting definition of his craft.

It took twelve years, however, for what the war had cost
him to find a reflection in his writing. With Martin du Gard,
as with his countrymen at large, the full emotional effect of
the slaughter was postponed for more than a decade. Like

[6] Introduction to *Oeuvres complètes de Roger Martin du Gard*,
Pléiade edition (Paris, 1955), I, xv.

them, he had at first sought refuge from tragic memories. Sufficiently content in his series of rural retreats, he had thrown himself into a new work—far larger than its predecessor, more psychological in emphasis, and only tangentially touching on public affairs. The new multi-volume novel, *The Thibaults*, was to be the story of two brothers of very different temperaments, "as divergent as possible, but deeply marked by the obscure similarities created by . . . a very strong common heredity." Such a subject allowed the author "to express simultaneously two contradictory tendencies" in his own nature: "the instinct for independence, escape, and revolt, the refusal of all types of conformity; and the instinct for order and proportion, the refusal of extremes," which he owed to his family origin.[7] The result was a substantial succès d'estime. By 1929 the first six parts had appeared; the quality of their literary workmanship and their psychological perception were undeniable. The narrative had reached the eve of the First World War; the volumes announced for the future would enlarge the account of family relationships into that wider depiction of contemporary history that Martin du Gard had only temporarily abandoned. His ideal seemed within his grasp, the Tolstoyan epic on the verge of realization.

On the first day of the year 1931, Martin du Gard and his wife were severely injured in an automobile accident. The two months of hospitalization that followed gave him an opportunity to rethink his writing in progress. This examination of conscience drastically altered the scheme of *The Thibaults*. Still more, it brought about in its author a spiritual change of course that broke his life's work in two.

On the surface all that Martin du Gard had decided to do was to reduce the scale of his novel—which he feared was losing its momentum—and to alter its conclusion. As a technical job alone this was difficult enough: it involved the

[7] Roger Martin du Gard, "Souvenirs autobiographiques et littéraires," *Oeuvres complètes*, I, lxxviii.

delicate process of attaching a new ending to the volumes already in print, while "trying to make the graft as unobtrusive as possible."[8] Beyond that—and not fully recognized by the author himself—there had occurred a shift in his own interests which was bound to alter the character and tone of the novel. History was crowding in upon him: the years of permanent crisis had begun. Events were forcing him back toward his prewar concern with ideology. And by the same process Martin du Gard himself—the diffident literary craftsman who had spent the decade of the 1920's almost totally removed from public controversy—was being pushed, like Maritain a few years earlier, into the arena of political debate. Toward the end of the twenties, he had made the acquaintance of André Malraux; the example of Gide was similarly drawing him to the left. The result was that the concluding volumes of *The Thibaults,* while they had the same cast of characters as their predecessors, became in effect a new novel, a novel of ideological engagement.

Seven years had elapsed since the publication of the last volume of the initial series. It was not until 1936—the climactic year of the Popular Front, the Spanish Civil War, and Maritain's *True Humanism*—that the sequel, *Summer 1914,* appeared. The three volumes which composed it were longer than their predecessors; they were more densely packed with events and, most notably, with political conversation. Their central plot concerned the unavailing effort of a group of international Socialists to stop the relentless course toward war in the weeks following the assassination at Sarajevo. At the end of *Summer 1914* one of the Thibault brothers was dead; the other was to perish in the *Epilogue* which closed the novel four years later. By that time their individual fate had become a matter of secondary importance: the war had dissolved their personal experience into that of Europe as a whole, whose disintegration had now taken over from them as the final dominant theme of the entire work.

With the "initial numbing effect" of combat service a

[8] *Ibid.,* p. xcvi.

decade and a half behind him, Martin du Gard had "felt
able, even impelled, to use war as his subject matter."[9] *Summer 1914* reached a wider audience than its predecessors.
Like Romains's *Verdun*, which appeared two years later, it
spoke to the anxieties of Frenchmen who had survived one
world conflict and now were living in dread of another. Its
international fame was established when it won its author
the Nobel Prize for literature in 1937. At the end of that year,
when Martin du Gard went to Stockholm to accept his
award, his ambitions might well have seemed attained: he was
only fifty-six years old, he had almost completed his epic,
and the world had recognized his achievement in the most
spectacular and satisfying fashion.

Whatever his public success, in private Martin du Gard
was racked by anxiety. He returned to Paris by way of Berlin,
where he was "overwhelmed" by a "hideous" atmosphere of
hatred and lies, of terror and submission.[10] To his intimates
he admitted that *Summer 1914* was an aesthetic disappointment, and it seemed clear that it had won the Nobel Prize
more for the current relevance of its subject matter than for
its literary qualities, which were inferior to those of the
earlier volumes of *The Thibaults*. In the course of its meta-
morphosis, the novel had very nearly turned into an anti-war
tract: overstuffed with the rhetoric of the political Left, it
had come close to foundering under its ideological freight.

Quietly, somberly, as the second war approached, Martin
du Gard worked away at his *Epilogue*. Finished a few months
before Hitler attacked Poland, it appeared in print during
the winter of the "phony war." Its tone could scarcely have
been more appropriate: the novel closed in unrelieved tragedy, with a barely perceptible glimmer of hope for the
generation that lay ahead. Sparser in construction and style
than *Summer 1914*, it resolved the themes of the earlier
volumes, it balanced and reconciled what had come before,

9 Denis Boak, *Roger Martin du Gard* (Oxford, 1963), p. 129.
10 Robidoux, *Martin du Gard et la religion*, p. 305.

through a "judicious harmony" that hovered on the edge of despair.[11]

Despite this recovery of his aesthetic equilibrium, Martin du Gard must have known that *The Thibaults* had fallen short of being the epic he had imagined. So he tried once more. In 1941, in the treacherous calm of Vichy rule, he conceived what he called his "summa," an omnibus work into which he could pour the enormous stock of notes on real or imagined people and events he had accumulated over a quarter of a century. The *Souvenirs du Colonel de Maumort* was to consist of the memories and current reflections of an elderly army officer living in retirement under the German occupation—a figure sufficiently close to Martin du Gard himself to provide a congenial vehicle for his own observations, but more of a grand seigneur, a freethinking spirit in the eighteenth-century manner, with a touch about him of Marshal Lyautey. At first *Maumort* seemed to be proceeding at a brisk pace; it gave precisely the stimulus its author needed to get him through the years of suspense and deprivation after the Germans had taken over the full occupation of the country. But this progress was deceptive: it did not go much beyond the preliminary organizational labor on which Martin du Gard always put such stress. When it came to the actual writing, the book failed to advance. By the end of 1943, Martin du Gard was admitting to himself and to Gide that he was engaged in little more than an elaborate game of literary therapy: the novel as such would never see the light.[12]

By this time, however, its author had reached a point in his own self-awareness at which his failure to carry through his second abortive epic had become a matter of secondary concern. His lagging progress on *Maumort* had gradually merged into a realization of the early waning of his creative powers. At the end of the German occupation and in the immediate postwar years, Martin du Gard's mind became

[11] *Ibid.,* p. 310.
[12] On the composition of *Maumort,* see "Souvenirs," pp. ciii–cxl.

more and more absorbed by his own aging and dissolution. As early as *Jean Barois*, he had been fascinated by the course of a premature senescence; now he was witnessing and meditating on his own. In *The Thibaults* he had twice described in clinical detail the processes of dying. The final decade and a half of his life he spent in a long preparation for death. His only remaining goal, he now saw, was to make a good end—to die with dignity and in control of his fears. And it happened, as he had wished, in August 1958, after eighteen years of nearly total silence. He saw himself in his last months as a traveler *"with no baggage,"* and without interest in his past achievements, awaiting the "night train, which does not come at a regular hour, but *which always passes through* before the end of the night."[18]

What are we to make of this truncated career? Was Martin du Gard, as he sometimes wondered himself, not really a novelist at all? He entertained the highest aspirations—as high as those of any French writer of the twentieth century. In the literary histories his reputation hovers between that of the immortals and that of the solid craftsmen who have not quite reached the summits at which they aimed. The very breadth and complexity of his interests condemned his efforts: he never found a literary form flexible enough to encompass all he wanted to say. History and religion—the twin obsessions of the 1930's and 1940's—defeated him: these and the pressure of the ideological themes with which he had been a pioneer but which he always handled with a certain awkwardness.

Martin du Gard had begun his mature life as a professional student of history, and a historian he in part remained. As a chronicler of contemporary society he had the qualities and the defects of that expert French training in documentary analysis to which Bloch and Febvre had reacted with alter-

18 Letter to Marcel de Coppet, March 18, 1958, "Textes inédits," *Hommage à Roger Martin du Gard: Nouvelle revue française,* VI (December 1958), 1162–1163.

nating respect and rebellion. His experience at the Ecole des Chartes had so molded his mind that it "became impossible" for him "to conceive a modern personality detached . . . from the society and history of its time." Such a conception helped to give his characters the substance and density his critics applauded. But it was dependent on the availability —and the digestibility—of a solid documentation. The method had worked admirably with *Jean Barois* and the Dreyfus Case: here Martin du Gard was dealing with events which as a very young man he had viewed only from a distance, and he could bring to them an optimum combination of sympathy and detachment. With *Summer 1914* he began to get into difficulties: he had almost no firsthand knowledge of Socialism, and no matter how hard he worked over his international ideologists, their conversations never quite came off; they remained contrived and externally observed. Finally, with *Maumort*, Martin du Gard was obliged to give up completely: he could breathe life and reality into the recollections of the Colonel's youth, but when it came to topical reflections on the Second World War and the occupation, he was at a loss; after the passage of a few months, he complained, everything he had written seemed platitudinous. Hence his stubborn refusal to deliver himself of the messages to his countrymen that were constantly being requested of him in the euphoria of liberation.[14]

Which is all to say that when he was personally thrown into the surf of history, he quickly lost his bearings. A similar difficulty perplexed his repeated efforts to delineate religious emotion. He himself had at first gone through the same succession of attitudes toward religion that he traced in his fictional protagonist Jean Barois. Having passed his childhood in a conventionally Catholic family environment, he had begun in adolescence to reject the literal truth of the Scrip-

[14] "Souvenirs," pp. xlviii–xlix, cxxiii–cxxvi; on this entire subject, see David L. Schalk, *Roger Martin du Gard: The Novelist and History* (Ithaca, N.Y., 1967). I have differed with a number of Schalk's conclusions.

tures and had learned to reinterpret the dogmas of the Church in terms of aesthetic and moral symbolism, that is, in the terms suggested by the turn-of-the-century theological movement which came to be known as Modernism. But with Martin du Gard this "symbolist compromise" had never given intellectual satisfaction: by the age of twenty at the very latest—far earlier than the imaginary Barois—he had lost his religious faith entirely. And by his mid-twenties, he had subscribed to the atheism and materialism of Félix Le Dantec, the same Le Dantec who had occasioned such profound spiritual distress in Jacques and Raïssa Maritain. Nor—again in contrast to Barois—did he ever return to Catholicism or relent in his hostility toward it. A quarter century after his original conflict with religion and at a time when most intellectually sophisticated Frenchmen had called off their war against the Church, André Gide found him "ensconced in his materialism like a wild boar in its wallow" and still obsessed with the teachings of Le Dantec.[15] And, after another quarter century had passed, one of his last public acts was to protest "vehemently" against the prayers that a Protestant pastor had read at the interment of Gide himself.[16]

Had this been all, Martin du Gard's attitude toward religion could be readily described as that of a belated nineteenth-century positivist. But there was also his personal kindness—on which both Gide and Camus laid stress—and the concern and respect he had for religious emotion. Unlike Barois, who left his Catholic wife, Martin du Gard remained closely attached to his own through more than forty years of a marriage in which their solitary manner of life made them unusually dependent on each other's company. Still more significant, he cherished the memory of his former teacher, the Abbé Marcel Hébert, who had introduced him to "Mod-

---

[15] Entry for March 1, 1927, André Gide, *Journal 1889–1939* (Paris, 1948), translated and edited by Justin O'Brien as *The Journals of André Gide* (New York, 1947–1949), II, 394.
[16] Robidoux, *Martin du Gard et la religion*, p. 367.

ernism" and had suffered cruelly when Pius X had condemned his stand. Throughout the writing of *Jean Barois*, Hébert served as Martin du Gard's counselor, although as the author noted in dedicating the novel to his teacher and friend, the latter could not fail to be wounded by its contents. When Hébert died in 1916, Martin du Gard wrote a memorial essay about him—the only finished writing he did during the empty war years. But it was to the "moral stature" of Hébert, to his "exemplary life," and not to his thought that Martin du Gard "gave his admiration"; perhaps the "key to his soul" was that he tried "to live like Hébert and . . . to think like Le Dantec."[17]

When Martin du Gard wrote of the Dreyfus Case, he described it in terms of an ethical ideal that had subsequently been perverted to partisan ends—which was the interpretation of the Affair that Péguy had propounded. And when two decades later in *Summer 1914* he told of the death of Jacques Thibault, it was as a moral sacrifice in the cause of peace and human fraternity. Similarly in the *Epilogue* to the story of the Thibaults, Martin du Gard's account—in diary form—of the physical decline and final stoic suicide of the older brother, Antoine, was an effort to show how an unbeliever could have as edifying a death as any Christian. Such was to be Martin du Gard's own end. In the last part of his life one of the rare new friendships he made was with another priest, this time a cleric with a solid intellectual regard for Catholic dogma, whose courageous death five years before that of Martin du Gard himself helped to give him strength to face the inevitable passing of the "night train."

This unremitting moral search, this ability to win the friendship of members of the clergy whose metaphysic was radically opposed to his, have persuaded Martin du Gard's Catholic interpreter to see in his writings the "under side" or mirror image of a religious attitude.[18] Martin du Gard never truly understood religion: throughout his literary career

[17] *Ibid.*, pp. 108, 113.
[18] *Ibid.*, p. 270.

he was handicapped by his inability to enter into the emotional universe of a believer. Yet he never gave up trying. Nor did he ever depart from a rooted conviction—against which his friend Gide strenuously protested—that outside religious faith there was no grounding for morality.[19]

"In the name of what?" Could there be a secular sanction for moral behavior? The question Martin du Gard ascribed to Antoine Thibault he never answered himself. Intellectually he was an ethical nihilist: in practice he was a man of exquisite moral sensibility. And similarly, when it came to the ideological commitments to which he felt drawn, he was unable to find a stance that suited his temperament. He alternated between an insistence that his business was to write novels and nothing else and sudden passionate plunges into controversy. During his years of military training, which he performed in the Norman capital of Rouen just after the turn of the century, he had become converted to the political Left by a group of young friends who followed the columns the Radical philosopher Alain published in the local newspaper. And throughout his life Martin du Gard remained a man of the Left in his nonconformist turn of mind and in the causes he espoused. Yet even here his attitude was not entirely coherent. While he professed his sympathy for Socialism and the Popular Front, there was nothing of the Socialist militant about him: his natural temper was conservative, and his way of life incorrigibly grand bourgeois.

His experiences in the First World War—about which he was as reticent as most sensitive Frenchmen of his generation—reinforced his leftward leanings. And a hatred of war remained the most abiding of his public attitudes. At first he could not bear the thought of a second major conflict. The unstated purpose of his *Summer 1914*, whose didacticism had undercut its aesthetic qualities, was to prevent a recurrence of mass slaughter. Two months before it appeared he had written of the Spanish Civil War: "I am hard as steel *for neutrality*. My principle: anything, *rather than war!* Any-

[19] Entry for October 20, 1927, *Journals of André Gide*, II, 415–416.

thing, anything! Even fascism in Spain! . . . even fascism in France! . . . *Anything:* Hitler, rather than war!"[20] And in his Nobel Prize acceptance address he expressed the hope that his writings might serve the cause of peace. Yet eventually, in common with so many of his pacifist-minded contemporaries, he was forced to admit that armed resistance to Nazi Germany was unavoidable. And after the Second World War began, he even voiced his regret that he had written *Summer 1914,* since it was now in danger of confusing the minds of young men leaving for military service.

Martin du Gard's public pronouncements, then, although sporadic and occasionally contradictory, had an underlying unity. It was not true, as a number of commentators have stated, that he broke silence "only once" on a matter of public controversy; a careful checking of the facts has proved that he spoke out not infrequently, and that the single occasion noted by one individual is different from that recalled by another. Besides his interventions in the cause of peace, he pleaded in behalf of social justice and human rights. During the occupation he sent a message of solidarity to the clandestine organization of Resistance writers, and four months before his death he joined Malraux, Mauriac, and Sartre in protesting to the President of the Republic against the use of torture in the Algerian War.[21]

By that time, with Gide and Valéry and Claudel all gone, Martin du Gard had become France's senior literary figure. Among the rising generation, Albert Camus in particular had generously recognized what his contemporaries owed to the author of *Jean Barois* and *The Thibaults.* The tragic pessimism of these novels had prepared the way for the new literature of heroism. Yet Martin du Gard himself never quite succeeded in striking the heroic note that came so naturally to his juniors. His characters hovered in a limbo of futile sacrifice: one Thibault brother, as the author himself explained,

[20] Letter to Marcel Lallemand, September 9, 1936, "Textes inédits," p. 1150.
[21] Schalk, *Martin du Gard,* Chapter 6.

died the death of an "imbecile" in quixotic protest against war;[22] the other asphyxiated by slow degrees through an unpardonable neglect of routine precautions against a gas attack. Both died bravely; both died uselessly; both died in failure and disappointment—as their creator had been disappointed in his aspiration to write an epic.

II. *Georges Bernanos and the Chivalric Ideal*

In the 1930's and early 1940's the spokesmen of the French literary Right excluded themselves almost automatically from the roster of writers whose work went beyond mere partisanship. Figures as divergent as Maritain and Martin du Gard—and subsequently Sartre and Camus and Merleau-Ponty—might all be classed as "men of the Left," but their political commitment was not the most interesting or permanently significant thing about them. On the Right it was otherwise: here partisanship set the tone that even in the finest literary craftsmen or most persuasive thinkers drowned out nearly everything else. Hence with the passing of the issues which once seemed of catastrophic urgency, their work has lost its relevance; it has been reduced to rhetoric and little more. The polemicists of the Right were masters of the French language; their prose had a drive and bite that few of their ideological opponents could match. By the same token, it offered the classic examples of the penchant toward verbal inflation, toward taking words for actualities, that was the central weakness of French political exchange throughout the era. Stripped of its topical interest, this prose rings hollow: its intellectual inconsequence and the ignorance of the contemporary world it betrays are exposed in all their glaring inadequacy.

One of these polemicists, however, stood apart from the others in the independence of his way of life and in the utter

[22] Letter to Marcel Lallemand, February 1, 1945, "Textes inédits," p. 1145.

integrity of what he wrote. Georges Bernanos is almost as difficult to classify as Gabriel Marcel. Like Marcel, he was a Catholic, but born in the faith, not converted to it. He shared with François Mauriac the distinction of being one of the two most influential Catholic novelists of the interwar years. And in addition to his novels he wrote a series of extended essays—couched in the form of appeals to his countrymen—which together give the most eloquent expression of the heroic ideal that these years produced.

Bernanos was thirty-eight when his first novel appeared, and over forty when he wrote the first of his major polemics. This long incubation period, reminiscent of Marcel's, suggests a life burdened by material difficulties and unremitting anxiety. Unlike nearly all the rest of his literary peers, Bernanos did not spring from a highly cultivated family. His parents were prosperous enough to give him a good education —his father was an upholsterer and interior decorator—but their origins were simple, and although they lived in Paris, where their son was born in 1888, they remained provincials at heart. Generations back, the Bernanos family had come from Spain; subsequently they had settled in Lorraine; but it was in Artois in the north of France that Georges's father bought the country house which was to become far more real to the boy than his Parisian home and was to put an indelible stamp on his subsequent literary creations.

If there was something Spanish about Bernanos in his vehemence and pride, his sense of honor and his love of risk, the sober, gray Artois countryside provided him with the setting for his novels and the image of the traditional France for which he stood. The local peasants remembered him as a "strong-limbed little boy, . . . with fragile nerves," delighting in rural adventures, but also given to sitting in a pine tree "to read or . . . to say mass and to address interminable sermons to an imaginary congregation."[28] For a boy of such a restless disposition, education was bound to be a spotty affair: he changed schools frequently, and never completed a

[28] Albert Béguin, *Bernanos par lui-même* (Paris, 1954), p. 28.

course of professional training. By the age of eighteen—in
1906—he had espoused the monarchist faith, and two years
later he enrolled in the Action Française, in whose noisy
ranks he distinguished himself by his zeal for rioting. Already
he was making a small reputation as a journalist. In 1913 the
Action Française sent him to Rouen to edit the local monarchist newspaper—an assignment that gave him a chance to
pit his talents against those of the formidable Alain.

On the outbreak of war, although he had been classified as
physically unfit for military service, Bernanos persuaded his
way into a cavalry regiment, where, like Martin du Gard,
despite numerous wounds and citations, he remained an enlisted man. But for Bernanos the war was something more
than empty slaughter. Not that he followed the jaunty line
of the professional patriots—in common with most front-line
soldiers, he found such effusions nauseating. Yet he could
not dismiss as meaningless the sacrament of misery he had
shared with his fellow Frenchmen—the war fought "without
hatred and without anger" which had marked him for life
as a man who carried about within him a daily familiarity
with death.

Before it was over he had married, appropriately enough, a
direct descendant of the brother of Joan of Arc, who was to
bear him six children. To support his growing family he decided that he required something more stable than journalism
and characteristically jumped to the opposite extreme, the
safe but incongruous life of inspector for an insurance company. Meantime, however, he had discovered that writing
was his vocation. The war had changed him from a reactionary brawler into a man of tragic seriousness who felt
obliged to "bear witness" to the suffering he had seen about
him.[24] Caught up in the postwar literary ferment, he had
come across Pirandello and Freud—required reading for a
man as subject as he was to devastating attacks of anxiety—
and he had steeped himself in the writing of Péguy. The last
of these, Bernanos found, never failed to respond to his need,

[24] *Ibid.*, p. 70.

and there was much in the younger writer's style that recalled Péguy—the conversational tone, the obsessive repetitions, the outbursts of cosmic anger, and the notion of religion as at once earthy, familiar, and infinitely majestic.

Immediately after the war Bernanos had began working on his first novel. And during the next few years he wrote away at it in cafés and railroad carriages as he pursued a harassed and nomadic life, sometimes alone and sometimes with his family. When *Under the Sun of Satan* finally appeared in 1926, it was an immediate critical success. It was followed over the next decade by four further novels, culminating in his most popular book, *The Diary of a Country Priest*. Mauriac had already accustomed the reading public to novels that were Catholic in inspiration, but he had kept them within the framework of secular bourgeois society. Bernanos broke more sharply with the literary past. With Mauriac religion was the presupposition behind the novels: with Bernanos it became the stuff of which they were made. They were dramas of sin and degradation, of Christian love and divine grace, and priests were frequently their leading characters. Indeed, the very writing of his novels was for Bernanos the spiritual equivalent of priesthood. Their incomparable power lay "in the gravity of a voice resounding with the echoes of a supernatural storm, in the strange light of a hidden sun which will burst forth only in death."[25]

The Diary of a Country Priest appeared four months before the outbreak of the Spanish Civil War. For reasons of economy, Bernanos was living at the time on the island of Majorca. The war in Spain interrupted his most productive period, tearing him away from his career as a novelist and drawing him into a passionate polemic that would continue unabated until his death.

"I have sworn to move you—with friendship or anger, does it matter which?" With the same phrase Bernanos began the two most powerful of his controversial essays, *La grande peur des bien-pensants* and *Les grands cimetières sous la lune*. The first of these, published in 1931, reflected his highly personal and ambivalent relationship to Charles Maurras and the Action Française. In 1919, Bernanos had ended his affiliation with this group: loyal to the idea of a monarchist seizure of power, he disapproved of Maurras's drift toward legal opposition within the framework of the parliamentary regime. But when the Papal condemnation of 1926 descended, it had on Bernanos exactly the opposite of its effect on Maritain. It made him rally behind his old comrades, who now appeared the victims of clerical treachery. Quixotic as always, Bernanos suffered agonies of soul in behalf of a movement in which he no longer fully believed. Not until 1932, when the worst of the storm was over, did he finally break with Maurras—and this time forever.

No wonder, then, that his *Grande peur des bien-pensants* was a puzzling and upsetting book. Its argument outraged nearly everyone. Cast in the form of a rambling and laudatory biography of the founder of French political anti-Semitism, Edouard Drumont, it assaulted not only the cherished values of the Left but the most influential attitude among the Catholic constituency to which Bernanos himself belonged. The Catholic voters of France, he maintained, had become timorous and prone to compromise. Deprecating their wondrous past, feeble in defense of their inherited faith, for thirty years they had looked for nothing better than to enjoy a safe lodging in bourgeois society, to adapt as unobstrusively as possible to the institutions and practices of the parliamentary republic. The bien-pensants, Bernanos argued, had lost the "heroic sentiment of justice and injustice."[26] They had forsworn the legacy of the embattled anti-Dreyfusards.

Such a bare sketch can convey little of the rhetorical force of Bernanos' tract. Its prose swept on in mighty gusts: its bravura passages against the Jews were studded with bizarre images, such as likening them to embalmers patiently pump-

[26] *La grande peur des bien-pensants* (Paris, 1931), p. 409.

ing out by the nostrils the gray matter of France itself.[27] But
this was not the Bernanos that a subsequent generation
would remember. His call to his fellow-Catholics went un-
heeded: the bien-pensants who did regain their militancy
wasted it on a philo-fascism which was never truly Catholic
in inspiration and which by the end of the decade Bernanos
had come to detest. His first major polemic, for all its
literary power, is now only a period piece, and its anti-Semitism an embarrassment to his admirers. Not so its successor,
which decades after the Spanish Civil War was still being
cited, along with George Orwell's *Homage to Catalonia*, as
among the most telling accounts of the tragedy by a foreign
observer.

Writing away in a fine frenzy in his Balearic retreat—his
publishers were now keeping Bernanos alive by paying him
immediately for each page of manuscript delivered—he found
himself in the middle of the Nationalist insurrection that had
rapidly taken over the island. Initially Bernanos was inclined
to favor Franco's cause: this, after all, was the Catholic side,
and one of his sons had even become a member of the Fa-
lange. But when he saw the atrocities that were being per-
petrated in the name of religion, Bernanos could not hold his
tongue. The mass shooting of suspected Republican sympathizers turned his stomach. He had seen, he reported, the
lorries go by, laden with men marked for execution:

> They rumbled like thunder on a level with the many-
> coloured terraces, freshly washed and running with water,
> gay with the murmur of country fairs. The lorries were
> grey with road-dust, the men too were grey, sitting four
> by four, grey caps slung on crosswise, hands spread over
> their tent-cloth trousers, patiently. They were kidnap-
> ping them every day from lost villages, at the time when
> they came in from the fields. They set off for their last
> journey, shirts still clinging to their shoulders with per-
> spiration, arms still full of the day's toil, leaving the

[27] *Ibid.*, p. 137.

soup untouched on the table, and a woman, breathless,
a minute too late, at the garden wall, with the little
bundle of belongings hastily twisted into a bright new
napkin: *A Dios! Recuerdos!*[28]

But what revolted Bernanos beyond anything else was the
part the Spanish Church clergy played in these massacres.
He had heard no word of protest from them. In a little town
near his, "two hundred inhabitants . . . had been dragged
from their beds in the middle of the night, driven in batches
to the cemetery, and shot down and burnt in a heap a little
further on. The personage whom good manners require that
I should refer to as Archbishop, had sent a priest round, who
stood with his boots paddling in blood, distributing absolu-
tions between the shootings." All Christian pity seemed forgotten. The world was "ripe for every kind of cruelty."
Soon the Stalinists, Bernanos predicted, would get used to
burning Trotsky's followers in public, and the Germans
would be doing the same to their Jews.[29]
    Was this last a sign of regret for what Bernanos had
written six years before? Although he never fully recanted
his anti-Semitism, he left Spain deeply shaken by the horrors
he had seen and appalled by the spectacle of violence that
writings like his own had helped to unleash. Once more the
experience of war at first hand had checked his polemical
fury. Back in France after three years' absence—it was the
spring of 1937—he found his country unrecognizable: here
also he detected an atmosphere of civil war.[30] From this
point on, Bernanos became less partisan in his polemic: he
was more concerned to aid in the reconciliation of the French
in preparation for the trials that he now knew lay ahead.
    At home, however, he could find no ideological comfort.
He had quarreled with his former allies, whom his *Grands*

---

[28] *Les grands cimetières sous la lune* (Paris, 1938), translated and
abridged by Pamela Morris as *A Diary of My Times* (New York, 1938),
pp. 66–67.
[29] *Ibid.*, pp. 90, 144.
[30] *Grand cimetières*, p. 116. This passage is omitted in the translation.

cimetières had scandalized, and he had no use for the Left, which in turn wanted nothing of him. In the summer of 1938 he migrated to South America. The reasons for this move were mixed and obscure: Bernanos was driven to despair by his government's failure to stand up to Hitler; he hoped that by turning to large-scale farming in the New World he would at last be able to support his family; he also apparently longed to carry out an exotic dream of childhood. First in Paraguay and subsequently—and more permanently—in Brazil, Bernanos took up the new trade of ranching. His material success was limited: he had never been good at the mechanics of living. But he became attached to Brazil and soon felt at home there. The endless wastes and the sparse scrub growth of the Brazilian interior gave him a second "metaphysical" landscape for his writings; he had always felt drawn to scenes of desolation, while the charms of the Mediterranean had scarcely touched him.

On the outbreak of the Second World War, isolated in a ramshackle house open to wind and weather, straining his ears for the scraps of news that came over a flickering radio, Bernanos began to keep a diary of his reflections. "We are going back to war," he wrote, "as to the house of our youth." With a heartbroken sensation of déjà vu, he contemplated the ordeal that was beginning. For Bernanos the idea of a second war was harder to bear than the first: this time he had no friends or comrades to sustain his courage. He was totally without illusion: his country was in no shape to fight, and the slaughter of ten or twenty million would make no difference at all. Only at the very end of his observations did Bernanos permit himself the glimmer of a hope that when the carnage was over the meek might at last inherit the earth.[81]

The diary concluded in the spring of 1940 just before the Germans struck in the West. It was not published until after Bernanos' death, under the title *Les enfants humiliés*—the

[81] *Les enfants humiliés: Journal 1939–1940* (Paris, 1949), pp. 9, 130–131, 210, 252.

children of humiliation—which Emmanuel Mounier had
chosen for it. In the intervening years, its author had regained
his combative spirit. The defeat of his country had resolved
his ideological uncertainties. Like Maritain in New York,
Bernanos in Brazil rallied his strength and pledged his allegiance to the Free French. His wartime messages, more particularly his *Lettre aux anglais,* joined the corpus of clandestine documents that circulated among the French Resistance.

After the Liberation, however, Bernanos was tempted to
remain in Brazil. It took a summons from De Gaulle himself
—"your place is with us"—to bring him home. He had been
back only six months when the General fell from power.
Once more Bernanos found himself alone, tilting against the
politicians of the Fourth Republic whom he liked no better
than those of the Third. His health was also failing. In March
1948—he had just turned sixty—he was taken to the hospital
for an operation *in extremis.* He was fully aware of his condition: "I am seized with the holy agony of death," he declared, almost with joy. At his funeral the only prominent
writer present was André Malraux, who in the last three
years of Bernanos' life had become his friend.

"I have dreamed of saints and of heroes, neglecting the
intermediate forms of our species, and I perceive that these
intermediate forms scarcely exist, that only the saints and the
heroes count." Bernanos was impatient with every sort of
moral mediocrity—an attitude entirely compatible with his
recognition that his own talents were not extraordinary and
that his life had been far from a model of good conduct; le
bon dieu, he knew, would understand him in the end. Had
he had his way, Bernanos would have liked "to sit down to
table every day . . . with old monks or young officers in love
with their job."[82] His notion of human greatness was archaic,
medieval, chivalric. It was because he had found a quality
of chivalry in the anti-Semite Drumont that he picked so odd

[82] *Ibid.,* p. 199; *Diary of My Times,* p. 233.

a political hero, and the loss of this quality was what he bemoaned among his countrymen.

To an attitude that an earlier or later period would have dismissed as merely quaint, the years of desperation gave topical relevance. In the two decades from the publication of his first novel until his death, Bernanos' writing spoke directly to his era. During his lifetime he thought of himself as neglected and misunderstood: today he appears representative of his age. But there was no lack of others who were also striking the heroic chord. What gave Bernanos his special appeal was the total simplicity with which he voiced sentiments that could so easily have turned into theatrical posturing.

The initial clue to an understanding of Bernanos is his absorption with death. During the First World War, he had experienced death all around him: he had seen men die; death had become almost a banality. The war had made saints of the patient, suffering soldiers—saints of "low quality," it was true, who would no more have aspired to true sainthood than to sleeping with the colonel's daughter.[83] (Such was the tone of tender gallows humor that Bernanos fell into when he wrote of his combat service.) In him, however, the war had merely confirmed a disposition with which he had been well acquainted since childhood: at the age of seventeen he had told his confessor that for many years he had been possessed by the fear of death, and that he had come to terms with it only by making the discovery that one might accept death as the "fortunate . . . close" to a life one had loved profoundly.[84] Thus Bernanos had begun the long and painful process—which by its very nature could never be complete—of turning into a source of creation the anguish that held him in its grip.

The other pole of his emotional universe was his image of childhood. There were "two periods in life," he knew, "when

[83] *Grande peur*, p. 74; *Enfants humiliés*, p. 11.
[84] Picon, Preface to *Bernanos: Oeuvres romanesques*, pp. xxvi–xxvii.

sincerity" could "be expected, childhood and the death agony," and these alone he found absolutely authenic. Both his novels and his essays were strewn with references to the world of childhood and to the demand he made of himself to remain faithful to what he had been as a child. "I write to justify myself," he once declared, "in the eyes of the child that I was."[85] Hence the world of grownups never seemed to him quite real. The actions of those generally considered responsible men struck him as without merit—or, in his more forgiving moments, no better than comical.

To think like a child was a great source of strength in an era such as the 1930's, when political rhetoric exuded hypocrisy and self-righteousness. Bernanos had a talent for blurting out the simple truths that the ordinary commentator on public affairs would have blushed to utter. But the fact that the world of responsible decision remained a mystery to him severely limited his grasp of contemporary history. He was nearly fifty when he began to discover the unworthiness of his ideological allies, and he never appreciated that there might be other ways of understanding Catholism besides the saintly and chivalric ideal he cherished. He had no comprehension of the social mission of the Church in its twentieth-century guise: he wrote mockingly of *Rerum Novarum*, of Marc Sangnier, and of Jacques Maritain. What he would have thought of the Second Vatican Council is only too easy to imagine.

Hence his version of the quest for heroism lacked a content that could be transmitted to others. He himself did no more than bear witness to the evil of his era—and evil to Bernanos always meant an inability to love. His archaic notion of rectitude might awaken glorious memories, but it could provide guidance only in the simplest of moral situations. His prose might be magnificent, but it had about it traces of conventional bombast which clashed with the honesty of his own thought. To the end—like a child lost in a strange city—

---

[85] Peter Hebblethwaite, *Bernanos: An Introduction* (London, 1965), p. 87; *Enfants humiliés*, p. 195.

Bernanos remained bewildered by the contemporary world. Two years before his death, in a sudden flash of self-knowledge, he had written a letter that might well stand as his epitaph:

> I cannot bear having lost the image of [my country] which I had formed . . . in childhood. Yet I shall not offer this suffering as an example to anyone. It is like . . . that of a dog who doesn't understand . . . what it misses, but who looks for its dead master everywhere and finally goes off to die on his tomb.[86]

III. *Antoine de Saint-Exupéry as Technician-Adventurer*

Antoine de Saint-Exupéry was frequently called a knight-errant. Yet the way he lived the chivalric ideal was twentieth-century through and through. With Saint-Exupéry we find ourselves in a new world of experience. All the figures we have been considering up to now were already mature men when the First World War broke out; though their period of achievement and fame came after the war, their minds had been formed during the long peace that preceded it, and they continued to treat as abnormal the era of tumult into which they had been thrown. With Saint-Exupéry and those still younger than he, such tumults were assumed as the givens of the human situation. Nostalgia for the past was out of the question: the point now was to rescue or to redefine whatever there was of human value that could be saved from the wreckage.

Although he was only twelve years younger than Bernanos —he was born in 1900—Saint Exupéry belonged to a different spiritual generation, the generation of those just too young to have had the experience of combat service. Had he been a year or two older, there seems little doubt that Saint-Exupéry would have rushed to enlist. His antecedents were aristocratic; he had been educated in elite Catholic schools

[86] Quoted in Béguin, *Bernanos par lui-même*, p. 144.

to a lofty conception of manliness and self-discipline; and
while he had lost his faith, he retained from his religious upbringing an ideal of heroism whose Christian origin was
unmistakable. His first intention was to attend the French
naval academy; then, having failed the admission examination, he began to study architecture—a passing interest but
one which left a permanent mark on his thought. In the
early 1920's he took up aviation: here he found the métier
that fitted him perfectly, and a flier he remained, with only
brief interludes in other occupations, until his death two
decades later.

When Saint-Exupéry became a commercial aviator, there
was nothing routine about flying. Indeed, it was to escape
the safety and tedium of bourgeois society that he and his
companions chose to be pilots. They were by necessity pio-
neers and adventurers, the men who staked out the air routes
that subsequent generations would take for granted. First in
West Africa, later in South America, Saint-Exupéry risked his
life as part of his daily task; he was in two bad crashes, and
his friend Mermoz perished in another. Such dangers and the
exhilaration of surmounting them provided him with the
themes for his books, only two of which, including the one
which established his reputation, *Night Flight*, published in
1931, could be called novels. The rest consisted of reminiscences of comradeship and loneliness, of deserts and mountains and exotic settlements, and of the unearthly landscape
above the clouds that no previous generation of writers had
witnessed.

The Second World War gave Saint-Exupéry a chance to
fly for his country. After the defeat of 1940, he made his way
to New York, where he spent more than two years writing
and nursing his impatience. With the Allied landing in North
Africa, he grasped the opportunity to return to combat. Over-
age and so stiff from his earlier injuries that he could not get
into a cockpit unaided, he insisted on going out on further
missions beyond the quota his superiors had grudgingly
granted him. He became the despair of his squadron; only a

man bent on challenging death could be as stubborn as he. His last flight was in late July 1944, six weeks after the execution of Marc Bloch and at the very moment when the liberation of France had become a certainty.

When Saint-Exupéry's plane disappeared to the north of Corsica—neither the aircraft nor his body was ever found— the manner of his death seemed to fit the life he had led. But in fact he had never cultivated the fascination with death which gripped Martin du Gard with icy horror, which nourished the religious faith of Bernanos, and which prompted men such as Malraux to hurl themselves against danger in order to be convinced of their own courage. With Saint-Exupéry risking one's life was simply part of the job. He glorified neither death nor a career of action for its own sake. Risk was no more than the unavoidable accompaniment of a task well performed.

This matter-of-fact, twentieth-century technician's attitude toward his métier was at least what Saint-Exupéry professed. But if that was all, why had he picked so hazardous an occupation? It was quite apparent that what appealed to him about flying was the extra moral effort, the possibilities of surpassing the human norm, that it called forth. For him, as for Bernanos, mankind's mediocrities scarcely existed. "A man was a mere lump of wax to be kneaded into shape." One had "to furnish this dead matter with a soul, to inject will-power into it," even at the cost of cruel sacrifice.[87] Thus Saint-Exupéry wrote of his superior Daurat, the real hero of *Night Flight*, who put the needs of his new air service above considerations of humanity and believed it his duty to send a pilot to his death by ordering him to fly in bad weather. And it was with a similar admiration that Saint-Exupéry related how his friend Guillaumet, forced down in the high Andes, had struggled through snow and ice for five days and four nights until at last he told his rescuers: "I swear that what I

[87] *Vol de nuit* (Paris, 1931), translated by Stuart Gilbert as *Night Flight*, Signet paperback edition (New York, 1945), p. 39.

went through, no animal would have gone through"—the "noblest sentence," Saint-Exupéry thought, that he had ever heard.[88]

Thus besides being a technically exacting profession which demanded of the pilot an intense self-discipline and concentration of energy, flying was an avenue toward the understanding of men and nature. A plane was a tool, but it was a tool like a peasant's plow which made of him who handled it something beyond a "dry technician"—a man in touch with "universal truth":

The airplane is a means, not an end. One doesn't risk one's life for a plane any more than a farmer ploughs for the sake of the plough. But the airplane is a means of getting away from towns and their book-keeping and rediscovering a farmer's reality.

Flying is a man's job and its worries are a man's worries. A pilot's business is with the wind, with the stars, with night, with sand, with the sea. He strives to outwit the forces of nature. He awaits the dawn as a gardener awaits the spring. He looks forward to his next landing as to a promised land, and he seeks his truth in the stars.[89]

Flying was also an exercise in comradeship. The greatness of the profession was that it bound men together, teaching them that the true luxury of life was not material goods but relations between human beings. Saint-Exupéry's passages about comradeship focus on the experience of participation with an intensity reminiscent of Marcel's.[40] But the kind of friendships which Saint-Exupéry described were restricted to men: women and children could have little place in the universe of adventure he celebrated; the most pathetic figure in his writing is that of a pilot's wife waiting in vain for her husband's return. It is true that Saint-Exupéry had the same

[88] *Terre des hommes* (Paris, 1939), translated (and rearranged) by Lewis Galantière as *Wind, Sand and Stars* (New York, 1939), p. 58.
[89] *Ibid.*, p. 227. I have altered the translation slightly.
[40] Simon, *L'homme en procès*, pp. 133–134.

grave respect for childhood as Bernanos, and during his years of inactivity in New York he wrote a children's book, *The Little Prince*. But children—and more particularly the figures of young girls who suddenly appear as though by a magic spell at intervals throughout his recollections—could never give more than a reprieve in a life of strenuous exertion; they offered the rare and privileged moments that showed the flier the alternative path, the way of living he had forsworn. For the life of action and individual happiness could not coexist; they were "eternally at war."[41]

There was, then, in flying itself, as in the chief who dispatched his pilots on desperate missions, a necessary cruelty. This was part of the eternal wisdom that Saint-Exupéry believed he had learned from his encounters with nature. One of the curious features of his writing was the way it accepted a type of suffering which most men of comparable sensitivity would find justified only in time of war or revolution. Saint-Exupéry could write without flinching about the practice of certain African desert tribes of leaving an old slave to die in the sand when he was past the age of useful employment, and he argued that one should try to understand those who made war before jumping to the conclusion that they were barbarians. On a temporary assignment as a newspaper reporter, he had a chance to witness the Spanish Civil War at first hand, and he came away from it with the conviction that the sacrifices each side offered to its version of the truth meant much more than the content of the ideology which either professed.

"What's the use of discussing ideologies? If all of them can be proved correct, all of them are also in opposition to the others, and such discussions make one despair of the salvation of man—when actually man everywhere . . . has the same needs."[42] Saint-Exupéry's basic attitude was non-ideological, even anti-ideological. In this respect once again

[41] *Night Flight*, p. 93.
[42] *Terre des hommes*, *Oeuvres d'Antoine de Saint-Exupéry*, Pléiade edition (Paris, 1959), pp. 252–254. These passages are omitted in the translation.

he recalls Gabriel Marcel. But in Saint-Exupéry there was less human warmth than in Marcel, and still more of a fastidious elitism. Saint-Exupéry's ideal, for all his long residence abroad, was not man the spiritual voyager but man the builder of civilization. An image of construction keeps recurring in his writings, the figure of speech of a technician who had once thought of being an architect. And the builders that Saint-Exupéry evidently had in mind were wielders of authority, convinced that they knew better than the run of mankind what was for humanity's own benefit, and quite prepared—like the founder of an airline—to sacri-' fice the individual's life or liberty to the great task at hand.

Such an attitude hovered dangerously close to what the fascists were saying. Despite Saint-Exupéry's hatred of fascism and his detachment from any specific ideology, his elitist sympathies and his aloofness toward his fellow-exiles in New York after the defeat of 1940 suggest a mentality not too far removed from that of the moderates at Vichy or the military men in North Africa who looked to Giraud rather than to De Gaulle—a mentality which drew a bitter rebuke from Jacques Maritain. Saint-Exupéry's grasp of political reality was never very solid; it was as precarious as his philosophical center of gravity, which oscillated between the visionary and the technocratic. This was notably true of his longest and most disputed work, *Citadelle*, which remained unfinished at the time of his death: some readers have found in it the final ripe statement of his wisdom; others—and more convincingly —dismiss it as a "bulky collection of oracular utterances, grave maxims, mystical aphorisms, and meditations on man" that adds nothing to his stature.[48] Saint-Exupéry's earlier writing had been stripped and supple; in *Citadelle* it acquired biblical or koranic cadences which left the course of the author's thought irremediably clouded.

When Saint-Exupéry disappeared over the Mediterranean, his friends discovered in his baggage certain typed pages of

[48] Henri Peyre, *The Contemporary French Novel* (New York, 1955), p. 180n.

Teilhard de Chardin that they at first assumed to be his.[44]
The confusion was only natural. Both were men whose mysticism had its point of departure and its justification in scientific or technical concerns; both were in the tradition of Pascal.
Saint-Exupéry always took a volume of Pascal with him on
his travels—in itself a sign that he belonged to a new generation of French writers. A Maritain or a Marcel had tried to
escape the cavern of spiritual desolation he found in Pascal:
Saint-Exupéry and his contemporaries welcomed it as the
bedrock on which they could ground their own efforts at
ethical reconstruction.

It was partly for this reason—because his thought echoed
the metaphysical questionings of his era—that Saint-Exupéry
enjoyed so large a reputation in his lifetime and immediately
after his death. What was known of his biography made him
an exemplary figure and gave his writings a significance disproportionate to their intrinsic worth. His concept of heroism
was purer—in the sense of being less theatrical—than that of
Bernanos or Malraux, but it also lacked the demonic force
that suffused their novels with the torment of an unbearable
anxiety. At its best Saint-Exupéry's writing was finely chiseled:
it contributed notably to the process of freeing French discursive prose from the grip of traditional rhetoric, and it
translated readily into the English version in which so many
of his readers first encountered it. All too often, however, its
content was either platitudinous or obscure: it could offer
little help in establishing a new style of thought for the
postwar era.

iv. *André Malraux as Artist-Adventurer*

As early as his second novel, *The Royal Way*, André Malraux had clearly posed his own ethical problem: "What is
one to do with one's soul if neither God nor Christ exists?"

[44] Clément Borgal, *Saint-Exupéry: mystique sans la foi* (Paris, 1964),
p. 8.

And the answer had come back no less clearly: "Heroism."[45]
Malraux had no doubt that God was dead; he suspected that
in the twentieth century the concept of man might be dead
also. In origin his thought was Nietzschean—in his last novel
Nietzsche himself made a brief appearance—and he likewise
acknowledged debts to Dostoyevsky and Barrès, Stendhal
and Michelet. And of course to Pascal: Malraux's finest
novel, *Man's Fate*, was a Pascalian exercise in human grand-
eur and misery. Besides all this, there was the world of fine
art; Malraux began studying the plastic arts at the age of
eighteen, and the editing of art books was the one regular
profession he ever pursued. Only those unacquainted with
his biography could be surprised when after the Second
World War he shifted his attention from fiction to the writing of essays on painting and sculpture.

About this biography, however, he remained strangely
reticent. He came of a family of ship outfitters in Dunkirk,
but he was born and educated in Paris, and he broke his ties
with home early in life. The dominating figure in his childhood seems to have been a grandfather, who in transposed
form appeared in two of his novels, *The Royal Way* and *The
Walnut Trees of Altenburg*, with his native Flanders first
shifted to Brittany and in the subsequent work to Alsace. It
was only in the latter—his final novel—that Malraux brought
himself to write at any length of family associations. But
beginning with *Man's Fate* the relationship between father
and son began to move into the center of his consciousness:
in 1930, three years before it was published, his own father
had committed suicide.

Whatever the reason, Malraux preferred to keep his early
life a mystery, and he apparently enjoyed the legend that
gathered around it.[46] Many of the details still remain un-
verified. Yet enough is authentic to suggest that nearly all
his novels grew out of his own forays into adventure. *The*

---

[45] Simon, *L'homme en procès*, p. 35.
[46] W. M. Frohock has skillfully separated fact from legend in the
first chapter of his *André Malraux and the Tragic Imagination* (Stanford, Calif., 1952).

Royal Way drew on his expedition in 1923 in search of ancient bas-reliefs lost in the Cambodian jungle; *The Conquerors* and *Man's Fate* reflected his work with Chinese revolutionists in the middle years of the decade; *Man's Hope* similarly—and much more immediately—derived from his experience as commander of a Republican air squadron in the Spanish Civil War; even *The Walnut Trees of Altenburg* began and ended with fictionalized reminiscences of his service with a tank division at the start of the Second World War. Only after that did legend cease to blend with fiction, and Malraux emerge as an indubitably historical character— as a colonel in the Resistance and in the final campaigns of the war, as Minister of Information in De Gaulle's provisional government of November 1945, and in his last and most protracted incarnation as Minister for Cultural Affairs after the General's return to power thirteen years later.

Malraux, born in 1901, was a year younger than Saint-Exupéry, having also just missed the experience of the First World War. And like Saint-Exupéry's, Malraux's novels celebrated the life of action as a means of defying death. But there was far more of anguish in the way his characters contemplated their own extinction and almost none of the resignation in confronting the forces of nature that permitted Saint-Exupéry's fictional pilots—and perhaps himself—to accept their end. There was rather the tragic conviction, which Malraux held in common with Martin du Gard and Bernanos, but in his case without religious tonality, that one's death delivered the verdict on all that had gone before and that the manner of a man's passing held the key to his courage and dignity. Malraux inaugurated in the French novel the stress on situations of trial at the limit of human endurance which was to become a central theme of Resistance literature; in this perspective, death posed the ultimate test.

"It is easy to die when one does not die alone."[47] If Malraux really intended to say something that his own view of

[47] *La condition humaine* (Paris, 1933), translated by Haakon M. Chevalier as *Man's Fate* (New York, 1934), p. 323.

man flatly contradicted, he meant it in the sense that comradeship alone might make the thought of death bearable.
For him, as for Saint-Exupéry, male friendships illumined and
justified the life of action he had freely chosen. But in Malraux's case the cult of comradeship was not restricted to an
elite of the daring. As one novel of adventure followed another, their cast of characters grew and their range of sympathy broadened. And by the same process the theme of
fraternity began to take over from a gratuitous defiance
of death. Malraux's most celebrated scenes were depictions of
the human solidarity forged in extreme situations—a group of
revolutionists awaiting their turn for execution at the end
of *Man's Fate*; peasants bearing down a mountainside on
stretchers the wounded aviators of *Man's Hope*; German
soldiers carrying on their backs to safety the Russian
"enemies" felled by their own gas attack, which was the
central episode of *The Walnut Trees of Altenburg*.[48] If Malraux became a semi-professional revolutionary and for more
than a decade worked in alliance with the Communist party,
it was not through any theoretical allegiance to the doctrine
of Marx: it was because the Communists seemed to offer the
most potent contemporary manifestation of the longing for
human fraternity.

One last comparison with Saint-Exupéry may suggest how
Malraux deepened and intellectualized the fictional material
that in the former's writing had remained no more than a
sequence of evocations. For Saint-Exupéry residence in exotic
places—and in particular his relationships with Moslems—
had prompted ethical relativism and a tolerance for behavior
which the West condemned as inhumane. This was a response that by the 1930's had become classic among educated
Europeans who had lived in Asia or Africa. Malraux readily
understood all that. But he was more concerned about the
intellectual effect—the cultural shock—which hit Europeans
when they realized that their own values depended on a sense
of history which was unique to their culture and which barred
them from the idea-world of the timeless cultures of the East.

[48] Joseph Hoffmann, *L'humanisme de Malraux* (Paris, 1963), p. 221.

The notion of cultural plurality that the anthropologists had introduced was spreading rapidly in the 1920's; everywhere it met resistance of varying intensity. But the French were perhaps the least ready to accept the idea of giving equal dignity to value systems radically different from their own: in the role they had assumed as custodians of the classic and humanist tradition for the entire West, they could not fail to react on this front also with a prickly defensiveness.

Here the attitude of the young Malraux was in notable contrast to that of most of his countrymen. He opted neither for cultural conservatism nor for a relativist irony or despair. His earliest essay—*The Temptation of the West*, published in 1926—was cast in the form of an exchange of philosophical letters between an Asian and a European. A decade and a half later, in *The Walnut Trees of Altenburg*, he gave eloquent expression to his personal reckoning with the theories of Oswald Spengler. Finally, in his studies of the fine arts, the "imaginary museum" he held before his reader's eyes was an effort to show that despite the diversity he recognized and valued, the masterpieces of painting and sculpture from all continents and ages could respond one to another and thereby re-establish a unified notion of mankind.[49]

Malraux lived contemporary history, both in the Far East and at home, not so much for the sake of the "surf" itself, as in an effort to dominate it by absorbing it into his own consciousness. Hence the paradox which threw so many of his readers off the track. If his novels were some of the bloodiest and most frenetic that the interwar years produced, they were also among the most cerebral. Nearly all their leading characters were intellectuals quite prepared to take time out from a scene of battle to speculate on the human condition.[50] From one of these conversations there emerged the clearest single formulation of what Malraux himself was

[49] *Ibid.*, pp. 60–61, 64–66.
[50] On this whole subject, see Victor Brombert, *The Intellectual Hero: Studies in the French Novel 1880–1955* (Philadelphia and New York, 1961), pp. 169–174.

after—and, significantly enough, from the lips of a historian
of art: "To transform into consciousness as wide an experience as possible."[51] Exotic adventure, revolution, the defiance of death—these opened avenues to understanding, but
they were not the main business at hand. This was to become
fully conscious of what man was, and in the end the lessons
of a life of action paled before what the monuments of man's
art could teach.

Once again, if his readers had followed with sufficient care
the deeper-running concerns that underlay the ideological
surface of Malraux's novels, they would not have been surprised by his rupture with Communism. This "apostasy"
was "slow, subterranean and imperceptible to all but the
closest observers."[52] Malraux had never submitted to the
confining discipline of party membership. But in the mid-
1920's he had worked with Communist revolutionaries in
China; in the early thirties he had stood side by side with
Gide among France's leading literary fellow travelers as the
French Communist party moved toward the Popular Front;
in the Spanish Civil War he had accepted Stalinist direction as the only force efficient enough to hold at bay the
intervention of the fascist powers. Yet this necessity had
troubled him profoundly: in *Man's Hope* he exposed his
own emotional struggle between the iron demands of wartime and his moral revulsion at Communist ruthlessness. It
is possible that the Spanish Civil War, with the imperative
call it made on Malraux's organizing energies, merely delayed a rupture which was already in the making. Sometime
after 1938—perhaps in the wake of the Nazi-Soviet Pact—
Malraux broke with Communism entirely.

Had Malraux been killed in the campaign of 1940, he
would have remained a hero to the French Left, and to

[51] *L'espoir* (Paris, 1937), translated by Stuart Gilbert and Alastair
Macdonald as *Man's Hope* (New York, 1938), p. 396. I have altered
the translation.
[52] David Caute, *Communism and the French Intellectuals 1914–
1960* (New York, 1964), p. 242.

Catholics the "despairing soul," the activist for his own sport, that Gabriel Marcel called him.[58] The image the more conservative public had of him was of an adventurer who was also something of a poseur and whose heroes—as his most famous phrase had it—wanted to put a "scar on the map." During the years of occupation and liberation, a new Malraux began to emerge. In terms of ideology, he had apparently made a volte-face; he had become a strenuous Gaullist— although the incompatibility between his earlier and his later allegiance was at first obscured by the fact that the Communists were cooperating with De Gaulle's provisional government. In terms of aesthetics, he was turning from fiction to the discussion of art, and his tendency to philosophize was growing more pronounced. Even his style was changing: what in his earlier novels had been staccato, nervous, overcharged, by *The Walnut Trees of Altenburg* had become cleaner and more static.

If this, his last, truncated novel (the Gestapo had carried off two thirds of it) most clearly marked the turning point, traces of a new evaluation of humanity had already been apparent in Malraux's novels of the 1930's. The revolutionists of *Man's Fate* were more fully presented than those of *The Conquerors*, and in this second work in a Chinese setting the struggle for human dignity replaced the theme of revolution for its own sake or as a test of man's courage. Still more pronouncedly in *Man's Hope*, the agony of an entire people was now what concerned the author most: the doings of extraordinary individuals were still in the foreground, but the Spanish peasants and workers were also visible, as opposed to the ordinary Chinese whose presence in the earlier novels had been insignificant. The autobiographical origin of this difference seems clear enough: Malraux's experience with Chinese Communism in the 1920's had been in great part play-acting; in Spain it was very real and very close to home. And along with this new feeling for human actuality had come the chastening effect of learning how revolutionists be-

[58] Quoted in Simon, *L'homme en procès*, p. 36.

haved when they were in power. If Malraux had ever subscribed to Marxism at all, it had been in the sense of a
generous vision, as the ethical myth into which Georges Sorel
had redefined it. When the vision became brutal reality,
the myth collapsed.[54]

Unfortunately, however, this ethical progression damaged
the quality of Malraux's novels. As his sympathies broadened,
his literary grasp grew less sure. *Man's Fate*, published in
1933, marked a point of optimum development between the
crudities of his earlier work and the aesthetic difficulties that
arose later on. In 1937, when *Man's Hope* appeared, the de-
terioration was already apparent: despite its majestic sweep
and the occasional glory of its set pieces, it was sprawling,
talky, and overcrowded with characters, with much of it so
close to the vocabulary of journalism and propaganda as to
be incomprehensible today. *The Walnut Trees of Altenburg*,
which was published in Switzerland in 1943, suffered from an
opposite set of defects: while its style had been notably disciplined, its plot was indiscernible, and the series of episodes
which constituted it were only tenuously related one to another. Its eccentricities suggested that what Malraux now
wanted to say no longer fitted the form of the novel.

For all its aesthetic faults, *The Walnut Trees of Altenburg* was in an intellectual sense the most interesting and
significant thing Malraux ever wrote. A fragmentary account
of the careers of an Alsatian father and son called Berger—
which was the name the author himself adopted as a Resistance leader—it was organized as a triptych within a triptych. The two outer panels told of the younger Berger's
tank service and his capture by the Germans in the campaign
of 1940. The central panel (set a generation earlier) dealt
with his father and was itself divided into three free-standing
episodes—the elder Berger's career of adventure as a Near
Eastern specialist in the service of the Young Turk leader
Enver Pasha; his attendance on his return to Europe at a
gathering of intellectuals in a medieval abbey, the Altenburg,
sponsored by his scholar uncle; finally, as an officer serving

[54] Hoffmann, *L'humanisme de Malraux*, pp. 212–213, 244.

in the German Army on the Eastern Front, his witnessing the gas attack already mentioned which was to turn into a manifestation of human fraternity across the barriers of national enmity. That Malraux should have written such a novel at all was remarkable enough. That it should have been almost totally free from anti-German feeling or ideological passion was more noteworthy still.

In Malraux's account both the elder and the younger Berger were seeking what was basic to human beings below their merely individual characteristics or their role as participants in "militant mobs": they wanted to discover what men were like when stripped of their cultural and ideological raiment. The father never quite found the answer: in the colloquy at the Altenburg he had replied with spirit to the Spengler-figure—or rather, the character modeled on Spengler's own guide to speculative anthropology, Leo Frobenius— who had argued that it was impossible to generalize about humanity; the elder Berger had held that under the cultural differences which were all that intellectuals were equipped to notice, there could be found something "fundamental" that made mankind one. He had not lived to complete this understanding—although the response of the German soldiers to the agony of the Russians facing them had given him the clue to what he was after. It was left for his son, in another world war and in the euphoria of escape from death, to learn at dawn, in the peace of a nearly deserted village and from the smile of an old peasant woman, the primeval joy in life that gave it meaning:

Let the mystery of man . . . emerge from that enigmatic smile. . . .

I now know the meaning of the ancient myths about the living snatched from the dead. I can scarcely remember what fear is like; what I carry within me is the discovery of a simple, sacred secret.

Thus, perhaps, did God look on the first man . . .[55]

[55] *Les noyers de l'Altenburg*, French edition (Paris, 1948), translated by A. W. Fielding as *The Walnut Trees of Altenburg* (London, 1952), pp. 23–24, 110, 224.

The greatest mystery is not that we have been flung
at random between the profusion of the earth and the
galaxy of the stars, but that in this prison we can fashion
images . . . sufficiently powerful to deny our nothingness.

Thus Walter Berger, the great-uncle of the narrator and the
host of the Altenburg, recalled what he had learned more
than twenty years before in helping to bring back from Italy
his friend Nietzsche, stricken with madness, who in the darkness of the St. Gothard tunnel had suddenly burst into
sublime song—a song "as strong as life itself."[56] Nietzsche's
inspired singing had seemed to cancel out his own insanity
and degradation; such, Malraux concluded, had been the
power of all great art since man first began to fashion images
in stone or clay. After 1945, laden with glory and weary of
adventure, he no longer sought in action the key to the
knowledge of man: he looked for it in the masterpieces of art.
The fictional colloquy at the Altenburg marked the transition.

Here the author had enlarged the vision of fraternity that
had possessed him since the writing of *Man's Fate* into an
even more sweeping aspiration toward the "humanization
of the world."[57] To elucidate this process was the underlying
purpose of his postwar volumes on the fine arts. And
similarly he was back to his old problem of cultural pluralism.
"We sense every great style," he specified, "as the symbol
of a fundamental relationship of man with the universe, of
a civilization with the value it holds to be supreme." Each
one spoke to the others with an equal dignity and timeless-
ness. The imaginary museum that it was now possible to put
together from photographs of the art of all civilizations and
all eras gave mankind a mirror for self-knowledge it had
never before possessed. Perhaps it would not yet be possible
to discover the "fundamental" which bound men together—

[56] *Ibid.*, pp. 72–74.
[57] *Ibid.*, p. 97.

but at least the search could begin. The old museums of Europe's capital cities had been "affirmations" of the aesthetic standards of a single culture. The new imaginary museum would be a cosmic "interrogation."[58]

Once again, however, Malraux's endeavor proved too great for the literary means at his disposal. Although his essays on art were splendid in conception, they were endlessly repetitive, and their style was clotted and portentous, elliptical and frequently obscure. Nor did he present his argument in an intellectually convincing form. His comments on the parallels and interactions among works of art were not the carefully-studied comparisons that the specialists would make but rather his own arbitrary reaction to his aesthetic experiences. He offered peremptory assertions, which the reader might accept or deny, but with which it was hard to engage in fruitful discussion. Such had always been Malraux's weakness. His writings overflowed with ideas: he displayed his cultural wares with the naïveté of a collegian anxious to receive full value from everything he has learned. Yet these ideas bore no clear relation to one another: they jostled each other on the page. Nobody denied that Malraux had a brilliant mind—but brilliance was a commodity of which his countrymen had never suffered a shortage. In his last and most ambitious incarnation—the one in which he tried to pull all his earlier interests together into a celebration of art as the redemption of humanity—Malraux remained a prestidigitator.[59]

However he strove to define a twentieth-century conception of man—however he reiterated the assertions on the far side of despair that he called his "tragic humanism"—his

[58] *Le musée imaginaire* (Paris, 1965), pp. 161–162. This is the third version of Malraux's initial book in his series on the fine arts. The first version was published in Geneva in 1947. The second formed Part I of *Les voix du silence* (Paris, 1951), translated by Stuart Gilbert as *The Voices of Silence* (New York, 1953).

[59] See Claude-Edmonde Magny, "Malraux le fascinateur," *Esprit*, XVI (October 1948), translated by Beth Archer for *Malraux: A Collection of Critical Essays*, edited by R. W. B. Lewis (Englewood Cliffs, N.J., 1964), pp. 125–127.

prose remained abstract and his creative world a solitude. In Malraux's universe women found little place and children none, while ordinary people figured as metaphysical symbols; his belated discovery of common humanity never became flesh and blood.

After the Second World War, despite his change of political allegiance, Malraux was honored as the great precursor of the novel of engagement and the literature of existentialism. After 1958, he served as France's official purveyor of culture. But the esteem he enjoyed was one of isolation, and his addresses to his countrymen became cloudier as he settled into his role of enchanter laureate. The old Malraux of death-defying heroism had been left far behind.

v. *Charles de Gaulle and the Epic as History*

With Charles de Gaulle we return to the generation of Bernanos—indeed the latter was one of the remarkable pupils whom the General's father had taught. Born in 1890, De Gaulle was a classic example of the patriotic young Frenchmen who came of age after 1905. Nourished on the literary imagery of Bergson, Barrès, and Péguy, yearning to find in action an outlet for his impassioned love of country, he entered the First World War with the fervor characteristic of his contemporaries—and survived. He survived, moreover, emotionally intact: his was not the profoundly wounded postwar existence of a Martin du Gard or a Bernanos. Like them, De Gaulle carried about within him the ineradicable sadness which the years in the trenches had instilled. But it was far from being a sadness of resignation. From his first day under fire—from his sudden horrified awareness that courage alone could not stand up to shells and machine-gun bullets—he had known that something was wrong with the way his generation had been prepared for combat. And after the war was over, unlike his fellow survivors who settled into lives of routine and forgetfulness, he resolved to think through the new methods of warfare that would spare his country another invasion and another sacrifice of its youth.

This search led him to the technique of armored warfare and the world of the machine—to the world of Saint-Exupéry. Despite the archaisms of his historical vision and his literary style, De Gaulle educated himself to be a modern man. And his long years of frustration reserved his energies for the future and made him seem younger than he actually was. A few months short of fifty in June 1940 when he assumed his role as national savior, he was sixty-seven when he returned to power—and the France he was to govern thenceforth was the new France of the twentieth century's third quarter. To the historian of social ideas De Gaulle bridges the gap between the generation of the First World War and the one which fought the Second, as his career links literature and the life of action.

Already the young De Gaulle was more sérieux about his patriotism than the run of his contemporaries. There was depth and independence to what he believed beyond a merely conventional respect for tradition. De Gaulle's religious life has remained a mystery: all that is certain is that he was a practicing Catholic; but his respect for Maritain suggests a concern for intellectual definition and the social teachings of the contemporary Church. His family sprang from the north of France—the countryside of Bernanos and of Malraux's ancestors—dignified people, part noble and part bourgeois, their northern gravity now and then enlivened by a streak of fantasy. Charles de Gaulle's grandmother had been a writer and editor, and his father was a teacher with a verve that made a lasting impression on the boys of good Catholic family who were his pupils. The elder De Gaulle's notion of French history was chivalric in the extreme; but he broke sufficiently with the prejudices of his milieu to allow himself to be convinced of the innocence of Captain Dreyfus. A half century later his son emerged as the one Frenchman who could hope to close the emotional fissure in French society that the Affair had left behind it.[60]

Charles de Gaulle celebrated no cult of death. Yet in the First World War he risked his life repeatedly, and it is unlikely that this model officer would have survived the conflict had it not been for the lucky accident that handed him, wounded and unconscious, into German captivity. There was also a fortunate symbolism in where he fell, at the supreme moment of the Battle of Verdun, in the defense of Fort Douaumont. In retrospect, the initial stages of De Gaulle's career seemed appropriately devised for the role ahead.

In the interwar years, however, little of this future was apparent. When in the early 1930's he wrote in the tones of a Vigny of the severe consolations of the professional military life, when he offered his self-portrait as a natural leader of men, steeling himself against career disappointments by cultivating his own ideas in the "secrecy" of his inner life, when he assured his readers that the sword was the "axis of the world," few among his countrymen were prepared to listen.[61] "No voice could seem stranger, more anachronistic than that of this austere, somewhat Jansenist young officer, whose historical pessimism refused to put up with the intellectual slackness that surrounded him. He who saw History as a perpetual and tragic confrontation of nations, how could he fail to feel the bitter joy of a solitary thinker?"[62] There was also something anachronistic in De Gaulle's fidelity to the teaching of Bergson, whom he cited repeatedly in his first book on military strategy. By the time his second such work, *The Army of the Future*, appeared, heroism was coming back into fashion. But it was a heroic ideal that required an exotic setting, or at the very least the stimulus of ideology. De Gaulle's particular combination of an old-fashioned military ethic with a modern technique of warfare cut

[60] On De Gaulle's youth and family background, see Paul-Marie de la Gorce, *De Gaulle entre deux mondes* (Paris, 1964), pp. 8–29, 40.
[61] *Vers l'armée de métier* (Paris, 1934), translated as *The Army of the Future* (London, n.d.), pp. 153, 158.
[62] La Gorce, *De Gaulle entre deux mondes*, p. 60.

across too many entrenched prejudices. The very fact that it was precisely what France required seemed to condemn it to neglect.

Nineteen-forty changed all that. The defeat of his own country had given De Gaulle the somber satisfaction of being proved right. In similar fashion the wager on the future which he offered from London had within three years established itself as the course that combined patriotic devotion with common sense. One by one his country's intellectual spokesmen rallied to his cause. Bloch worked for the Resistance; Maritain and Bernanos sent in their adherence from overseas; Saint-Exupéry overcame his hesitations when he heard De Gaulle speak in Algiers in the winter of 1943-1944; Malraux found his "ideal-type" hero, "made real but enlarged," the hero of "active intelligence, . . . combining mind and will."[68] The unattainable epic had become history.

But in order to fulfill their historic function great deeds must be celebrated. De Gaulle's conviction, dating back to before the First World War, that he would one day perform a service which would be "noted" by his countrymen—a conviction expressed in the very first paragraphs of his memoirs —made it inevitable that he would write those memoirs. Among the national leaders in the second war De Gaulle alone wrote a set of recollections which also rank as literature. Even Churchill's are not comparable to them. For, as the General himself remarked, the British statesman put his memoirs together in piecemeal fashion with the help of a team of researchers; his own were "composed" all by himself, with careful attention to conciseness of thought and to the balance of phrase and structure.

When the first volume appeared in 1954, France's senior historian recognized a kindred mind. Lucien Febvre found in De Gaulle's writing a tone of orgueil—of haughtiness in its old and worthy sense of holding the head high. Greeting the General as a poet, Febvre declared that the author of the

[68] David Wilkinson, "Malraux, Revolutionist and Minister," *Journal of Contemporary History*, I, No. 2 (1966), p. 49.

memoirs had "rediscovered, recreated" the "harmony . . .
of the purest French style."[64] Such might be the verdict of
most older readers. But the younger generation could not
refrain from a smile at the seventeenth-century turns of
phrase, the studied figures of speech, with which De Gaulle
had adorned his account. Even the soldier-historian had not
shed the trappings of an inherited rhetoric.

There was also in the memoirs a curious quality of optical
illusion. Begun in the quiet of De Gaulle's retirement from
politics after 1953, they were not completed until he was
back in power. Yet the aesthetics of their composition demanded that they close on an elegiac note of "bitter serenity."
"The end of an enterprise, the end of an epoch, the end of a
life"—everything returned to the "great adventure of the
war," and the memoirs themselves were cast in the form
of a "monument . . . to the glory of that privileged era."[65]
So, as inevitably as he had begun, De Gaulle was obliged to
finish with a picture of himself patiently waiting in his
garden at Colombey-les-Deux-Eglises:

> Old Earth, worn by the ages, wracked by rain and
> storm, exhausted yet ever ready to produce what life
> must have to go on!
> Old France, weighed down with history, prostrated
> by wars and revolutions, endlessly vacillating from great-
> ness to decline, but revived, century after century, by the
> genius of renewal!
> Old man, exhausted by ordeal, detached from human
> deeds, feeling the approach of the eternal cold, but
> always watching in the shadows for the gleam of hope.[66]

[64] "Psychologie de chef: Charles de Gaulle et ses mémoires," *Annales*, X (July-September 1955), 375–377.
[65] La Gorce, *De Gaulle entre deux mondes*, p. 516.
[66] *Mémoires de guerre*, III: *Le salut 1944–1946* (Paris, 1959), translated by Richard Howard as *The War Memoirs of Charles de Gaulle*,
III: *Salvation 1944–1946* (New York, 1960), p. 330.

CHAPTER

5

The Marriage
of Phenomenology and Marxism

THE DEFIANCE OF DEATH, the imprint of one's passage through history by the recording of lofty deeds—these were not the only manifestations of the heroic ideal in the years of war, occupation, and Resistance. There was also the thirst for social justice. As the war went on and the rigors of Nazi rule deepened, the forces opposing it drew closer together and became more conscious of the moral goals they had in common. As the moment of France's liberation approached, the question of how new this new France would be took on a bitter urgency. Under the menace of deportation, torture, or summary execution, the activists of the Resistance began to cross the barriers that had separated class from class; sharing similar fears and hardships, they talked of a republic which would at last make real the word "fraternity" that had figured so long and so platonically in the national motto —a republic "pure et dure," honest and compassionate, but implacable toward traitors and the exploiters of the poor.

Thus regarded, the Resistance ranked along with the Dreyfus Case and the First World War as the third great spiritual revolution which the French had traversed in a half century. And like its two predecessors, the experience disappointed those who had hoped that the nation as a whole would be transfigured by it. Quite predictably its effect was restricted to an elite drawn in disproportionate numbers from intellectuals and militants of the working class. On these, however—and more particularly on intellectuals—its effect was decisive; like the Dreyfus Case two generations earlier, the Resistance provided a criterion of reference, the base point from which to judge past and future. Under this kind of scrutiny, the ideologies of the Right collapsed, and with them the verbal elegance that their leading spokesmen had cultivated. In the perspective of the Resistance, such refinements had a suspicious ring: they seemed calculated to obscure with polite turns of phrase a world of misery and social strife. The writing that emerged from the Resistance tried to mirror in all its crudeness and horror a human reality which the sufferings of war had disclosed.

For at least a half decade after the war's end, the writers who had been résistants dominated the literary and philosophical landscape. In their minds and in the minds of their followers, an anti-fascist record alone counted; the parallel and contemporaneous experience of service at Vichy had best be forgotten as a shameful hiatus in the nation's history. In such circumstances fair-mindedness could hardly be expected. Yet to lump together as unprincipled reactionaries *all* the intellectuals who had rallied to Marshal Pétain was to refuse to understand the special kind of self-abnegation which had led a minority of men of good will to serve a cause that in the end brought them only disrepute. At Vichy there was a little of everything, even of Socialism in its pacifist guise. More especially in the period in which the Marshal had enjoyed a quasi-independence from German control—the beginning of 1941 to the spring of 1942—there had flourished a style of corporative or technocratic thinking which was to be revived (and in part vindicated) with the advent of the Fifth Republic sixteen years later. None of such theorizing, however, occupies a very large place in the history of French social thought: it was neither notably original nor of major influence on public policy. The most charitable judges of Vichy's would-be reformers have characterized them as a heterogeneous collection of malcontents, united only by a

conviction that parliamentary democracy was the root of all
evil, and condemned by internecine discord to inefficacy and
historical neglect.[1]

Yet the apparent triumph of the Resistance way of thought
was also the source of its undoing. In France, the memory of
the Resistance was celebrated at least as intensively as elsewhere on the Western European continent; it became a cult,
a social myth in the style of Georges Sorel, whose majestic
features would be tarnished by confrontation with subsequent
reality. Out of the Resistance, directly or indirectly, came
nearly every "advanced" social movement or current of ideas
that stirred French opinion from the end of the war to the
mid-1950's. Within the confines of the intellectual avant-
garde, its victory shielded it from self-criticism and from an
examination of the assumptions on which that victory had
been based. So once again provincialism threatened: a self-
righteous rigidity settled on the veterans of the Resistance
as they became aware of a growing incomprehension and
hostility among their fellow citizens or their intellectual
counterparts abroad. The result was renewed isolation: the
curious combination of neo-Marxism and phenomenological
abstraction that set the tone for post-Resistance social
thought was eventually to figure as at once the last, the most
eccentric, and the most influential of the moral explorations
on which the French intellectuals had embarked over the
course of a crowded generation.

1. *The Intellectual Legacy of the Resistance*

The pride of the Resistance can only be understood in terms
of the humiliation that had gone before. The collapse of 1940

[1] See Robert Aron, *Histoire de Vichy 1940–1944* (Paris, 1954),
translated (in slightly abridged form) by Humphrey Hare as *The Vichy
Regime 1940–44* (London, 1958), pp. 145–158; Stanley Hoffmann,
"Aspects du régime de Vichy," *Revue française de science politique*, VI
(January-March 1956), 46–48; René Rémond, *La droite en France de
1815 à nos jours* (Paris, 1954), pp. 227–230. Compare the more
severe judgment in Henri Michel's authoritative *Vichy: année 40* (Paris,
1966).

was without precedent: not even in 1870 had the national self-esteem been so cruelly wounded. Marc Bloch's *Strange Defeat* tried to explain it in terms of a failure of nerve and technical imagination on the part of France's governing classes. André Malraux's *The Walnut Trees of Altenburg* similarly depicted the moral disarray of the crowds of leaderless soldiers whom the Germans had gathered in as prisoners, an account echoed in harsher detail in the third volume of his *Roads to Freedom* that Jean-Paul Sartre published in 1949. Such was the verdict of the résistant writers: France's old elite had abdicated through a failure to live up to its public responsibilities.

It was only gradually, however, that the militants of the Resistance began to think of themselves as an alternative elite. Initially the mood was one of elegy and meditation, of reserving one's energies for an uncertain future. Thus André Chamson, who was subsequently to emerge as a maquisard major, reflected in the treacherous quiet that followed the defeat:

> I hate this silence that servitude imposes on us, but today it alone can shelter the truth. We must bear our country's misfortunes as our own private sorrows, . . . in the silence of our meditations. . . . The drama of France has thus become, as it were, a personal drama which each of us carries about within himself, according to his merit and his strength. But the meditation of a people that wants to rediscover its greatness cannot forever remain silent. It needs a thousand voices to attain . . . the conviction of a liberation to come. I hope that these voices will be prepared in this same silence. . . .
>
> To live only in the spirit, yet in fidelity, in memory, and in hope—that is still to serve. . . . My sole purpose is to maintain within me the potential for a greatness that lies beyond me, and to be ready to fulfill what the future may bring.[2]

[2] *Ecrit en 1940* . . . (Paris, 1940), pp. 10, 18.

Less than four years later, the same Chamson reported to the headquarters of his former commanding officer, General de Lattre de Tassigny, now once more in France at the head of the army that was liberating the South. The Resistance major had been ordered to bring back with him the irregular troops he had collected in the region of the Dordogne. On the way he had encountered another writer turned guerrilla chief, and they had merged their forces. De Lattre was curious as to the identity of this new Resistance commander: the name "Colonel Berger" meant nothing to him. "There is no Colonel Berger," he objected, "in the French Army." "But there is an . . . André Malraux in French literature," Chamson answered triumphantly.[3] Thus began the last of Malraux's adventures in the pursuit of his heroic ideal.

Those such as Chamson and Malraux who had enrolled for active military service, first in the irregular formations of the maquis and after the summer of 1944 in De Lattre's liberating army, had neither time nor inclination for the ideological writing that was to give the Resistance its characteristic stamp. The task of clarifying the objectives for the future devolved on the editors of clandestine newspapers and on a handful of older men whose appeals circulated surreptitiously among the résistants. For Catholics the work of Bernanos and Maritain enjoyed a prestige compounded of moral sympathy and literary esteem; the latter in particular became a spiritual adviser *in partibus* to young men and women who were interpreting their faith in terms of an active social mission. Similar injunctions could be found in the personalist message of Emmanuel Mounier.[4] This kind of teaching met in mid-course the new tendencies that the Socialists were expressing. For like the Catholics, the Socialists in the Resistance were shedding their political dogmatism and their

[3] Robert Aron, *Histoire de la libération de la France* (Paris, 1959), pp. 666–668. This passage appears neither in the English nor in the American translation of Aron's book.
[4] Henri Michel, *Les courants de pensée de la Résistance* (Paris, 1962), pp. 151n., 387.

distrust of those whom the ideological quarrels of the past
had relegated to the opposite side of an invisible barricade.
From the prison in which the Marshal's government had confined him, Léon Blum had given his followers the cue. The
critique of his own and his party's conduct that he composed
in 1941 offered friendship to the Catholics and all others
among his countrymen who shared Socialism's humanist
goals. For the future Blum envisaged that his own party
would dissolve itself into a wider grouping in which Marxist
doctrine would be virtually forgotten.[5]

Two months after he had completed his ideological examination of conscience, Blum was brought to trial. With his
own thoughts clarified, he felt free to turn the tables on his
accusers. Blum's defense at Riom combined logic with passion, and personal charm with polemical dexterity: summoned to answer for the defeat of his country, he transformed
the proceedings into a rehabilitation of French democracy.
Even those who had opposed Blum when he headed the Popular Front government of 1936 could not refrain from admiring the bravery of a frail and elderly statesman whose religious
origin exposed him to particular dangers: once more, as in
the case of Captain Dreyfus, a Jew was on trial, and once
more he had justice on his side.[6] The text of Blum's defense
joined the writings of Maritain among the corpus of clandestine documents that gave courage to the Resistance.

However exalted their tone, older men such as these
offered counsels of moderation. Of necessity they clashed with
the more activist policy which the Communists espoused.
The latter were proud of their role as the "parti des fusillés"
—the party whose militants suffered the greatest losses because they took the greatest risks. As the liberation drew near,
the strength and prestige of the Communists grew steadily.

[5] A *l'échelle humaine, L'oeuvre de Léon Blum*, V (Paris, 1955),
translated by W. Pickles as *For All Mankind* (London, 1946), pp.
136–138.
[6] See the spirited description in Joel Colton, *Léon Blum: Humanist
in Politics* (New York, 1966), Chapter 15.

Jealous of their organizational independence, they kept their own formations only loosely linked to the rest of the Resistance and to De Gaulle's provisional government in Algiers. Some intellectuals found these tactics annoying; a larger number were willing to give the Communists the benefit of the doubt. Even Bernanos argued that the popularity of Communism was due to a moral default on the part of those who were supposed to stand for spiritual values: people had "become Communists in the same way as the young priests and the young French nobles of the eighteenth century were enraptured with *The Social Contract* and Jean-Jacques Rousseau." The best way to check the spread of Communism, a number of Resistance writers agreed, was "to go beyond it" by offering an ideal that would have an even greater moral appeal. The goal should be to build alongside Communism "a social edifice as revolutionary as its own, but fraternal and authentically French."[7]

Inspired by similar considerations, many of France's leading men of letters were willing to associate themselves for a time with the Communist-led Comité National des Ecrivains, which proved the most successful of the front organizations that Communism launched during the Resistance years.[8] Some apparently joined because they were unaware of the committee's ideological guidance; others agreed to affiliate because they knew of no competing group that covered so wide an intellectual spectrum. The case of Jean-Paul Sartre is instructive: as early as 1941 he had tried to form his own circle of Resistance writers; lacking specific tasks and in the face of Communist hostility, the group had failed to make headway and had eventually been dissolved; three years later, when the Communists changed their tack and asked Sartre to join the committee they were launching, he was happy to

---

[7] Cited in Michel, *Pensée de la Résistance*, pp. 280–281.
[8] David Caute, *Communism and the French Intellectuals 1914–1960* (New York, 1964), pp. 150–152.

associate himself with people who gave some promise of efficient performance.[9]

Reinforcing the argument from effectiveness which was the Communists' most telling point, was the fact that the non-Communist writers were racked by self-doubt. The majority were sufficiently schooled in the examination of their own motives to realize that they were far from being heroes. For the most part they continued to lead lives in which danger and sacrifice had only a small place. As Merleau-Ponty recalled this era:

> How many heroes are there among the men who today take pride in . . . having resisted? Some were civil servants and continued to draw their salary, swearing in writing—since they had to—that they were neither Jews nor Masons. Others . . . agreed to seek authorization for what they wrote or staged from a censorship which let nothing pass which did not serve its purpose. Each in his own way marked out the frontier of the permissible. "Don't publish anything," said one. "Don't publish anything in the newspapers or magazines," said another. "Just publish your books." And a third said, "I will let this theater have my play if the director is a good man, but if he is a servant of the government, I will withdraw it." The truth is that each of them settled with outward necessity, all except a few who gave their lives.[10]

The result was a settled conviction of ethical ambiguity. In the poisoned atmosphere of German occupation, the Communists alone seemed sure of their course. Risking more and more certain of their ideological goals, they enjoyed a clearer conscience. The lack of self-assurance which so many non-

[9] On this sequence of events see the second volume of Simone de Beauvoir's memoirs, *La force de l'âge* (Paris, 1960), translated by Peter Green as *The Prime of Life* (Cleveland and New York, 1962), pp. 382–383, 396–397, 424–425.
[10] "La guerre a eu lieu" (originally published in June 1945), *Sens et non-sens* (Paris, 1948), translated by Hubert L. Dreyfus and Patricia Allen Dreyfus as *Sense and Non-Sense* (Evanston, Ill., 1964), p. 146.

Communists felt vis-à-vis their Communist Resistance comrades may help explain the enormous reluctance to separate
from them—amounting in some cases to a psychological impossibility—that such writers experienced after the inaugura-
tion of the Cold War.

For all the heroism and sacrifice that went into it, the
social thought of the Resistance lacked specific content. Most
of the time, it did not go beyond a reiteration of the principles
of fraternity, moral regeneration, and the transcending of
factional quarrels. The economic policy the Resistance writers
advocated lay somewhere between a nondogmatic socialism
and the techniques of the welfare state; in this sphere alone
their thought left a visible trace on official practice in the
postwar years. Elsewhere the social doctrine of the Resistance
was more a state of mind—a mystique—than a tangible
program.

To find the permanent legacy of the Resistance in French
intellectual life, one has to look rather at its effect on
ideological or philosophical tendencies which were already
present in the prewar years. Here the wartime experience
emphasized or gave prominence to earlier attitudes that now
took on a new relevance. Such was particularly the case with
social Catholicism, Marxism, and the complex of philosophical teachings that came to be known as existentialism.

The comradeship of the Resistance notably reinforced the
leftward course of French Catholic thought. And it added to
this tendency a tolerant understanding of Marxism which
had earlier been restricted to the circle around Emmanuel
Mounier. In the wake of the liberation, Mounier's review
Esprit emerged from its prewar isolation: its following among
Catholics increased; non-Catholics read it with a new sympathy. Indeed there began to appear an ecumenicism of the
Left, what hostile critics called a new bien-pensant attitude,
a conformism of shared ideological assumptions. Thus Jean
Lacroix, an associate of Mounier, could write in terms of a
friendly three-way exchange among Marxism, existentialism,

and Catholic personalism. And in comparing the three, he treated Marxism with comradely respect: he took the tortuous reasoning of the Leninists at its face value; he stressed in the Marxist canon the principles most congenial to the religiously inclined—its ethical definition of the class struggle, its hatred of disorder, its conviction of the dignity of labor, and its un-remitting endeavor to "humanize" the raw material which nature offered. The proper course for those outside the Marxian fold, Lacroix concluded, was not "to refute Marx-ism" but "to ask that it recognize" the transcendent element in human history "without which its own basic intention could not be accomplished."[11]

Although Léon Blum might be ready to dismiss the Marxian teachings as useless and outmoded, his attitude was not shared by most intellectuals of the Left. To Blum and the older generation Marxism brought back distasteful memories of sectarian quarrels with the Communist party. To the younger generation it was a new intellectual experience, whose inspirational virtues they had learned at first hand during the Resistance years. Marxism in France was preponderantly, though not exclusively, the ideological preserve of the Com-munists. These had interpreted the doctrine in varying fash-ion as the tactical requirements of the moment dictated. But the reading of Marx that had proved most rewarding was in terms of a patriotic tradition of strong popular authority—a tradition descending from Auguste Blanqui in the mid-nine-teenth century and ultimately from the Jacobins of the Great Revolution. This interpretation had the advantage of being recognizably French.[12] And it coincided admirably with the combination of patriotic and ideological appeals that was the characteristic language of the Resistance. The Resistance gave Marxism in its idiosyncratic French form an intense topical relevance.

[11] *Marxisme, existentialisme, personnalisme: présence de l'éternité dans le temps* (Paris, 1949), pp. 15, 19, 26, 28–29, 47–48.
[12] George Lichtheim, *Marxism in Modern France* (New York, 1966), pp. 11, 17, 23.

As for the third member of the ideological panel—existentialism—its intellectual link with the Resistance was clearly delineated in its own literature. The existentialist emphasis on situations of moral extremity and on the need for personal commitment in ambiguous circumstances had already been present in the philosophy of Gabriel Marcel and in the novel of the 1930's; themes such as these had given the work of André Malraux its tone of anguished urgency. But what in Malraux had been the frenetic gamble of a band of adventurers, the clandestine struggle against the Nazi occupation had made the daily routine of thousands of men and women who had never thought of themselves as heroes. There was pungent irony in the fact that it took the experience of German rule to give living actuality to an austere and intellectually difficult pattern of thought which was itself an import from Germany.

Among the new bien-pensants of the Left, nostalgia for the Resistance dominated the first postwar decade. Along with it went a sense of overwhelming disappointment that the nation as a whole had failed to respond to the breath of change. After a few months of economic experiment—after the nationalization of public services and a vast extension of the social security system—France returned to the familiar procedures of middle-class parliamentary democracy. General de Gaulle relinquished his authority at the beginning of 1946; the quasi-dictatorship he had wielded as the residuary legatee of the Resistance came to an end in a collision with the old political parties. Sixteen months later De Gaulle's most formidable Resistance rivals—the Communists—were less ceremoniously evicted from the government. The Cold War had begun: for seven years the French were to live under American protection, with the threat of a third world conflict hanging over them and their economy precariously supported by aid from the United States.

Realistically considered, it was not surprising that the majority of the nation refused to follow the Resistance lead.

The latter, after all, had never been more than a devoted minority: most people, in common with the run of mankind throughout history, had adopted an attitude of attentisme—of wait-and-see. The final victory had proved the résistants right—but this did not necessarily endear them to the rest of their countrymen. Indeed, it was perhaps this historical vindication itself that made the veterans of the Resistance distasteful to their fellow citizens: the apathetic majority could not forgive the heroic minority for the air of moral superiority with which their triumph in 1944 and 1945 had endowed them. And such an air seemed doubly unjustified in view of the political incompetence so many of the résistants had displayed.

By 1947—or by 1950 at the very latest, when a bitter controversy erupted over forced labor in the Soviet Union and the Korean War broke out—the Resistance writers had irremediably split. A few, of whom Malraux was the shining example, followed De Gaulle in protest against the ineffectiveness of parliamentary government. A larger number, of whom Albert Camus was to become the most celebrated, adjusted more or less grudgingly to the rule of the political Center and to dependence on the United States. But the characteristic intellectuals of the Resistance-inspired Left opted neither for Gaullism nor for parliamentary democracy; they similarly tried to avoid a clear choice between East and West. Those who most punctiliously cherished the Resistance inheritance advocated a neutralist policy, which in practice leaned toward the Soviet Union, since its proponents refused to break their ties with the Communist writers and strenuously combated the governmental line of political moderation and Western solidarity. Such a stand could not fail to alienate the greater part of the intellectual community in Great Britain and the United States: as the 1950's opened, the French once more seemed to be retiring into cultural isolation.

Nineteen-fifty to 1953 were the years of most severe ideological tension. With the outbreak of the Korean War, it was

not too farfetched to predict a Russian occupation of Western
Europe, and many French writers asked themselves in desperation how they would behave in a situation whose ambiguity made that of the Second World War look childishly
simple: their ideological sympathies inclined them toward
the Soviet Union; their love of liberty and middle-class way
of life bound them to the United States—and they certainly
had no intention of becoming "collaborationists." At a later
date such moral dilemmas were to sound ridiculous; at the
time they were perfectly serious and responsible. Fortunately
for the peace of mind of the French intellectuals, in early
1953 Stalin died; the following summer the war in Korea
came to an end; and by the mid-1950's the beginnings of
economic expansion and prosperity were already apparent.
France in fact was over the worst of its postwar difficulties:
the new society was on the way. But it took another seven or
eight years to liquidate the inheritance of a generation of
ideological strife: the intellectuals remained embattled until
well into the 1960's.

In the middle years of the previous decade there had appeared two books which from radically contrasting standpoints summed up the ideological conflicts of the immediate
postwar era. Simone de Beauvoir's *The Mandarins* and Raymond Aron's *The Opium of the Intellectuals* both dealt with
the politics of the French literati—and more particularly with
the attitude of the literary Left toward Marxism and the
Soviet Union. Their authors had in common a self-confident
rationalism, a taste for polemic, and a close acquaintance with
Jean-Paul Sartre, whose activities, whether directly reported
or in thinly disguised form, provided the central focus for
both accounts.

The Mandarins, published in 1954, was an *apologia pro
vita sua*, cast in the form of a novel, by Sartre's lifetime companion. As a work of art, it was disappointing—cumbersome,
contrived, and repetitious. The intellectual exchange in its
dialogue was frequently dazzling, but just as often wordy
and self-conscious. *The Mandarins* succeeded most where it

tried least—not as a novel, but as journalism of a high order, an imaginative rendering of a milieu that had been observed with both sympathy and penetration. As a portraiture of intellectuals in postwar France, it had no equal.

The comparison with traditional Chinese society its title implied had long been a staple in the game of cross-cultural comparisons—fine cooking, the cultivation of one's garden, a disabused philosophy of life: the elements of the parallel were thoroughly familiar. The stress in this case was on the similarity between the two societies in ascribing the supreme personal status to a self-perpetuating literary intelligentsia. But the ironic promise of the title was never fulfilled: Simone de Beauvoir reserved her humor for the rich and their hangers-on who stood outside the privileged circle. Within— toward the world of the mandarins themselves—her tone was one of muted respect. Indeed, the author herself apparently failed to realize the full force of a title which had been suggested at the last moment by a friend. The protagonists of her novel did not picture themselves as the heirs of an ancient cultural tradition: they figured in their own minds as revolutionaries of the pen.

Yet the subjects they discussed were those over which French intellectuals had been battling for two and a half centuries: the presumed general principles of mankind that found their embodiment in public ethics. And the manner of discussion was irreproachably Cartesian—that is, in terms of sharply defined opposites and lapidary formulations. Nor did Simone de Beauvoir question the validity of a type of abstract reasoning which could lead by apparently rigorous steps to the curious conclusion that the United States was about to "subjugate" the European continent. She never challenged the central assumptions of the leftward-oriented mandarinate among whom she lived. Her unremitting conversational exercises went on within a circle which was both personally and intellectually self-contained.

Hence the pedantic solemnity with which it took its most trivial doings—hence its conviction that what it had to say was of supreme importance for the rest of humanity. In the mental universe of *The Mandarins* there opened a widening gap between expectation and actuality: the aim was as universalist as ever, but in the particular circumstances of the postwar era its result was parochialism. Simon de Beauvoir's novel was at its best in depicting the pathos of French intellectuals cut off from their counterparts elsewhere in the Western world. In the early 1950's cultural communication was breaking down: to the British and Americans the French seemed unrepentantly doctrinaire and intellectualist —they themselves accused the "Anglo-Saxons" of slipping ever deeper into the quicksands of adaptability and empiricism. For Simone de Beauvoir the choice was clear: while giving her ideological opponents their due as men of good will striving for peace and justice according to their lights, her support of necessity went to a neutralist position tinged with philo-Communism.

Raymond Aron made the opposite choice. His Resistance credentials were as good as Simone de Beauvoir's—he had spent the war years as a Free French journalist in London— and his experience was considerably more cosmopolitan. In the early 1930's he had been the first of his generation of intellectuals to go to Germany for philosophical study: out of this experience he had produced two basic works which had introduced the French public to contemporary German sociology and to the neo-idealist philosophy of history.[18] In the following decade his long residence in Britain had given him fluency in English and a ready familiarity with Anglo-American thought. Sartre had been his friend at the Ecole Normale Supérieure; immediately after the liberation the two were once again closely associated. But by 1947 the Cold War

[18] *La sociologie allemande contemporaine* (Paris, 1936), translated from the second edition (1950) by Mary and Thomas Bottomore as *German Sociology* (Glencoe, Ill., 1957); *Introduction à la philosophie de l'histoire* (Paris, 1938), translated by George J. Irwin as *Introduction to the Philosophy of History* (Boston, 1961). For an over-all assessment of Aron as a political thinker, see Roy Pierce, *Contemporary French Political Thought* (London and New York, 1966), Chapter 8.

had driven them apart. Predictably enough, Aron sided with
the English and Americans. Still more, he cut his ties completely with the French Left, attacking as a dangerous
"mystification" the Marxist assumptions of his former friends.

At the very start of his *Opium of the Intellectuals*, published in 1955, Aron signaled his break with the ideological
"family" within which he had come to intellectual maturity;
under current conditions he questioned whether the terms
"Right" and "Left" any longer conveyed a clear meaning,
and he was quite sure that Marxism was having the soporific
effect on the French intellectuals which its creator had a century earlier attributed to religious faith among the masses. In
France—or perhaps better, in Paris—or still more narrowly,
in the neighborhood of Saint-Germain-des-Prés, where the
intellectuals of the Left had their headquarters—a shared
Marxist faith inspired a type of family quarrel that was incomprehensible across the Channel or the Atlantic: in Britain
or the United States people discussed Marx's sociology or
economics "without much passion, as . . . important works"
marking a certain stage "in the development of scientific
knowledge"; in France the same theories were treated as
gospel. More especially—and in Aron's view, most noxiously
—the result of such ideological bemusement was an "idolatry
of history." To the intellectuals of the Left, history had a goal
—the triumph of the proletariat; in its name the most revolt-
ing crimes could be pardoned or condoned; the vision of an
"inevitable future" had blunted the French critical sense and
turned abstract philosophers into "fanatics."[14]

Aron was on firm ground when he reproached his fellow
intellectuals with attributing to "history" a course and an
aim that ideological faith could descry. His own studies had
tried to bring his countrymen abreast of a critical philosophy
of history—German, Italian, or English in origin—which re-
nounced such aspirations, relegating them to the realm of

[14] *L'opium des intellectuels* (Paris, 1955), translated by Terence
Kilmartin as *The Opium of the Intellectuals* (London, 1957), pp. xi,
57, 135, 156–157, 190.

poetic insight or moral uplift. Aron was also quite correct in suggesting that the French intellectuals, "accustomed to speaking for the whole of mankind, ambitious for a role on a planetary scale," were trying "to camouflage the provincialism of their controversies under the debris of the nineteenth-century philosophies of history"—in brief, that their attitude was a curious compound of "nostalgia for a universal idea" and "national pride." Yet in explaining why these intellectuals behaved as they did, he in effect found a justification for them. In the "frozen" state of French society, Aron surmised, France's writers could take little comfort from the external circumstances of life about them. Not until those circumstances became more "worthy of their ideal" would they be reconciled, like their counterparts in Britain and America, to the society in which they lived.[15]

But precisely this had been the point of disagreement all along. In the early 1950's, French society offered a discouraging prospect to anyone who yearned for social justice and human fraternity: the good things of life were still in short supply; the class struggle was very real. True, the signs of change were already apparent: at the very time that Aron and Simone de Beauvoir were writing, the great transformation was beginning. Yet few were able to discern it: in the opening years of the 1950's the most penetrating students of contemporary France were till describing its society in terms of stagnation;[16] even Aron, who had every reason to stress the change, referred only glancingly to the "forces of regeneration . . . ripening under the crust of conservatism." In the late 1940's and early 1950's, it was very difficult for a morally sensitive Frenchman to accept the conditions he saw around him; it was only a step from this to sharing the anger of working people against a government that seemed invariably to side with the propertied classes and was holding in a state

[15] *Ibid.*, pp. 64, 247, 318.
[16] See, for example, Herbert Lüthy, *Frankreichs Uhren gehen anders* (Zürich, 1954), translated by Eric Mosbacher as *The State of France* (London, 1955).

of political quarantine the party that alone inspired much confidence among the poor. And the way in which intellectuals translated their anger was by subscribing with wholehearted recklessness to the doctrine of Karl Marx.

Moreover, from some standpoints the French writers were more farsighted than their compeers in Britain or America who on economic matters or the state of affairs in the Soviet Union seemed so much better informed than they. The French were more alert to the threat of a thermonuclear conflict, and they had a far better appreciation of the horrors of colonial warfare and of the explosive potential within the movements of liberation in Asia and Africa. Taught by their country's experience of eight years of fruitless repression in Indochina—which was to be followed almost immediately by an equally long and even more distressing war in Algeria—the French intellectuals early awoke to the importance of what was just beginning to be called the underdeveloped world. At home, their ideological pronouncements might sound more and more old-fashioned; in the colonies and the ex-colonies they could still evoke a response. As the French intellectuals of the Left sank into obsolescence in their own land, their words gained a new relevance overseas. Such was notably the case with the most talented and influential of them all, Jean-Paul Sartre.

II. *Jean-Paul Sartre: The Idealist Phase*

Shortly after the liberation, Sartre and the existentialist philosophy that was associated with his name suddenly mushroomed into a colossal intellectual fad. The term "existentialism" began to be applied in all kinds of inappropriate contexts, as a word of scorn for the conservatives, as a badge of pride for the young. Sartre himself had every reason to be surprised by his new-found fame. Before the war he had lived only on the margin of the influential cliques that dominated French literary life. However prodigious his talents might appear later on, he had never been acclaimed as a boy genius, and public recognition had been slow in coming; most of his time he had spent as an obscure lycée professor—he was thirty-three when he enjoyed his first literary success. This was just a year before the war broke out, and it was not until the occupation period that he became the center of a circle of like-minded friends and admirers. In these years he and Simone de Beauvoir and a few others would gather at the Café de Flore near Saint-Germain-des-Prés—to exchange opinions, to keep warm in winter, but chiefly to write, to write with an indefatigable single-mindedness that epitomized their commitment to their craft. To his younger friends Sartre ranked as a great "awakener": he spoke to them in direct and colloquial language, eliciting from them what they "really were" under the veneer of their education as civilized Frenchmen. Sartre's manner might be blunt: he refused to take refuge in the polite formulas that usually covered over basic disagreements. But he was also very kind: a wealth of testimony from this period concurs in stressing his generosity. Subsequently, when the tourists and sensation-seekers had driven Sartre and his friends from the Café de Flore, the latter were to recall these first years with nostalgia as a "time of purity."[17]

Sartre was only four years younger than Malraux—he was born in 1905—and the themes of their fictional work had much in common. But their contrasting rates of intellectual maturation set them worlds apart. By the time Sartre began to produce the books that brought him fame and influence, Malraux had already spent a decade and a half at the very center of the French literary scene; when Sartre was finally ready to launch his ideological adventures, Malraux was about to renounce his own and to retire into aesthetic contemplation. Jean-Paul Sartre was slow in recognizing where his

[17] Jacques Guicharnaud, "Those Years: Existentialism 1943–1945," *Yale French Studies*, No. 16 (Winter 1955–1956), translated by Kevin Neilson for *Sartre: A Collection of Critical Essays*, edited by Edith Kern (Englewood Cliffs, N.J., 1962), pp. 16–19.

thought was leading him. His intellectual and emotional biography was both unusual and complex, and he required a long time to sort out its elements. When he was almost fifty, he reached the conclusion that his previous work had been based on a misapprehension; a few years later, he decided to write of his childhood and to try to explain to himself and others how it had all come about.

This was a novelty in French literature—an autobiography that went only to the age of ten and was unashamedly psychoanalytic in inspiration. Sartre's understanding of psychoanalysis had its serious gaps (more of that shortly), but at least he did his best to confront his childhood and to find in it the origin of the ambiguity which was to figure so prominently in his published work. Thus he could write of his early years that they were "paradise" and that he "loathed" everything about them. He also ascribed his lack of a super-ego to the fact that he had never known his father.[18] The latter statement deserves to be treated with skepticism: examples of self-punishment are strewn wholesale throughout Sartre's career. He may have grown up with only one parent—his father, a naval officer worn out by a tropical ailment, died two years after his birth—but he had a maternal grandfather whose image dominated his early years.

A majestic figure, this Charles (or Karl) Schweitzer, a retired Alsatian professor and the uncle of Albert Schweitzer. His full beard made him look like God the Father: he summed up in his person the good conscience of the intellectual class, the sentimental humanism which was to be the butt of his grandson's sharpest attacks. The ideology of the Schweitzer household was behind the times even for its own era; Sartre later complained that he had spent his childhood in the intellectual atmosphere of the reign of Louis-Philippe, and that he had had to jump over eighty years in order to get abreast of his own generation. This highmindedness, however, was without religious tonality: Charles Schweitzer was a Prot-

[18] *Les mots* (Paris, 1964), translated by Bernard Frechtman as *The Words* (New York, 1964), pp. 19, 34, 164.

estant and his wife a Catholic; the two influences canceled
out, leaving the boy Jean-Paul with the conviction that
religion was of no particular importance—he came by his
atheism quite painlessly. At least that is what he later claimed:
his writings, on the contrary, suggest a long, unconscious,
subterranean struggle with a hidden deity.

The household gods were, rather, the masters of literature
and the arts; it was their priesthood to which the young
Sartre found himself already consecrated by right of birth.
Charles Schweitzer decreed that his grandson should become
a writer, and this the latter dutifully did. The one injunction
he never rebelled against was the precept "Thou shalt write";
still more, he "internalized" it and made it his own. Words
ruled his childhood, as they did his mature years. The inevitable title for his autobiography was *Les mots—The Words*
—as his "natural habitat" was a Parisian apartment with a
view over the roofs of the city: only here could he breathe
the "rarefied air of belles-lettres." As for the world of nature,
it meant absolutely nothing to him.[19]

Charles Schweitzer was also something of an actor: he
found satisfaction in his noble poses. And in the atmosphere
of adoration with which his grandparents and his mother
enveloped the boy, the little Jean-Paul was virtually forced
to be a comedian also. He felt obliged to produce the charming actions or turns of phrase his "audience" expected of
him. When he finally realized that he was an "impostor," his
world became a desolation.[20] It is curious that Sartre himself
did not stress more explicitly in his memoirs the origin of an
obsession with "bad faith" which was to become the central
feature of his philosophy.

Here literature stepped in to save him. Shy and bookish,
Sartre found few other children to play with in the Luxembourg Gardens. Years later, when his mother had remarried
and the family moved to La Rochelle, he felt similarly cut

[19] *Ibid.*, pp. 22–24, 33, 49, 51, 59–63, 98–103, 154–156, 163–165,
178.
[20] *Ibid.*, pp. 83–86.

off from his more robust schoolmates. At home he had discovered that he was de trop—superfluous—another concept
which joined his special philosophical vocabulary. Writing
gave him a reason for living—forgiveness for the fact of his
existence; it was a mask for the grace that others would ask
of death or religion, a way to wrench his life free from the
play of chance.[21] Behind the strenuous pace of literary exertion which Sartre imposed on himself lay what one of his
closest associates called the "calm" and "secret horror" his
childhood had left with him. It was responsible for the dark
side of his writing, the insistence on the distasteful aspects
of existence, that made so many of his readers think of him
as irritable and pessimistic rather than the gay, enterprising,
universally curious man his intimates knew and loved.[22]

One more element in Sartre's childhood deserves mention.
As Alsatians the Schweitzers were bilingual. In his incarnation as Karl, Charles Schweitzer occupied his academic
retirement by running a language school which specialized in
teaching French to visiting Germans. These students, hearty
and sentimental like their teacher, where frequent guests at
the family table. Thus the young Jean-Paul was familiar with
the sound of German from his earliest years. By childhood
exposure he seemed predestined to translate the German
philosophical speculation of the first postwar period into
terms that would make sense to Frenchmen just emerging
from a second world conflict.

By that time—by the time he became a celebrated philosopher in his own right—he had returned to Paris from
La Rochelle; he had prepared for the Ecole Normale Supérieure at one of the capital's elite lycées; he had passed the
agrégation in 1929—having failed it, significantly enough, on
his first time round; he had met in Simone de Beauvoir the

21 *Ibid.*, pp. 96, 134–135, 193, 251.
22 Francis Jeanson, "Un quidam nommé Sartre," *postface* to new
edition of *Le problème moral et la pensée de Sartre* (Paris, 1965), p.
325.

partner who shared his life and thought and to whom he could pour out his half-formed reflections; and in 1933, a few months after Hitler came to power, he had gone off for a year to Germany as Aron's successor at the French Institute of Berlin.

Here he plunged with characteristic energy into the phenomenology of Eduard Husserl. Aron had brought back from Berlin tidings of a type of speculation which seemed to be precisely what Sartre was seeking—a philosophy of the concrete, which focused intensively on appearances themselves without regard for conventional abstract categories. One night the two were drinking together at a bar in Montparnasse. " 'You see,' " said Aron, pointing to his glass, " 'if you are a phenomenologist, you can talk about this cocktail and make philosophy out of it!' Sartre turned pale with emotion. . . . Here was just the thing he had been longing to achieve for years."[28] With the discovery of Husserl, he was launched at last. In Berlin Sartre also read Scheler and the rival existentialists Jaspers and Heidegger. But a close study of the last of these did not come until 1939, when he was preparing himself to compose the major work that was to adapt Heidegger's thought to the French intellectual context.

Sartre's reading of Freud was more spotty. According to Simone de Beauvoir's account, he knew only *The Interpretation of Dreams* and *The Psychopathology of Everyday Life*. What he had understood of psychoanalytic theory attracted him at the same time as it aroused in him a deeply rooted resistance. While admiring in Freud an expert explorer of human conduct, Sartre rejected Freud's formulation of the unconscious as a threat to the metaphysical freedom which was at the heart of the philosophy he was himself elaborating; in its place he put his own concept of bad faith. For the next decade and a half Sartre was to remain an unreconstructed rationalist, ready to find an intellectual affinity in the "poetic" version of psychoanalysis propounded by Gaston Bachelard, but for the most part faithful to the "lucidity" of

[28] Beauvoir, *Prime of Life*, p. 112.

his Cartesian inheritance.[24] Not until the mid-1950's, in the gravest crisis of his entire intellectual life, did he return more humbly to Freud for guidance.

It never seemed to occur to Sartre that he might himself have benefited by psychoanalytic therapy. Yet the evidence of unresolved childhood suffering was amply apparent. As a young man Sartre remained profoundly wounded—wounded by his mother's remarriage when he was eleven years old and by the almost simultaneous and "brutal" discovery that he was far from handsome. He was also haunted by fantasies of illegitimate birth which were to appear again and again in his imaginative writings: one of Sartre's younger friends found in this absorption with "bastardy" the hook on which he could hang his own effort at an amateur psychoanalysis.[25] At the age of thirty Sartre was troubled by hallucinations of lobsters pursuing him.[26] Eventually the lobsters disappeared—lucidity triumphed—but the emotional vulnerability remained.

As Heidegger had followed Husserl in Sartre's intellectual biography—with Freud trailing considerably behind—so Marx arrived later still. By the 1930's Sartre had acquired a few summary notions of Marxian theory, but until the war he remained basically nonpolitical and ideologically uninvolved. While he had rejected with scorn the facile rationalizations of the bourgeoise, he had nothing to put in their place beyond a highly individual form of intellectual anarchism. In 1936 he cheered for the Popular Front—but strictly as an outsider: he did not even bother to vote. Then came Munich to shake him into an awareness that armed resistance to Hitler was unavoidable.[27] And a year later, when the war broke out, he was called up for military service.

During the winter of the phony war, which he spent in enforced idleness with a noncombatant unit in Alsace, Sartre

[24] *Ibid.*, pp. 23, 106–107, 425.
[25] Francis Jeanson, *Sartre par lui-même* (Paris, 1955), pp. 61–62.
[26] Beauvoir, *Prime of Life*, pp. 169–170, 177–178.
[27] *Ibid.*, pp. 211, 268.

had time to think through what he would do when the conflict was over. He determined that he could no longer stand aside from politics: he must "assume his situation" by engaging himself in ideological action; any other conduct would be an evasion, a flight into bad faith. Within less than a year, Sartre had an opportunity to put this new understanding into practice. Captured by the Germans in the great defeat, he threw himself with enthusiasm into the totally novel experience of a prisoner-of-war camp. He was exhilarated by the taste of community living; he stimulated the flagging morale of his fellow prisoners, organizing the production of an anti-German play he had written.[28] When he was released a few month later, he similarly did his best to bring together his literary friends in one of the earliest of the Parisian Resistance groups; later, as we have already observed, he worked with the Communist writers. After the liberation, Sartre established a new review—*Les temps modernes*—that combined literature and politics; and as the Cold War opened, he helped to found a neutralist political movement. This venture—which aimed at aligning the intellectual Left both alongside the Communists and independent of them—succeeded no better than Sartre's first wartime effort; in just over a year it had collapsed utterly, torn apart by its own internal inconsistencies. The experience had a sobering effect: Sartre realized that as a neophyte in politics he had acted precipitately and with insufficient ideological preparation. It was only then that he was ready for a full-scale encounter with Marx as a guide to the second phase of his public career.

Meantime Sartre had become famous as the grand master of French existentialism. It is odd that the identification which was to adhere to him most closely was not applied until late in the war, when he had already been publishing philosophical studies for seven years, and then almost

[28] *Ibid.*, p. 342; Simone de Beauvoir, *La force des choses* (Paris, 1963), translated by Richard Howard as *Force of Circumstance* (New York, 1965), pp. 5–6.

casually. Gabriel Marcel, who had preceded Sartre along a similar path, seems to have been the first to refer to the latter as an existentialist. Sartre thought of himself, rather—to the extent that he was willing to accept a label at all—as a phenomenologist, and only after the war did he issue anything resembling an existentialist manifesto. His fifth and most influential philosophical work, published under the occupation in 1943, was, as its subtitle put it, no more than an "essay in phenomenological ontology."

Being and Nothingness was read straight through by very few of Sartre's contemporaries. When it first appeared, it made little impression on the public, and the reviewers and professional philosophers took their time about discussing it. It was not until Sartre had found a general audience with his plays and novels that people turned back to his philosophical treatise in search of the abstract assumptions which lay behind his imaginative work. What they discovered most of the time only confused them. To readers accustomed to the graceful, limpid style of a Bergson, *Being and Nothingness* was hard going: it was portentously long, and its author had not hesitated "to create new expressions, to do violence to syntax," to weigh down his prose by "piling words on top of each other," and to pursue his argument long after he had made his main point.[29] Still more, the book was so idiosyncratic both in conception and in execution that the French public might be pardoned if it found little connection between Sartre's philosophical speculations and what existentialism had come to mean as a literary movement.

Throughout *Being and Nothingness* Sartre gave full credit to his German masters Husserl and Heidegger—and to Hegel, who was only later to move to the center of his thought. He made passing reference to Bergson and Proust as having gotten into insoluble difficulties through their inadequate theories of memory, and, among his near-contemporaries, to Malraux and Saint-Exupéry; in the former he admired the

29 Jeanson, *Problème moral*, pp. 136–137.

union of thought and action which was most fully expressed
in *Man's Hope*; in the latter he believed he had discovered a
concrete illustration of Heidegger's effort to fuse subject and
object in a totality of human endeavor.[30] But in Sartre's work
there was none of the fascination with death that had gripped
the generation of novelists only a few years his senior. For
Sartre death was something merely external: it was—to use
one of his favorite expressions—"absurd."

His whole elaborate ontological structure rested on the
radical distinction he drew between consciousness, which he
identified as for-itself (pour soi), and the phenomenal world,
including the existence of the individuals who experienced
such consciousness, which he consigned to the realm of being-
in-itself (en soi). The eccentricity of this distinction lay in
the fact that although the for-itself enjoyed all the philosophical prestige imaginable, it had no attributes of its own:
consciousness as such was a negative quantity—hence the
word "nothingness" in the book's title. Being-in-itself might
constitute the totality of the universe, but by its density and
massiveness it was always threatening to drag down the for-
itself to the level of a routine and depressing existence. Thus
Sartre's major assertions all referred back to a single source.
Everything he valued—"for-itself, nothingness, human consciousness, freedom, free choice"—was ultimately, in his
system, "one and the same thing."[81]

It was Sartre's deepest conviction that the for-itself was
radically free. He admitted only grudgingly the limitations
imposed on human actions by external circumstances, and he
found the true barrier to one person's liberty of choice in the
freedom of someone else. The result was a concept of human
relations whose bleakness was almost without precedent.
Each individual consciousness pursued its existence in isola-

[30] *L'être et le néant* (Paris, 1943), translated by Hazel E. Barnes as
Being and Nothingness (New York, 1956), pp. 131, 170, 431.
[81] Wilfrid Desan, *The Tragic Finale: An Essay on the Philosophy of
Jean-Paul Sartre*, Torchbook paperback edition (New York, 1960), p.
101.

tion from the others. Each was prey to an "anguish" which Sartre defined not as fear of what others might do, but as dread of one's own potential for good or evil. Anguish was man's recognition of his freedom: it was the simplest and most profound of his self-definitions. The majority of mankind could not stand such an awareness: they fled for refuge to a state of bad faith, which again needed to be distinguished from untruth or falsehood, since it meant lying to oneself rather than to others. But even the minority who tried to become fully aware of their condition could not manage to live with what the conventional moralists called sincerity. Sincerity was an illusion, an "impossible task." For how could a man remain true to what he had been in the past without converting himself into a fixed "thing" which the very definition of consciousness denied?[82]

In a universe thus constituted, relations between human beings could be only those of conflict—of one freedom pitted against another. Love was as much an illusion as sincerity: what the lover was really after was to subjugate his partner. Similarly the experience of community—of "we"—was never direct: it had always to be mediated by a third relationship. In the conflict of rival freedoms that was the texture of human existence, there could be no more than temporary truces and understandings; respect for the freedom of another was an "empty word," since every attitude one might adopt to express such respect would end by being a violation of the freedom in question.[83]

Far from regarding each other with mutual respect, human beings cast baleful glances which stripped one another of their comfortable disguises. Man's characteristic reaction to the "look" that someone else turned upon him was to feel naked and ashamed.[84] In the Sartrian universe shame was the token and measure of human inadequacy; it suggested the

[82] *Being and Nothingness*, pp. 29, 43, 47–50, 62–63, 525.
[83] *Ibid.*, pp. 364, 366, 375, 409, 429.
[84] *Ibid.*, pp. 288–289.

impossibility of living, as the bourgeois humanists had thought they were doing, at peace with one's fellow men and in the enjoyment of a good conscience.

A concept of being which was so unsparing in its dissection of motives, an ontology which gave no quarter to ethical evasions, had obvious affinities to classic psychoanalysis. Yet when at the end of his long study Sartre defined his own concept of "existential psychoanalysis," it became apparent that his philosophy was irreconcilable with Freud's central insight. Sartre gave the Freudian school full credit for being the only one among his predecessors to start from the "same original evidence" and to try to get at the "more profound structures" of human consciousness. But this search, Sartre contended, had stopped in mid-course: Freud had limited himself to the exploration of his patients' past; he had not gone on to examine the future toward which their emotional configurations were directed. More specifically he had not tried to understand the "fundamental project" that gave meaning to the life of each of them—and man's "project" was to loom ever larger in Sartre's thought as he became increasingly absorbed with the social realm.

Freud had failed to recognize this orientation toward the future, Sartre argued, because he had remained absorbed by the unconscious. He had not sufficiently examined what he meant by the "censorship" that prevented intolerable thoughts from arising to full awareness. More closely examined, the censorship itself proved to be a conscious self-deception—an aspect of bad faith. Sartre's concept of bad faith, as we have already observed, virtually forced him to reject the Freudian "hypothesis of the unconscious": the unconscious gave human beings an alibi for failing to accept the consequences of their inner dishonesty.[85]

In the Sartrian moral universe there was no room for excuses—as there was none for remorse or regret. There was only a sense of "overwhelming . . . responsibility"—the

[85] *Ibid.*, pp. 52–53, 458, 564, 570, 573.

sense that man, "condemned to be free," carried the "weight of the whole world on his shoulders."[86]

Such, in broad outline, was the argument of *Being and Nothingness*. Under its ponderous manner, it was in fact a highly personal self-revelation. Its very vocabulary betrayed the author's anxieties and his unremitting effort to resolve them through literary or philosophical formulations. Sartre, as one of his younger admirers described him, was an obsessive who delivered himself of his obsessions for his readers' profit or expense.[87] He was an intellectual who turned the full force of his intellect upon his own person, who was driven by his inner furies to play a "hellish game with consciousness."[88] Throughout his work lurked the fear of being entrapped, imprisoned, confined. The most pervasive of his metaphors was the viscosity or stickiness of being-in-itself in which the weightless, transparent for-itself was forever in danger of foundering. To such contamination Sartre's characteristic reaction was nausea—as *Nausea* had been the title of the novel with which he had first come to the attention of the reading public. This metaphysical disgust could on occasion extend to the entire corporeal aspect of existence; at one point in *Being and Nothingness* Sartre referred almost casually to the "nauseous character of all flesh."[89]

As the mythic carriers of fleshly values, women thus became automatically suspect: Sartre's critics have repeatedly drawn attention to the harsh treatment he dealt them in his plays and novels, where they figured as soft, damp, porous, and once even as a "swamp." If the flesh (or life, or existence) was dense and viscous—in short, female—the intellect was hard and sharp and male. Between these two realms, there could be neither emotional nor intellectual understanding. "A mind which thinks in Cartesian geometrical terms,

---

[86] *Ibid.*, pp. 553, 555–556.
[87] Jeanson, "Un quidam," p. 307.
[88] Victor Brombert, *The Intellectual Hero: Studies in the French Novel 1880–1955* (Philadelphia and New York, 1961), p. 197.
[89] P. 357.

which fixes all life in concepts that have the brittle clarity of crystal, . . . can designate the transcendent force of life only as Not-Being, Nothingness."[40]

Sartre had welcomed the density and concreteness of phenomenological speculation as an antidote to the intellectualism of his French philosophical upbringing. But in the course of converting to his own uses what Husserl had taught, he had landed himself in an intellectualism of another kind. In seeking to break out of an old and familiar prison, he had confined himself in a new one of his own construction. This was what Gabriel Marcel—who was uniquely qualified to judge the viability of Sartre's philosophical venture—concluded after a reading of *Being and Nothingness*. While expressing his admiration for the fashion in which its author had delineated the phenomenon of bad faith, Marcel wondered whether Sartre had not in the name of freedom itself condemned his thought "to move in an infernal circle." Beyond that—and this for Marcel was the "most serious question" the book raised—how could a work that set out "from premises which in another age would have been called idealistic" have reached "conclusions which a materialist would not disclaim?"[41] Under Sartre's novel formulations, Marcel, as an obstinate "spiritualist," had detected a crypto-materialism. By the time *Being and Nothingness* was written, the old dichotomy between idealism and materialism (or perhaps better, positivism) had been largely overcome: both philosophers and social scientists had tried to go beyond such nineteenth-century distinctions by focusing on practical procedures that might furnish provisional verification to the constructions of the intellect. In this perspective, Sartre's method marked a step backward: the radical distinction he drew between the for-itself and being-in-itself split apart once

[40] Theophil Spoerri, *Die Struktur der Existenz* (Zürich, 1951), a selection from the chapter on Sartre translated as "The Structure of Existence: *The Flies*" for *Sartre: A Collection of Critical Essays*, p. 59.
[41] *Homo Viator: Prolégomènes à une métaphysique de l'espérance* (Paris, 1945), translated by Emma Craufurd as *Homo Viator: Introduction to a Metaphysic of Hope* (London, 1951), pp. 179, 183.

more the realm of existence and the realm of pure thought.

In Cartesian fashion, Sartre offered his readers an either-or choice. If they found the notion of consciousness without attributes too much for them, they could always opt for the viscosity of corporeal existence. It was here, after all, that life and action went on. The other face of Sartre's ultra-idealism was a concept of being which readily lent itself to the most extreme materialist interpretations.

The Sartrian for-itself was something totally new. Although it might at first glance resemble the mind or the soul or the ego or the consciousness of the Western philosophical and psychological tradition, it was actually distinct from them all, since it lacked definition—or rather, was defined in terms of nothingness. Hence it was necessarily impersonal. It had to be so—for to give it "the slightest granule of being" would mean to "provide something for deterministic influence to take hold of" and thereby to destroy the freedom of "pure and translucid consciousness." Sartre's uncompromising search for freedom ended in its own negation. "In his absolute process of emptying the for-itself" of all content, he "killed it."[42] With conciousness reduced to nothingness, materialism was the only remaining recourse.

Yet in fact Sartre did not succeed in holding to his own philosophical definitions. Ostensibly he had abolished the individual ego, but under a series of transparent disguises it crept back into his prose. Without an ego, without a notion of human individuality, his whole idea of "existential psychoanalysis" would have been impossible. Quite apparently the still-undiscovered Freud of the new discipline would have to work on something more tangible than a negative quantity. This was an aspect of his reflections that Sartre had not yet thought through: his discussion of existential psychoanalysis read like a dangling addendum to his finished work.

Sartre was quite right in discovering an affinity between his own speculations and the procedures of psychoanalysis.

---

[42] Desan, *Tragic Finale*, pp. 153, 158.

But he had the matter turned around. It was not that he needed to define a new kind of psychoanalytic procedure; Freud's successors were already doing that by sending out investigations in the directions he had simultaneously discovered. It was rather that Sartre—and the other writers who dealt in existential categories—could reveal to the more sophisticated of the post-Freudians their own implicit philosophical assumptions, how without knowing it they had been "unofficial existentialists all along." Sartre's teaching had in common with classic psychoanalysis an insistence on the "unsparing truths" that confronted human beings with the necessity for decision. Both stressed the "anxiety about existence itself" which might go under many names—clinical or philosophical—as one or another symptom cried out for attention. Whether one called it "anomie, estrangement, dread, despair, depersonalization, alienation, abandonment," or anything else, it invariably referred back to an emotional state in which the "darkness of the world" caused "even shadows to disappear."[48] This Sartre had understood: the most telling passages in his whole long book gave it eloquent expression. And this was what his readers retained after they had given up wrestling with his special vocabulary.

Thus what was viable in Sartre's rendering of psychoanalysis had little or nothing to do with his newly-coined abstractions. The same was true of the moral and political implications of his philosophy. From the start there had been something arbitrary about Sartre's ontological categories. And they became more arbitrary still when he began to extend them to the realm of ideology.

There was no necessary connection between Sartre's philosophy of being and any specific political faith. Nor were his readers on the right track when they tried to pick out of his plays and novels a coherent sequence of moral declarations. Sartre had originally made his reputation with his novel

[48] Avery D. Weisman, M.D., The Existential Core of Psychoanalysis: Reality Sense and Responsibility (Boston, 1965), pp. vii, 215, 231–233.

Nausea in 1938. Then after the publication of *Being and
Nothingness* he had returned to imaginative literature—with
plays such as *The Flies* and *No Exit* which were produced
in Paris during the final months of the German occupation,
and with the first two volumes of his novel *Roads to Freedom*.
Like Gabriel Marcel, Sartre found emotional stimulus in
shuttling back and forth between philosophy and the theater.
Some of his plays carried an implicit message: in *The Flies*
an audience trained to the special alertness of the oppressed
could detect an undertone of Resistance rhetoric. But there
was no one-to-one correlation between what Sartre said in his
philosophical works and the lines the actors delivered in his
plays. In his imaginative writings Sartre was concerned,
rather, to show his characters "in situation," to demonstrate
how they forged their own reality at the moment of choice.[44]
The Resistance had provided the maximum and unrepeat-
able example of such testing. Yet even in the plays or novels
where it was not evoked at all, Sartre left his characteristic
mark in the delineation of a situation of moral extremity: his
protagonists were heroes of "the impossible," who walked
straight into an "impasse with tragic honesty."[45]

At the end of *Being and Nothingness*, Sartre undertook to
follow it with an ethical sequel. And in the last few pages of
this book he sketched out the themes that the subsequent
work would discuss. But the second treatise never material-
ized. As happened with the final volume of *Roads to Freedom*
for which the public waited year after year in vain, Sartre
neglected his promise to his readers in favor of topics that
seemed of greater current urgency. In both cases, a gradual
shift in his thought made it impossible for him to redeem
his earlier pledge. By the mid-1950's, Sartre was no longer in
the mood to give a systematic account of the existentialist
ethic.

In its absence, a lecture he delivered in the autumn of
1945 had to suffice. This ethical sketch—which was subse-

[44] Jeanson, *Sartre par lui-même*, p. 12.
[45] Brombert, *Intellectual Hero*, pp. 202–203.

quently published under the title *Existentialism is a Humanism*—was Sartre's response to the awkward situation in which his sudden fame had placed him. As the war ended, existentialism became the topic of the hour. The word was bandied about everywhere; it was, Sartre protested, even turned to purposes of cultural nationalism, as evidence that a much-tormented France was once again in the literary vanguard. At first Sartre tried to refuse the epithet "existentialist" that Gabriel Marcel had applied to him; he was quite ready to grant that his was a "philosophy of existence," but he failed to understand what it meant to be an existentialist. Eventually, however, since everyone else pretended to know— most of them mistakenly—the only recourse seemed to be to accept the label and to try to explain in the simplest possible terms its application to human conduct.[46]

Sartre's lecture, then, was an effort to set straight those who had distorted his thought. According to his most authoritative expositor, Francis Jeanson, Sartre subsequently decided that he had made an "error" in staking out a moral position which was not yet firmly established in his mind. And Jeanson himself, with the older man's blessing, undertook to rectify the situation by stressing in an analysis of his own the openness, the ambiguity, and the total lack of a moral imperative in the existentialist ethic.[47] At the time, however, it is hard to see how Sartre could have avoided some kind of reply to his critics and vulgarizers. By 1945 he had become a public figure; he had been torn from the sanctified obscurity in which his grandfather had taught him that the masters of literature dwelt. His words were now common property; the best that he could do was to join in the process of vulgarization.

Existentialism, Sartre explained, was not a humanism in the old sense of a categorical imperative and the good conscience of the bourgeoisie. It could be called such, however,

[46] See Simone de Beauvoir's account in *Force of Circumstance*, pp. 38–42.
[47] *Problème moral*, pp. 36, 284–285.

in the more basic meaning of a doctrine which made "human life possible" by awakening men to their responsibilities. Starting from a total denial—of God, of conventional morality, of "human nature"—the existential ethic refused to embrace a comfortable skepticism. It taught, rather, that every man was responsible not merely for himself but for all his fellowmen—and that each of the unavoidable choices one made was also a choice for all humanity, since it participated in the creation of the still-undefined entity known as man. Such choices, if "authentic," were necessarily good: the only true evil was bad faith. And they were also choices for freedom: men of good faith could not fail to choose freedom. There might be no such thing as human nature, but there was a "human condition" that made mankind one. Thus every man of good faith must necessarily seek the freedom of everyone else.[48]

This was a long way from the bleak world of universal conflict which *Being and Nothingness* had described. Although Sartre continued to assert that his doctrine was pessimistic in origin and that hope was not necessary to ethical engagement, he now discovered an "optimistic toughness" at the bottom of his despair.[49] *Being and Nothingness* had insisted on the futility of existence: in passages which were to become catchwords, Sartre had declared that man was a "useless passion" and that to "get drunk alone" or to be a "leader of nations" was equally vain.[50] Yet at the very time he was putting these thoughts on paper, Sartre was deeply committed to the ethical goals of the literary Resistance. His abstract reflections and his practical activity were going in separate directions. In his lecture of 1945, Sartre tried to bridge the gap between the two, to establish a philosophical justification for the new imperative which had inspired his Resistance work. But he succeeded only in part. Sartre's moral

[48] *L'existentialisme est un humanisme* (Paris, 1946), translated by Bernard Frechtman as *Existentialism* (New York, 1947), pp. 12, 18–21, 25–26, 45, 53–54.
[49] *Ibid.*, pp. 37, 39–40.
[50] *Being and Nothingness*, pp. 615, 627.

statements lacked the intellectual power of his ontology and
had the effect of blunting the harsh outlines of what he had
written earlier. In the world of practical action, he was still
adrift.

Sartre's emotional sympathies, his doctrine of universal
freedom, inclined him toward the Left—and toward a Left
which professed its revolutionary character. But this leftism
lacked content: it was a temper of mind rather than a fully
developed ideology. Sartre's grapplings with Marx were still
in the future. And he was to come to Marx not by the ordinary route of party activity, but through the mediation of
another philosopher, younger and less well-known than he,
Maurice Merleau-Ponty.

III. *Maurice Merleau-Ponty: From Meditation to Ideology and Back*

Until the Second World War, the intellectual appreciation
of Marx in France lagged notably behind what it had been
in Germany in the Weimar period or in Italy before the advent of Mussolini. The leaders of the French Socialist and
Communist parties had satisfied themselves with summary
notions of Marxian theory and felt free to interpret that
theory in a characteristically French fashion. For the Socialists this meant a generous, nondogmatic humanism in the
style of Jean Jaurès—a way of thought to which Léon Blum
remained true throughout his life. The corresponding Communist interpretation was in the Jacobin-Blanquist vein which
proved so appealing during the Resistance years. The Socialist party included many professors and littérateurs, but almost
no theoreticians of Marxism. The Communists had begun
with a number of adherents or sympathizers who professed
to be such, but by the end of the 1920's most of these had
dropped out, and none had risen to a position of leadership
in the party. In France there was no counterpart to the To-
rinese circle around Antonio Gramsci that gave Italian Com-

munism its characteristic openness and intellectual tone.
This lack of an intellectual tradition in France helps explain
why the French Communists became so woodenly Stalinist
and why they were so much slower than the Italians to
inaugurate an ideological "thaw" after Stalin's death. To the
extent that the French—either inside or outside the Communist party—had an intellectual understanding of Marxism,
it was predominantly Leninist with a Stalinist gloss.[51]

At the turn of the century, the French had participated
only slightly in the philosophical and sociological critique
of Marxism which was to end in the absorption of a "rela-
tivized" Marx into the mainstream of Western thought.
While Pareto and Croce among the Italians, and in Germany
Max Weber, had offered analyses of Marxism that were
widely read and accepted, in France Sorel had remained intellectually isolated and Durkheim had never gotten beyond
a few pregnant references to Marx's emotional appeal.[52] It
was to be a full generation before the French began to catch
up with the Germans and Italians. Predictably enough, the
process was inaugurated in 1936 with the lectures on Hegel
of an émigré, the Russian Alexandre Kojève, to an audience
that included some of France's most influential future intellectuals. Thus the young French of the 1930's came to
Marx in the authentic chronological and philosophical sequence; they did not go directly to him, skipping over Hegel
as irrelevant to the times, as was so often the case in this
period of economic depression in Britain or the United States.
Concomitantly, however, the approach via Hegel made the
French understanding of Marxism excessively abstract and,
in philosophical terms, idealist. And the penchant for Germanic abstraction was reinforced when a few years later, and
more particularly during the occupation period, a reading of
the thoroughly non-Marxist Husserl and Heidegger prompted
an interpretation of Marxism in existential terms.[53]

All this might have ended in the tender-minded under-

[51] Lichtheim, *Marxism in Modern France*, pp. 34, 80.
[52] See my *Consciousness and Society* (New York, 1958), Chapter 3.
[53] Lichtheim, *Marxism in Modern France*, pp. 84–85.

standing of Marx based on his own early manuscripts of a Hegelian cast that was to attain such popularity in America in the 1960's, had it not been for the intrusion of still a third foreign influence. Antonio Gramsci's writings became known only slowly in France; but the work of his rival as the greatest of Lenin's heirs, Georg Lukács, joined the Central European philosophical onslaught that was shaking up the French in the war and postwar years. The book the French read was Lukács' essay of 1923, *Geschichte und Klassenbewusstsein*—history and class consciousness—which had displeased the leadership of the Third International and which its author had subsequently repudiated. In it Lukács had extended Marxism in two directions: he had simultaneously gone back to Hegel in his idealist and literary conceptualization and had moved forward into his own time in an effort to push Leninism to its logical consequences. The result was a view of Marxist action which was even more forthrightly elitist than Lenin's. In Lukács' view the position of greatest prestige and responsibility in a revolutionary situation devolved on the "intellectual workers"; for it was up to them to instill into an inert proletariat an authentic class consciousness—and, if all else failed, by a resort to terror.[54]

Thus Lukács' book of a quarter century earlier suggested how the French could combine the Hegelian source and the Leninist derivative of Marxism into an understanding of that theory which was both idealist and revolutionary, humanist in tone, but with a tolerance for terror. Such an eclectic doctrine was not what the French Communist party taught. But it provided an optimum meeting ground for writers formally affiliated with the party and those who stood outside it in an attitude of sympathy. Its lofty philosophical vocabulary made it intellectually respectable; its "toughness" gave the party, in practice, the last word; in the meantime it offered the writers themselves a key role in the revolution to come.

Among those who had attended Kojève's lectures on Hegel

[54] See the analysis of Victor Zitta, *Georg Lukács' Marxism: Alienation, Dialectics, Revolution* (The Hague, 1964), pp. 183–193.

and studied Lukács with the greatest care was Maurice Merleau-Ponty. One of the curious features of the vicissitudes of
Marxism in postwar France was that its most sophisticated
interpreter and critic should have been an heir of the phenomenological tradition whose original writings seemed to have
nothing to do with ideology.

Merleau-Ponty, by his own account, had never gotten over
an inordinately happy childhood. Like Sartre, he had felt
himself adored by his mother, and he apparently escaped the
need that Sartre experienced later on to reconsider this idyllic
memory. The social origins of the two were also divergent:
Merleau-Ponty came of the grande bourgeoisie and retained
the manners of the gently-bred, while Sartre insisted on the
modesty of his own middle-class milieu and on his independence from polite conventions. It was characteristic of
Merleau-Ponty that he performed his combat service as an
officer—something that was less common among French intellectuals in the Second World War than it had been in
the First. And he likewise differed from most of his counterparts in his attitude toward religion: although he shared
their atheism, he had lost his Catholic faith only in late
adolescence, and he subsequently refrained from the aggres-
sive or insulting tone toward the Church that was normal
among his acquaintance; the rare occasions on which he
referred to religious matters revealed a thorough familiarity
with the Catholic tradition and an awareness of the intellectual changes that were taking place within French Catholicism.[55]

Merleau-Ponty, born in 1908, was three years younger than
Sartre, but their careers at the Ecole Normale Supérieure
had overlapped. Here they had known each other only at a
distance. Subsequently Merleau-Ponty had started out, as

[55] Remy C. Kwant, *The Phenomenological Philosophy of Merleau-
Ponty* (Pittsburgh, 1963), pp. 128–129; Maurice Merleau-Ponty,
"L'homme et l'adversité" (originally published in 1952), *Signes*
(Paris, 1960), translated by Richard C. McCleary as *Signs* (Evanston,
Ill., 1964), p. 242.

Sartre did, teaching philosophy in a succession of lycées. The difference between them—again in character—was that while Sartre never submitted a doctor's thesis and after the war gave up teaching to concentrate exclusively on his writing, Merleau-Ponty followed the normal French pattern of academic advancement, eventually reaching the very top of the country's intellectual establishment. In 1945 he was appointed professor at the University of Lyons; four years later he was called to Paris; and after only three years at the Sorbonne, he received in 1952 a chair at the Collège de France—where Bergson and Febvre had lectured before him, and where Lévi-Strauss was to arrive a few years later—a recognition of the extraordinary position in French intellectual life he had attained in just over half a decade.

From the philosophical standpoint, he and Sartre had followed parallel paths. During the 1930's, they had pursued a similar course of reading and reflection quite independently of one another. Not until the war and Sartre's release from German captivity did they become once more acquainted, and as co-workers in Sartre's original abortive effort at a Resistance organization discover that they had in common the words "phenomenology" and "existence." "Too individualist to . . . pool" their research, they "became reciprocal while remaining separate"; the influence of Husserl was both what divided them and what made them friends. The result was a mixture of sympathy and ineradicable difference in their philosophical approaches which perplexed their students and admirers. In this early period of their association it was Merleau-Ponty rather than Sartre who was mainly responsible for the distance between the two. The younger man preferred to keep his reflections to himself and was thrown off his track by extended discussion. Sartre, on the contrary, loved talking with Merleau-Ponty, as "ventilation" for his own thought, and had a way of referring to their relationship as a team which the latter subsequently resented.[56]

[56] Jean-Paul Sartre, "Merleau-Ponty" (originally published August–September 1961), *Situations*, IV (Paris, 1964), translated by Benita Eisler as *Situations* (New York, 1965), pp. 230–232.

In terms of technical philosophy, Merleau-Ponty's reputation rested on two substantial works, *La structure du comportement*, published in 1942, and his doctor's thesis, *Phénoménologie de la perception*, which followed three years later. In the latter work in particular he traced the view of human existence that lay behind his subsequent social thought—a view that considered mind and body as inseparable and stressed the preconscious origin of man's conscious activity. A foe of both rationalism and empiricism in the forms in which he had encountered them in his own philosophical training, Merleau-Ponty was in no sense an apologist for unreason. It was rather that he had been impressed early in life with the inability of any formulation—whether abstract or experimental—to give an even remotely adequate account of the infinite complexity of interpersonal relationships. Like Marcel, Merleau-Ponty felt that he was groping his way in a universe which gave up few of its secrets—but in his case a universe in which religious faith offered no guidance. The human world was the sphere of contingence, of ambiguity: in ultimate terms it was unintelligible. Existence was suffused with meanings—but these were human meanings devoid of absolute truth. Such a philosophy combined an extreme subjectivism with a radical objectivity in the delineation of phenomena: its basic attitude was wonder at the marvelous variety of man's adventure. To the end of his life Merleau-Ponty remained hostile to any philosophical or historical theory that tried to climb above the phenomenal world and attain a bird's-eye view; his own final position has been summed up in the single expression "en-être"—which can be translated quite literally by the American colloquialism "being with it."[57]

Merleau-Ponty had become a Pascalian in adolescence before he had read a word of Pascal himself.[58] This affiliation

[57] Introduction to *Signs*, p. 21; Remy C. Kwant, *From Phenomenology to Metaphysics: An Inquiry into the Last Period of Merleau-Ponty's Philosophical Life* (Pittsburgh, 1966), p. 227.
[58] Sartre, "Merleau-Ponty," *Situations*, p. 228.

implied a negative attitude toward Descartes and at least a beginning of sympathy for Bergson. In Merleau-Ponty's view, as in that of Maritain, Descartes's great mistake had been to consign mind and body to two distinct realms of being: in his own philosophy they were one; man was a "body subject," both spiritual and material, whose "soul" was no more than the "higher level of the subject's self-organization" and whose conscious activity was marginal in importance to what went on at the preconscious stage. For such a philosophy language offered the clue to all the levels of human existence; man as "speaking subject" epitomized the unity of mind and body in a single movement of self-expression.[59]

This unity Bergson had understood. What Merleau-Ponty prized in Bergson was the boldness of the innovator who had rejected the standard notion of philosophy as a panoramic world-view and had redefined it as thought inherent to the matter at hand; he had no taste for the official "Bergsonism" of his own youth, the master's teaching that had been half-accepted by the Catholic Church and watered down almost beyond recognition.[60] Merleau-Ponty's abiding concern was to find an intellectual method which would attain to an inner understanding of the human world.

Such had also been the aim of the German philosophers and social theorists of the turn of the century. And in purpose, if not in vocabulary, Merleau-Ponty was their legitimate heir. He shunned the word "idealism," which to him, as to Sartre, had a narrower meaning than it did in Germany, recalling unpleasant memories of neo-Kantian teachings in the French lycées. But his work in fact linked up with German twentieth-century idealism in its emphasis on "comprehension"—Verstehen—a method that found "amid the multiplicity of facts a few intentions or decisive aims." Merleau-Ponty had little use for the conventional French notion of

[59] Kwant, *Phenomenological Philosophy of Merleau-Ponty*, pp. 11–13, 18, 47, 50, 61.
[60] "Bergson se faisant" (originally published in 1960), *Signs*, pp. 182–184.

sociology: he was critical of the Durkheim tradition and scornful of a "myth about scientific knowledge" which expected wonders from the "mere recording of facts." His own idea of sociological study was close to how Dilthey and Weber had defined it: it should be expressed in terms of "ideal variables," intellectual constructions which would reflect the vast interrelatedness of human experience, and it should be made continually aware of its limitations through the vigilance of philosophical method. As opposed to the pretensions of the sociologists, Merleau-Ponty found the French historians more modest and realistic in their aims, and he expressed his admiration for the reconstitution of the mentality of a vanished age that he had found in Lucien Febvre's study of sixteenth-century disbelief.[61]

Merleau-Ponty's interest in the social psychology of the past, his concern for the phenomenon of language and for preconscious processes, led him effortlessly to Freud. Like Freud, he found in the pathological and the disturbed a key to the functioning of "normal" humanity. But his chief philosophical tie to psychoanalytic theory was his concept of the "body subject"; in this respect he went farther than Freud in breaking down the old dualism between mind and body. For Merleau-Ponty, Freud was the pathfinder who had inaugurated a new and ampler view of man's relation to his physical equipment; in place of the nineteenth-century idea of the body as a "bit of matter" or a "network of mechanisms," he had substituted the notion of a body that was "lived in," where spirit and matter were engaged in a never-ending process of mutual exchange. This new sense for the life of the flesh was the first aspect of contemporaneity that Merleau-Ponty called to mind when just after the half-century mark he was asked to delineate the characteristic philosophical attitudes that the past fifty years had brought into currency.[62]

[61] "La métaphysique dans l'homme" (originally published in 1947), *Sense and Non-Sense*, pp. 88–93; "Le philosophe et la sociologie" (originally published in 1951), *Signs*, pp. 99, 110.
[62] "L'homme et l'adversité," *Signs*, pp. 226–229.

Marxism was not one of these: it was a legacy from the previous century. But for Merleau-Ponty, as for so many French intellectuals of his generation, Marxism in a nuanced and modernized form was the presupposition that lay behind his speculations about the social world. In this case also, as in that of psychoanalysis, his phenomenological interest in the human body had a direct connection with the theory of a respected predecessor. For in Marxism Merleau-Ponty discovered an understanding of what he called the "flesh of history," the interaction between the material infrastructure of existence and the ideas which human beings had formed about it, a relationship which had escaped nearly all of Marx's intellectual competitors.[63] Reduced to its essentials, Marxism simply meant that "nothing can be isolated in the total context of history, . . . with, in addition, the idea that because of their greater generality economic phenomena make a greater contribution to historical discourse." Or—to put the matter in terms of human action—while Marxism was not in principle an optimistic philosophy, its central idea was that "another history" was "possible," that there was "no such thing as fate," and that man was free—indeed, should strive —to build a future which "no one in the world or out of the world" could know whether or what it would be.[64]

For Merleau-Ponty, then, Marxism was a way of thought that remained open to man's infinite possibilities. And far more clearly than Sartre, he established its connection with what he was perfectly willing to call an "existential philosophy." Hegel and Marx, he argued, had been proto-existentialists without knowing it: the former had founded his "militant philosophy" not on the passive subjectivity of the idealists but on the dynamic idea of intersubjectivity; the latter had gone beyond his explicit system to posit a concept of human relations in which men made their own meanings as they engaged their lives in liberating actions. Properly understood, Marxism had nothing abstract about it: it dealt

---

[63] Introduction to *Signs*, p. 20.
[64] "Autour du marxisme" (originally published in 1946), *Sense and Non-Sense*, pp. 112, 119.

in concrete relationships among men and social classes, and
the morality it taught was one of authentic responsibility
and passion as opposed to the formal ethics of the schools.[65]

Thus defined, Merleau-Ponty's Marxism was quite capable
of a wide and nonsectarian appeal. Yet alongside formulations
that were irreproachably permissive, he allowed himself to
interject a scattering of lapidary expressions that conceded
nothing to the skeptical. Until very late in his philosophical
career, Merleau-Ponty invariably referred to a "proletariat"
whose existence and ethical value stood unquestioned: it is
curious to find a man ordinarily so critical of abstract
entities applying this word in almost as crude a sense as
would a party believer. Still more, he whose notion of historical interpretation was usually so refined could on occasion
speak of Marxism not as one philosophy of history among
others but as *the* philosophy of history—a philosophy so
indispensable that if one should have to abandon it, reason
in history would cease to exist, leaving "only dreams or adventures."[66]

Apparently Merleau-Ponty was initially unaware of the
extent of the cleavage within his own thought. It became
apparent to him under conditions of maximum ideological
tension five years after he began to apply his Marxist reasoning to the world of political action.

In the months following the liberation, Merleau-Ponty
was much sought after by the French Communist intellectuals. They knew very well that at that time he was not
one of their kind. Before the war, Sartre surmised, he may
have been closer to their way of thinking, until the Moscow
purge trials, which were to figure prominently in his subsequent writings, raised awkward questions in his mind.

[65] "La querelle de l'existentialisme" (originally published in 1945–
1946), *Sense and Non-Sense*, p. 82; "Marxisme et philosophie" (originally published in 1947), *Sense and Non-Sense*, pp. 133–134; *Humanisme et terreur: essai sur le problème communiste* (Paris, 1947),
pp. 118–119.
[66] *Humanisme et terreur*, p. 165.

Evidently the Communists respected in Merleau-Ponty the rigor of an intellectual method impervious to shifts in the party line—a "severe and disillusioned" Marxism of expectant waiting.[67]

This ideological expertise became a precious asset when in 1945 Sartre and his friends founded *Les temps modernes*. As editor, Sartre knew that he needed political guidance; and Merleau-Ponty was willing to furnish it, on the condition that his own role be left undefined. In effect, he served as co-editor of the new review, charged with responsibility for its ideological orientation. In theory, he was merely an ordinary member of the editorial board: he courteously rejected Sartre's repeated offers to place his name alongside his own on the cover of the magazine, and he insisted that Sartre approve everything he wrote. In this fashion the younger man provided himself with an escape hatch for the future: more conscious than Sartre of their deep-running temperamental differences, he apparently already feared the rupture that was to come a half decade later, and he took his precautions in advance.[68]

The book which according to Sartre's own account gave him the "push" that tore him loose from his political "immobility" was Merleau-Ponty's *Humanisme et terreur*.[69] Published in 1947, just as the Cold War, already latent for two years, was becoming manifest, it angered nearly all ideological camps. The Communists disliked its cool and realistic analysis of Stalinism; the democratic Center objected to its attitude of neutrality between East and West and the preference it gave to the goals of the Soviet leaders, if not to their current practice—*Humanisme et terreur* was one of the prime targets of Raymond Aron's *Opium of the Intellectuals*. Reread in the less charged atmosphere of two decades later, Merleau-Ponty's tract—for such it unashamedly was—may seem not nearly so provocative as it did when it

[67] Sartre, "Merleau-Ponty," *Situations*, pp. 237, 242–244.
[68] *Ibid.*, pp. 248–252.
[69] *Ibid.*, p. 253.

first appeared. Basically, it was the most sophisticated
apologia for Soviet Communism to come out of the late
1940's in any Western country: as a plea for suspended judgment, for giving the Soviet Union the benefit of the doubt,
it was to accord far better with the European temper of the
1960's than with the era of maximum political passion which
immediately followed it publication.

In the series of loosely-joined essays that made it up,
Merleau-Ponty pursued three related arguments of steadily
widening scope. The narrow and immediate purpose of
Humanisme et terreur was to answer Koestler's *Darkness at
Noon*. The Moscow purge trials, Merleau-Ponty contended,
were not the crude dramas of sensitive intellectuals pitted
against brutal commissars that Koestler had depicted. More
particularly in the case of Bukharin, whose testimony Merleau-Ponty analyzed in detail, such a trial was the confrontation of two clashing interpretations of Marxism, in which
prosecutor and defendant recognized the common ground on
which they stood and in which the latter was given a chance
to "save his revolutionary honor" by phrasing his recantation
in Marxist terms. Both parties knew that terror was essential
to the making of a revolution, as to its preservation. Beyond
that—and here Merleau-Ponty's argument broadened into its
second phase—the Soviet leaders were more honest than
those of the West in admitting to their own terrorist practices. In their colonies the British and the French pursued
without saying so a policy of repression comparable to Stalin's.
Even at home—and this was Merleau-Ponty's cleverest and
most resented thrust at his compatriots—the trials of French
collaborationists after the war had borne a disquieting resemblance to the harsh political justice that the Soviet courts
had handed out in the 1930's. "To know and to judge a
society," Merleau-Ponty argued, "one must reach to its
depths, to the human tie which binds it together and which
depends not only on juridical relationships but also on the
forms of labor and on the way people love, live, and die.
. . . A regime that is liberal in name may in fact be oppres-

sive. A regime which recognizes its own violence *might* contain more true humanity."[70]

All this being so, the best attitude to adopt toward Communism was a "practical" one of "understanding without adherence and of free examination without belittling." Its aim should be to make clear what the ideological situation actually was, "to underline the real terms of the human problem, beyond the paradoxes and contingencies of current history, to recall to the Marxists their humanist inspiration, . . . and to the democracies their fundamental hypocrisy" —in short, to take advantage of the margin of safety, the "minimum of play" that was still left in the course of events, in the hope of finally saving the peace of Europe.[71]

Such was the third and widest circle of argument in *Humanisme et terreur*. Three years after its publication, the "minimum of play" vanished, and Merleau-Ponty began to regret his own work. By the mid-1950's, he was ready to grant that his "Marxism of expectant waiting" had erred in directing all its attention at the excesses of anti-Communism and in neglecting to attack the "crypto-Communism" which was so prevalent among Merleau-Ponty's own acquaintance.[72] This was certainly the book's major weakness: it loaded the dice against the Western democracies while trying to "understand" the crimes of Stalin; it equated Britain's timid and heartless policy of keeping Jews out of Palestine—a policy that was about to be abandoned—with the systematic terror practiced in the Soviet Union. When he finished *Humanisme et terreur*, Merleau-Ponty had failed to answer a fourth question he had set himself—the extent to which Communism still lived up to its "humanist intentions"—and he had failed to do so because in the terms of "expectant waiting" in which he had put the problem, it was in fact unanswerable.[73]

What had changed Merleau-Ponty's attitude was the out-

[70] *Humanisme et terreur*, pp. x, 40–44, 51.
[71] *Ibid.*, pp. 159–160, 196, 202.
[72] *Les aventures de la dialectique* (Paris, 1955), pp. 306–309.
[73] *Humanisme et terreur*, pp. xiv, 200.

break of the Korean War. His reaction to this event, like that of so many other French intellectuals, in retrospect seems disproportionate. He went into a deep depression and made bitter jokes about a future life of exile in which he would work as an elevator man in New York. Too honest to take refuge in the comforting rationalization that the North Korean attack was only a surface appearance and that the real aggressors were the American puppets in the South, Merleau-Ponty recognized that the launching of a military offensive by a Communist state had knocked out a major prop from under his earlier argument. In *Humanisme et terreur* he had pleaded for an attitude of understanding toward the Communist regimes on the grounds that they had not in fact attacked their neighbors; now one of them, with the apparent blessing of the Soviet Union, had done just that. Communism's humanist "mask" had been torn away: Stalin's Russia stood revealed as a "Bonapartist" tyranny.[74]

For months on end Merleau-Ponty nursed his chagrin and disillusionment, turning his anger in upon himself and shaken by remorse for what he had earlier written. *Les temps modernes* ceased to publish articles on politics—which was inevitable, since its two directing spirits differed on the meaning of the war (Sartre had quickly come around to the standard interpretation of the French Left that the South Koreans and the Americans were the guilty parties). In long, inconclusive conversations they tried to save their friendship and their collaboration on the review; Merleau-Ponty's role sank to that of a self-effacing partner whom delicacy of feeling and personal loyalty alone kept from resigning outright. In 1952 he swallowed in gloomy silence the series of articles entitled "Les Communistes et la paix"—the Communists and the peace—with which Sartre announced his conversion to a thoroughgoing sympathy with the party. It was not until a few months later that a minor editorial disagreement between the two at length induced Merleau-Ponty to abandon *Les temps modernes* entirely. Shortly thereafter his mother died.

[74] Sartre, "Merleau-Ponty," *Situations*, pp. 275, 279.

By 1953—the year of dawning hope for the peace of Europe and the world—Merleau-Ponty seemed almost totally bereft, delivered over to a slow internal self-destruction.[75]

Two years earlier, at the height of his post-Korean discouragement, he had written of the contemporary world that it was becoming inexplicable in terms of conventional ideology. Hovering in a limbo that was neither quite peace nor quite war, it was a prey "less to the antagonism of two ideologies than to their common disarray" before a situation of which neither one could give an adequate account; international affairs were confused because the ideas on which they were ostensibly based were "too narrow to cover" their "field of action."[76] The implication was that Merleau-Ponty had relinquished every vestige of Marxist faith and had found nothing to put in its place. In 1955, however, he pulled together his courage for another try. He published a second collection of Marxian essays, entitled *Les aventures de la dialectique*, in which he tried to salvage what he could of his earlier allegiance while defining Marxism in an even more skeptical and relativist fashion than he had in *Humanisme et terreur*.

If this earlier work was the most expert Marxian polemic to appear in postwar France, *Les aventures de la dialectique* was the ablest recapitulation of the intellectual catching-up process which had gone on among French Marxists in the 1940's and early 1950's. Its publication marked the fact that the "French discussion had recovered the level of the earlier German one"—and "with the advantage of additional political experience."[77] Its author did not announce it as a systematic treatise; it was rather a collection of "samples," of "soundings," a "continual rumination" on the problems which Marxism raised. This body of political theory, Merleau-Ponty explained, was as impossible to verify as any other; the only difference was that it knew it was such and that it had

[75] *Ibid.*, pp. 273–274, 276, 279–298.
[76] "L'homme et l'adversité," *Signs*, pp. 238–239.
[77] Lichtheim, *Marxism in Modern France*, p. 80n.

"explored the labyrinth" of human affairs more thoroughly than had its rivals.[78]

The sequence from one to another of the essays which made up *Les aventures de la dialectique* was half left to the reader's imagination; Merleau-Ponty's "rumination" was characteristically elusive. But there gradually emerged the underlying theme of the need to understand Marxism in radically relativist terms as a theory of the consciousness of events rather than a truth immanent in those events themselves. Thus it was indicative of what was to follow that Merleau-Ponty began with an essay on a non-Marxist, Max Weber, singling him out as a new type of liberal who had recognized the material and emotional limits within which liberal principles operated, and who had taught the "best" among the Marxists to understand their theory with rigor and consistency.[79] Merleau-Ponty's discovery of Weber seems to have come just at the time he needed him most to help him over the transition from his earlier to his later political views. A footnote in *Humanisme et terreur* suggests that in the mid-1940's his knowledge was limited to Aron's secondhand account. By the time he came to write *Les aventures de la dialectique*, however, he had studied Weber's writings thoroughly and with transparent sympathy. Merleau-Ponty's essay, entitled "The Crisis of Understanding," is one of the most perceptive brief treatments of Weber there is. In his moment of maximum ideological perplexity he had evidently found comfort in encountering a kindred mind as scrupulous and tormented as his own.

From Weber, Merleau-Ponty went on to Lukács—the early Lukács of *History and Class Consciousness* who still remembered that he had been Weber's pupil. In Merleau-Ponty's interpretation, Lukács had gone a step beyond Weber: he had abandoned the lingering nostalgia for unconditional truth which had haunted his former teacher and had propounded a method which asked nothing beyond the

---

[78] *Aventures de la dialectique*, pp. 7, 11.
[79] *Ibid.*, pp. 15, 42.

meanings that events themselves prompted. But this subjectivist "Western Marxism" had been stifled in embryo;
the leaders of the Third International, after forcing Lukács
to recant his errors, had retreated to the safer ground of the
rough-and-ready positivism that Engels and Lenin had
bequeathed to them. *History and Class Consciousness*—"this
cheerful and vigorous essay," which had revived the "youth
of the Revolution and of Marxism"—marked the measure
of what Communism had given up, the extent of its subsequent resignation.[80]

After such a promising beginning, *Les aventures de la
dialectique* diverged, rather disappointingly, into an unnecessarily exhaustive refutation of Sartre's essays on the Communists and peace, which occupied nearly half the volume.
The subterranean "ruin" of dialectical reasoning begun by
Lukács' recantation and which Merleau-Ponty had subsequently traced through the conflict between Stalin and
Trotsky, he now found out in the open in the attitude of
Sartre. His former friend, Merleau-Ponty argued, had abandoned all pretense to Marxian method: he took on faith that
the Communist party represented the oppressed of the earth
—whose status he was unable to define as that of any recog-
nizable proletariat; he turned history into a "melodrama
daubed in crude colors" in which the only criterion for
political judgment was the anguished expression on the faces
of the poor; he blurred all previous intellectual distinctions in
a reckless "ultra-Bolshevism" where the extremes of realism
and idealism met and merged. If Sartre was serious in his
skepticism of Marxist dialectics, then the logic of his position
would be just the opposite of the subordination of his
own judgment to the party line that he seemed to be proposing—it would be to evaluate Communist behavior step
by step, in an agnostic and nominalistic temper. And this was
how Merleau-Ponty himself concluded his book: in an
epilogue which tried in vain to tie together its heterogeneous

[80] *Ibid.*, pp. 44, 61, 80.

predecessors, he outlined the politics of a "new liberalism," a "non-Communist Left" which would renounce revolution as an end in itself while making practical progress toward social equality at home and ideological coexistence abroad.[81]

A tame ending for a philosopher who had once been so pungent an ideologist and one marked by the disabused good sense that nearly always characterized Merleau-Ponty's later political writings. But it was not quite so tame as it might appear in bald résumé: Merleau-Ponty specified that the new liberalism he proposed had nowhere yet been put into practice; when it did materialize, it would follow Weber's "heroic" practice of respecting ideological enemies and treating them as equals. To the end of his life—as Sartre himself generously granted—Merleau-Ponty refused to subscribe to the conventional anti-Communism of the 1950's. And he continued to find, along with Sartre, the new horizon of ideology and social thought in the awakening of Asia and Africa.

Did he remain, then, in any sense a Marxist? One can certainly find a number of nostalgic references to Marxian theory—notably the use of the term "proletariat"—scattered through *Les aventures de la dialectique*. And it is also worth recalling that even in *Humanisme et terreur* Merleau-Ponty had kept his ideological distance from Marxian dogmatics. But the difference between the two books was unquestionable: while the first was sure-footed and almost cocky, the second was tentative and "ruminating." Nor was this change limited to a re-evaluation of Communist practice: it entailed also a rethinking of Marxian theory. His own earlier attitude, Merleau-Ponty now recognized, had been based on a priori moralizing; it had propounded a concept of revolution as "absolute action" which had smacked of "Kant in disguise." It had not been a genuine philosophy of history—not even a Marxist philosophy of history properly understood. By 1960, as Merleau-Ponty explained in one of the very last of his

[81] *Ibid.*, pp. 134–135, 138, 198, 207, 225, 227, 246, 248–249, 279, 302–304.

published essays, Marxism had entered a "new phase" in which it could still "orient analyses and retain a real heuristic value," but in which it was "no longer true *in the sense in which it believed itself true.*" In the course of a century it had "inspired so many theoretical and practical undertakings," had been the "laboratory for so many . . . experiments," even among its enemies, that it would be "simply barbarous" to speak of it in terms of "refutation" or "verification." In the second half of the twentieth century, the works of Marx had become "classics," which like other such classic writings were not to be taken literally, but in relativist terms, as a "second order of truth." Under these conditions it was pointless to ask a man or for a man to ask himself whether he was still a Marxist, since the question was incapable of a yes or no response.[82]

That was as much light on the subject as Merleau-Ponty ever dispensed. We can go no further with it until we examine the last phase of this thought, a phase of return to meditation.

Les aventures de la dialectique stood isolated among Merleau-Ponty's later reflections. It marked a final weary effort to dispose of a bundle of concerns that now lay far behind him. His first period of intellectual effort had been one of intense phenomenological reflection which had produced his two major technical works. This had been followed by a half decade in which he had plunged into the ideological controversies of postwar society and in which he had been strongly engaged by Marxist theory and practice. After 1950 —and still more markedly after the death of his mother in 1953—Merleau-Ponty withdrew once more to a life of reflection and to a growing interest in metaphysics. From this third period of his philosophical life there remain the collected essays he published under the title *Signs* in 1960, just a year before his sudden and totally unexpected death, and

---

[82] *Ibid.*, p. 312; Introduction to *Signs*, pp. 9–11. I have altered the translation slightly.

the posthumous and unfinished volume *The Visible and the Invisible*, which offered the outline of his final meditations.

In his last phase, Merleau-Ponty's writing became even more subtle and elusive than it had been before. Rejecting surface clarity—he detested what he called Sartre's "cursed lucidity"—he had always given his work the "character of a living search" rather than of a finished production; when he began writing a book, he was never quite certain where he was coming out.[83] Perhaps he had read too much German in his youth: his sentences went on endlessly, and it was some-times impossible to distinguish the main statement from the qualifications that surrounded it. These eccentricities grew more marked as his intellectual self-confidence waned. A "calculated inexactitude," an "enveloping complexity," a "glittering density" of expression—such, in the view of one of Merleau-Ponty's younger associates, were the special attributes of his late style.[84]

Yet among these complexities of his last phase we can discern at the very least a steadily growing interest in the unconscious. Toward the end of his life Merleau-Ponty drew closer to psychoanalytic theory: at the Sorbonne he lectured on child psychology; at the Collège de France he gave a course on "passivity" which included a detailed treatment of memory and dreams. For "classic" phenomenology, as for Sartre, the unconscious was an inadmissible concept. Merleau-Ponty admitted it, although he preferred to call it by other names. And so with the rest of the psychoanalytic vocabulary: again and again we find that a term of Merleau-Ponty's translates readily into Freudian language. But a final, irreducible difference remained: for Freud the body was primarily libidinal—for Merleau-Ponty libido was only an additional aspect of corporality; Freud began with an internal perception of emotional processes—Merleau-Ponty, despite his quarrel

[83] *Ibid.*, p. 24; Kwant, *Phenomenological Philosophy*, p. 9; *From Phenomenology to Metaphysics*, p. 229.
[84] Paul Ricoeur, "Hommage à Merleau-Ponty," *Esprit*, XXIX (June 1961), 1115.

with Descartes, remained sufficiently rooted in the French philosophical tradition to start his reflections with the perception of the external world. Beyond that, it would have gone against his temperament to become too closely identified with any single school; he preferred to situate himself at a crossroads of social thought, leaving his own allegiances veiled in enigma until the last.[85]

To be with it—en-être—this final definition of his metaphysical understanding was perfectly compatible with psychoanalytic method. So was the emphasis he placed on internal comprehension in his reflections on history and in his new respect for the work of Max Weber. Indeed, in Merleau-Ponty's late formulations, Weber tended to blend with a Marx understood in the French philosopher's own categories. Both were depicted as waging an unremitting two-front war against idealism and positivism. Both were applauded as social thinkers almost unique in their understanding of the coherence of body, mind, and external world in a totality of human experience. Not all of this celebration was free of ambiguity: the "relativism beyond relativism"—and beyond both Marx and Weber—which Merleau-Ponty had found in Lukács was never adequately explained; the implication was that the events of history themselves vouchsafed meanings to those who scrutinized them with sufficient care and skepticism. But this was to ask a great deal of history—far more than a professional historian would be inclined to demand. Perhaps the weakest point of Merleau-Ponty's social thought was a lingering tendency to write of history in awe-struck terms, an ineradicable penchant, despite his philosophical sophistication, to look for an immanent logic in the course of human affairs.

Sartre was quite sure that such a logic existed—and just before Merleau-Ponty's death he published a large book to prove it. The latter never had a chance to comment on

[85] André Green, "Du comportement à la chair: itinéraire de Merleau-Ponty," *Critique*, XX (December 1964), 1017–1018, 1032–1034, 1036–1037, 1040, 1046.

Sartre's *Critique of Dialectical Reason*. But unquestionably he would have objected to most of it. The perplexing thing about the relationship between the two was not that they parted, but that they managed to hold together so long. Although both had come out of the school of Husserl, what they had drawn from the German phenomenological tradition was very different: to Merleau-Ponty, who thought of experience in a dense net of interrelationships, the radical distinction Sartre drew between the for-itself and being-in-itself was totally unacceptable. Moreover, their personal and philosophical temperaments had little in common: where Sartre, by his own admission, was dogmatic, Merleau-Ponty was nuancé. It would be tempting, but quite incorrect, to regard them as a team in the style of Febvre and Bloch; it would be more accurate to say that they served as half-friendly, half-antagonistic foils to each other's intelligence. The only valid parallel to the Febvre-Bloch relationship was that in each case the younger man was both the better thinker and the less well known in his own country. There was a monstrous injustice—against which Sartre himself was the first to protest—in the widespread impression among the general public that Merleau-Ponty was his junior partner or possibly even his disciple.

When Merleau-Ponty was stricken by a fatal heart attack in early 1961, he and Sartre were in the course of arriving at a careful reconciliation. The younger man's energetic critique in *Les aventures de la dialectique*, far from making matters worse, had cleared the atmosphere, since he had finally delivered himself of the personal and intellectual resentments he had kept suppressed for a full decade. On the Algerian War, the two former friends stood once more together in condemning the official policy of repression.[86] Whether they could have become close again is more than doubtful—or perhaps it is better to say that they had never been truly close at all.

[86] Sartre, "Merleau-Ponty," *Situations*, pp. 244, 318–320.

When Merleau-Ponty was struck down, his friends could scarcely believe the news. At the funeral no one gave a memorial address, and "no one . . . regretted it," since no eulogy would have been adequate to lament a philosophical voice irremediably cut off in full speech.[87] There was no question that Merleau-Ponty had much left to say; but there was doubt as to whether he still had the desire to say it. His death was tragic; but precisely what kind of tragedy it was remained unclear. Had he died in the plenitude of intellectual vigor, or had he rather, as Sartre suspected, been succumbing for more than ten years to a slow process of internal destruction? Discouraged he unquestionably was, but the nature and extent of his weariness remained locked in his own heart.

Whatever the answer, Merleau-Ponty after the mid-1950's was lost to French social thought. Whether or not he recovered from his ideological disappointments, he almost entirely abandoned the field of political and methodological criticism. The result was a catastrophe for French intellectual life. The best speculative intelligence that France possessed —the philosopher who had almost "broken through" to a new comprehension of the social universe—removed himself from the scene just at the moment he could have been of greatest help in guiding his countrymen to an understanding of the unfamiliar society they were entering.

IV. *Jean-Paul Sartre: The Marxist Phase*

With Merleau-Ponty out of the way, Sartre was left in *de facto* control of the ideological field they once had shared. Just as the former's confidence was faltering, the latter came into full possession of his own; at the very time that Merleau-Ponty hesitated and withdrew, Sartre overcame his previous scruples and hurtled headlong into the political struggle. He who had once been his younger friend's pupil in matters ideological now felt qualified to pronounce on all subjects

[87] Ricoeur, "Hommage à Merleau-Ponty," p. 1115.

of public controversy. Thus in the early 1950's the political
paths of the two crossed each other bound in opposite directions: as Merleau-Ponty declared his disillusionment with
Communism, Sartre vowed eternal hatred for the bourgeoisie.
And the irony of the matter was that Sartre was "less of a
Marxist than Merleau-Ponty: indeed in a fundamental sense
no Marxist at all."[88]

For Sartre the decisive year was 1952—the year in which
he began to publish his essays on the Communists and peace.
The course of events since the outbreak of the Korean War
had convinced him that the United States alone threatened
to drag humanity into a third world war; the Soviet Union
and its dependent Communist parties were striving to preserve the peace—hence it was only logical for him to urge the
working people of France to trust in their Communist
leaders (although he himself would continue to maintain his
personal freedom from party discipline). This line of action
had been anticipated the previous year in one of the most
influential of Sartre's plays, *The Devil and the Good Lord*,
in which it was apparent that the spokesman of revolutionary
violence and ruthlessness was expressing the sentiments of
the author himself. Three years before in another ideological
play, *Dirty Hands*, the moral verdict had been left unclear.

It would be quite wrong, however, to suggest that Sartre
had in any sense sold out to Communism. He had always
disliked and continued to protest against the Communist
practice of twisting reality to party ends, and he remained as
stubborn as in the past about telling unpleasant truths; in
1956 he jeopardized his whole rapprochement with the
party by denouncing the Soviet suppression of the Hungarian
revolt. Nor was his judgment of events in the early 1950's as
extravagant as it might appear later on: in the United States,
with Senator McCarthy leading the pack, the forces of know-
nothing nationalism were in full cry; in France, by virtue of a
tricky new electoral law, the Left had been reduced to im-

[88] Lichtheim, *Marxism in Modern France*, p. 98.

potence, while the institutions and personnel of the Fourth Republic were sinking into political squalor. By the middle of the decade, of course, the international outlook had improved: with Stalin dead, and the Korean War and the French war in Indochina both at an end, the peace of Europe was no longer in danger; in 1956 the Americans made no move to aid the Hungarians who had taken up arms. At this point, when Sartre's scruples over Hungary might have tempted him to reconsider his alignment with Communism, events outside Europe supervened, confirming his earlier choice and prompting a rapid reconciliation with his Communist friends.

Like Lenin before him, Sartre discovered the underdeveloped world when he needed it most to buttress a faith that seemed increasingly inapplicable to European conditions. Beginning in 1951, when he made his first trip to the Soviet Union, he systematically visited the lands under revolutionary regimes—more particularly Cuba and China—and other non-European nations with a high revolutionary potential such as Brazil. Here his "ultra-Bolshevism" expressed a bitter reality: the anguished look of the poor was patent for all to see. Moreover, the neo-colonial wars waged by the Western powers provided ample reason for indignation. From 1954 to 1962, the question of Algerian independence mobilized Sartre's ideological energies; after 1965 it was the turn of the American war in Vietnam. Throughout the 1950's and 1960's, and wherever he went in the non-European world, Sartre pledged his solidarity to the revolutionary struggle.

In 1958 he was with the demonstrators in the streets of Paris, singing out the *Marseillaise* in protest against the return to power of De Gaulle. Two years later he was a leading figure among the "121"—the intellectuals who announced their support of the Algerian rebels and asserted the right of French citizens to civil and military disobedience in an unjust war. Summoned before his country's courts, he sent back an answer that turned the charge on his accusers; he refused to cut short his stay in Brazil, where he was committed to a

lecture tour, and he denied the moral legitimacy of the
French government, defying it to impose whatever sanctions
it chose. This was the moment at which Sartre came closest
to political greatness, as he voiced the shame and anger of
professors and writers, of pastors and priests, revolted by the
tortures and barbarities that France's war of repression had
entailed.

Back home at the end of 1960, Sartre found himself
officially unmolested: De Gaulle's government had quite
sensibly decided that it would be folly to make a martyr of
him. But the unofficial violence of the right-wing extremists
was mounting: in 1961, Sartre was obliged to change his
residence repeatedly, and his apartment was devastated by a
plastic bomb. In February of the following year he was again
in the streets, joining his voice to those protesting the callous-
ness of the police toward anti-war demonstrators and the
government's delays in bringing the Algerian conflict to an
end. This was the last and largest of the ideological displays
that had punctuated the postwar years; a million Parisians
had turned out. And then, just at the moment of greatest
bitterness, peace descended. The spring of 1962 brought the
liberation of Algeria and the end of France's three decades
of political strife.

It all happened so fast that the French themselves failed
to understand how an atmosphere of latent civil war could
have changed almost overnight into one of ideological torpor.
In fact such a demobilization of spirits had long been in the
making. For the better part of a decade the French had
been enjoying the most extended period of prosperity they
had known since 1914: the old antagonisms were dissolving;
the traditional political cleavages were losing their relevance.
But the Algerian War had masked the change, prolonging
France's civil hostilities into an era which was basically alien
to them. With the war over, the new France was suddenly
revealed.

Yet Sartre carried on as though nothing had occurred. He
now considered himself as enrolled for life in the worldwide

struggle for freedom, and he had no intention of desisting merely because his countrymen at home had grown more satisfied. In 1964 he declined the Nobel Prize for literature on the ground that a writer should not allow himself "to be turned into an institution"—although he added that if the Algerian War had still been in progress, he would have accepted the award as honoring the cause to which he was pledged. On the verge of sixty, Sartre was too old to reconsider his assumptions or to learn a new ideological language. This fidelity to the established direction of his political thought was manifest in the bulky treatise with which he rounded out the inner dialogue that *Being and Nothingness* had begun—his *Critique of Dialectical Reason*.[89]

In the *Critique* Sartre finally engaged himself with Marxism as an intellectual discipline. Earlier, when he had taken ideological lessons from Merleau-Ponty, his convictions had been more passionate than reasoned, and his declaration of sympathy with the Communists, as his former mentor had pointed out, was insufficiently buttressed by logical argument. His *Critique* was not announced as an answer to Merleau-Ponty's essays on Marxism; but the word "dialectics" in both titles suggested that Sartre intended to defend his "ultra-Bolshevism" against the most subtle and competent of its detractors.

Although the full *Critique* was not published until 1960, its origins dated back to 1957, when a Polish review—inspired by the new intellectual freedom that Poland had won in the previous year—asked Sartre to write an account of the state of existentialism in France after more than a decade of public notoriety. This invitation gave Sartre a chance to think through the relationship between his earlier ontology and his later ideological allegiance. The result of his reflections, sub-

[89] For this sequence of events see Simone de Beauvoir's account in *Force of Circumstance*, Chapters 7–11, and the judicious analysis in Caute, *Communism and the French Intellectuals*, pp. 249–257; Michel-Antoine Burnier, *Les existentialistes et la politique* (Paris, 1966), is far more partial to Sartre.

sequently published in slightly altered form in *Les temps modernes*, figured in a third guise under the title "Search for a Method" as an extended preface to the *Critique* itself.[90]

This work apparently gave Sartre more difficulty than any of its predecessors. It involved him in what he called writing "against himself"—presumably meaning against his own inclination—and he complained that he had to "break bones in his head" to bring his thought around to where he wanted it to come out. He wrote the book at a dizzy pace: abandoning his usual practice of pausing and making corrections as he went along, he sat writing for hours and days on end, jumping from page to page without taking time to reread what he had written. He cut short his sleep and kept himself going with a variety of pep pills until his health began to buckle under the strain. His eyes were veiled with weariness; his speech became confused; on occasion he went nearly deaf. Finally his doctor sounded the alarm, and Sartre consented to take some rest.[91] The impression he gave was of a man forcing himself to complete a burdensome task and writing as fast as he could to get it over with. And the style of the book betrayed the effort it had cost. It was incomparably more cumbrous than anything Sartre had written earlier: reviewer after reviewer declared it unreadable.

If its execution was labored, its purpose was simple and direct—to fit Marxism and existentialism together. The former, Sartre declared at the very start, was the "one philosophy of our time which we cannot go beyond," and the latter no more than an "enclave" within it. Marxism figured as the third and last of the classic philosophies of the modern era—the first two having been the rationalism that had sprung from Descartes and Locke, and the German idealist tradition of Kant and Hegel. After these great "moments" had come the time of the epigoni, whose work deserved to be

[90] This is the only part of the *Critique de la raison dialectique*, I, *Théorie des ensembles pratiques*, which is available in English: *Search for a Method*, translated by Hazel E. Barnes (New York, 1963).
[91] Beauvoir, *Force of Circumstance*, pp. 385, 451–453.

called "ideology" rather than true philosophy. Such was existentialism. Yet existentialism ranked as an ideology with a pressing claim to attention, since its purpose was to rejuvenate the teaching of Marx.

In substance, Sartre claimed, Marxism was a very young philosophy: its implications had only begun to be developed. But under the ministrations of the orthodox it had stopped in mid-passage: the Stalinists had turned it into a cult of fixed ideas. The task for existentialism, then, was to restore to the Marxist method its feeling for the specific and the actual—to rediscover a "supple, patient dialectic" that would cling to the contours of human events. Such a dialectic would follow a "progressive-regressive" course not unlike that pursued in psychoanalysis: it would first discover the "project" which gave an individual life its meaning and then trace that project to its remote sources in the past. This method of "comprehension"—Verstehen—would convert Marxism into a new "anthropology" which would be "historical and structural" at the same time. And when the conversion had been completed, existentialism, having done its work, could simply disappear—a process of self-dissolution that Sartre's own book was intended to hasten.[92]

So much for the methodological preface. The bulk of the *Critique* itself consisted of an exhaustive account of the struggle of man's ontological freedom against the resistance of matter and circumstance, of the vast realm of the "practical-inert" which was eternally dragging it down. For Sartre the fact of scarcity gave the key to human history. It was the origin of violence, in that it explained why men killed each other or permitted each other to die. Violence was "interiorized scarcity, . . . that by which everyone sees in everyone else the Other and the principle of Evil."[93] Against the

[92] *Search for a Method*, pp. xxxiv, 7–8, 22–23, 30, 126, 133–134, 150–153, 175, 181.
[93] *Critique*, p. 221; I am following the translation of Wilfrid Desan (p. 94), whose meticulous analyses in *The Marxism of Jean-Paul Sartre*, Anchor paperback edition (Garden City, N.Y., 1966), are indispensable for finding one's way in Sartre's inordinately difficult book.

brute fact of scarcity, men as individuals were powerless. Try as he might—and the *Critique* was the laborious record of his efforts—Sartre could not avoid recognizing that human freedom was less complete than he had imagined when he had written *Being and Nothingness.*

He now saw that such freedom became actual only when men grouped themselves together for mutual assistance. The group, then, furnished the bridge between his earlier and his later view of man, and he strove desperately to keep the individual in the center of his account as he traced the growing complexity of human organizations. Such bodies, he found, had an inevitable tendency to ossify: only an unremitting vigilance could protect them against succumbing to the inert. And among them political parties were by their very nature particularly exposed to degeneration. One of the most curious features of Sartre's reasoning was that while he made no effort to deny the ravages of bureaucracy where Communism was in control—while he readily granted that a Western-type society was preferable from the standpoint of spontaneity—an idealized image of a Communist party such as history had never seen provided the underlying theme for the whole latter part of his book.

It was here that Sartre's congenital passion burst the dikes of dialectical reasoning within which he had tried to confine it. As the *Critique* advanced, the revolutionary romanticism which the public knew from his more journalistic writings came tumbling back in. Some passages breathed a Jacobin fervor: true to the rhetoric of 1793, Sartre spoke of terror as "the very bond of fraternity." Elsewhere, borrowing a term of Malraux's from *Man's Hope*, he celebrated the moment of "apocalypse" when a series of isolated individuals fused into a group inspired by a single aim. Hope and terror, freedom and violence, Sartre explained, were not the antitheses which reactionary authors made of them: they were dialectically linked together in a relationship so complex that it took him more than twenty pages to explain it; the tortured character of the prose itself suggested a strenuous effort at rationalization.[94] For in Sartre's view, revolutionary violence was both inevitable and moral—that is, in conformity with "history." Far more than Merleau-Ponty, Sartre delivered himself over to the illusion that there was such a thing as an underlying course of human events and that he was capable of charting it. Hence the equanimity with which he envisaged the sacrifice of life or liberty in the service of a promised future; he apparently felt that his rooted convictions about the inalienability of man's ontological freedom grave him a special license to condone the terroristic practices of the revolutionary Left.

In a similar flood of passion, Sartre poured out once more his old hatred of the bourgeoisie. It was a class, he declared, forever guilty of "massacres"—"avorteuse, affameuse et diviseuse"—the alliteration suggesting the linked crimes of reducing the birth rate and starving and dividing the poor. Such charges might still carry weight in the world of former colonies; in France itself they had lost touch with reality. And the same was true of the magnificent passage—in a literary sense one of the few in which the old Sartrian verve came through—that sketched the portrait of the bourgeois of "distinction," cultivating a set of tastes as divergent as possible from those of ordinary men, down to and including the well-displayed frigidity of his wife! A judgment so transparently personal can readily be ascribed to the particular quirks of the author's emotional biography—but what are we to do with the parallel assertion that the analytic method itself is as characteristic of bourgeois humanism as the dialectic is by definition anti-bourgeois?[95]

No more than his Marxist predecessors who wrote an equally complicated prose did Sartre ever make clear what he meant by dialectical reason. Nor was he much more precise about the related term "praxis"—which might refer simply to pragmatic behavior or might function in a more sinister fashion as a polite term for amorality. If dialectics

[94] *Critique*, pp. 391, 429–450, 689.
[95] *Ibid.*, pp. 717, 727, 741.

meant a supple method, which refused to be limited by
either-or alternatives and which took account of the ramify-
ing interrelatedness of human emotions and actions, all well
and good. But this was no discovery requiring special con-
gratulation. For more than a generation it had been the
common coin of social study everywhere in the West—
everywhere, that is, except possibly in France. Here the
"lucidity" of Cartesian reasoning had never really relinquished its hold, and Sartre himself in his earlier writings
had been faithful to that tradition. By the time he composed the *Critique* he had come up against the limitations of
Cartesian thought. But it was one thing to recognize in the
mind the inadequacy of a certain style of reasoning and something far more difficult to apply that recognition in his own
work. When the style of Sartre's *Critique* was not merely
turgid—which was most of the time—it displayed the same
"cursed lucidity" as in the past. His treatise suggested an extended lecture to himself about being less Cartesian, and one
to little avail, since the formulas of this self-correction remained as categorical as before.

It was curious that Sartre failed to recognize a predecessor
in Georges Sorel, whose polemic against the literal-minded-
ness of orthodox Marxism had anticipated his own, and whose
apologia for violence had been similarly phrased in terms of
a liberating myth. Perhaps Sartre could never forgive Sorel
his flirtations with the political Right and his admiration
for Mussolini. In any case, the twentieth-century writers
he cited with the greatest esteem were for the most part of
a younger generation and more respectable from the standpoint of social science. Among sociologists there was Max
Weber, among anthropologists Claude Lévi-Strauss, and
along with them a distinguished roster of French historians
including Georges Lefebvre, Marc Bloch, and Fernand Braudel.[96] Such were the contemporary students of human society
in whose work Sartre found anticipations or reflections of his
own concerns. But his references to them were confined to a

[96] *Ibid.*, pp. 116, 187, 236–238, 246, 381–382, 487–490, 743.

passing comment or an unnecessarily lengthy paraphrase; they failed to establish any intrinsic connection between twentieth-century social science as its most perceptive practitioners had understood it and the venture on which Sartre himself was embarked. These bows to contemporary scholarship figured as highly un-Sartrian endeavors to legitimate his *Critique*—to prove that it had an impeccable pedigree. At their worst, they were simply dragged in; at their best, they indicated that Sartre, like Merleau-Ponty a few years before, was participating in the generalized French experience of catching up with social study abroad (and with the progress of historical writing in France itself). But Sartre's digestion of the new material was incomplete. He never satisfactorily integrated it with his personal synthesis of Marx and Descartes.

Even this latter was tenuous in the extreme. Sartre's marriage of Marxism to his earlier philosophy entailed a number of sacrifices. It meant tacitly abandoning his former distinction between the for-itself and being-in-itself; it implied a denigration of the contemplative life in favor of revolutionary action; and it made impossible the writing of the work on ethics he had earlier announced—since the claims of praxis now overrode everything else.[97] If Frenchmen of the generation preceding Sartre's—men like Bloch and Febvre—had lived with too good a conscience to question their own values, in his case the process had been just the reverse: he had become so obsessed with the concept of bad faith, he had delivered himself over so totally to his conviction that he, like every other bourgeois intellectual, was ultimately at fault, that in the end he found no norm to live by beyond a desperate commitment to the cause of the oppressed—a commitment which left little scope for intellectual nuances. And by the same emotional imperative Sartre had been driven to compose a whole bulky treatise to rationalize his choice.

In the end the *Critique* boiled down to a "complicated way of talking *about* phenomena with which historians and

[97] Desan, *Marxism of Sartre*, pp. 251, 255, 282.

sociologists" were "perfectly familiar."[98] It was neither Marxism nor social science—nor did it offer the prolegomena to
a new understanding of man. Both amateurish and old-
fashioned, it closed rather than inaugurated a major phase
in French intellectual history.

If this is the case—if Sartre's greatest ideological effort
can be written off as a pretentious failure—it may seem pointless to spend so much time on him, indeed to devote more
extended attention to him than to any other French intellectual who wrote in the years of desperation. Such is the
conclusion of most Anglo-American commentators, who are
quite ready to dismiss Sartre with a few patronizing references to a confused mind. But to do so is to miss the point
entirely—at least to the historian of ideas. For Sartre had in
no sense a second-rate intellect. His interests were as wide
as those of any man of his era; he wrote successfully in at
least four different genres—the novel, the drama, the essay,
and formal philosophy; with a different temperament he
could have become a French Goethe. The point, rather, is to
ask what there was in his emotional constitution and his relationship to society that made a man of such extraordinary
gifts take the road he did.
    At the start one needs to insist—again with Anglo-Amer-
ican detractors in mind—that there was nothing base or
self-interested about Sartre's alignment with Communism. It
brought him little credit and much abuse. The only tangible
benefit he derived from it was the pleasure of being royally
entertained in Moscow or Havana or Peking. In return he
received an unending stream of calumny, sarcasm, and dis-
tortion of his thought—not all of which came from the
political Right. When the 1950's opened and Sartre set out
on his ideological adventures, he was just entering middle
life and his fame was securely established; his subsequent
forays abroad only damaged the reputation he had already
won.

[98] George Lichtheim in *The New York Review of Books*, VI
(January 28, 1965), 9.

The conclusion seems inescapable: Sartre's relation to Communism and revolution was inspired by an inner need for atonement—a need to take upon himself the sins of the French bourgeoisie. Whether one chooses to call this attitude heroic or masochistic is immaterial: the evidence of self-punishment remains. The agonies he underwent in composing his *Critique of Dialectical Reason* may stand for all the rest. And even when he was not writing "against himself," Sartre behaved as a man driven by an inner compulsion toward words: he wryly admitted that he went on working at a furious pace decades after he had lost all conscious sense that anyone was ordering him to do so. If Sartre attacked so savagely the crypto-Puritanism of the traditional French bourgeois, it was certainly in part because he knew (and detested) the tyranny of such sentiments in his own heart.

Eventually the words themselves became vehicles of his moral asceticism. In the mid-1950's, Sartre's literary efforts bifurcated. After a struggle with his conscience which the recollections of his associates leave obscure, he evidently determined that literature—in the sense of style and composition—was no longer so important as he had once thought. In effect, he chose to sacrifice his position as a writer to what he regarded as his role in history. Hence the careless, utilitarian cast of his later writings; hence the crabbed style of his *Critique*. But at the same time—and most fortunately for posterity—he kept intact a corner of his literary pasture, which he tended rather more carefully than he had before. If he now devoted the bulk of his writing to polemical ends, he preserved a smaller segment of it as the domain of that "pure" literature which had originally started him on his way. It was to the second category that his autobiography of childhood, *The Words*, belonged—in the sense of craftsmanship as fine a work as he had ever composed.

This little book, published just four years after the *Critique*, seemed to take back or refute much that his Marxian treatise had asserted. After speaking with bemused irony of his "idealist" phase as a "long, bitter-sweet madness" from which he had recovered a decade before, Sartre went on to question the ideological commitment that had succeeded it. His pen, he now recognized, was not really a sword; he was well aware that intellectuals like himself were powerless; he no longer quite knew what to do with his life. But he was resolved to go on writing. It was, after all, his métier: there was no other way in which he was equipped to live.[99]

It is possibly unfair to judge an author by the moment of self-abandonment in which he delivers himself over to the mercy of his readers. Yet in Sartre's case, as in that of so many others, we have no more direct evidence available. Perhaps we can put the matter most charitably by suggesting that the whole ideological phase of Sartre's life—the *Critique* and all the rest—was based on a fundamental skepticism to which the autobiography finally gave expression. As a young man Sartre had thought in terms of the absolute: that had vanished with his idealist style of thinking, and no corresponding imperative had taken its place. There had come instead a more particularist and down-to-earth conviction that even in the absence of any fixed ethical norm, "innumerable tasks" remained to be performed. Alternatively—this time in terms of Sartre's self-definition—he had once thought of himself as a very special kind of person: a mandarin by hereditary right. Now he was cured of that illusion: he was ready to take his place in the ranks of mankind along with other men. But the only way in which he could serve his fellows was by writing in their behalf; and so he would continue to write—and in the fashion that had become habitual to him, in the tone of a peremptory summons to duty.

Thus absolutist thinking went out by the door and came in again through the window.[100] The result, while illogical, had an undeniable dignity and even charm. Sartre meant quite literally what he had said in his lecture on existentialist ethics two decades before—that he (in common with everyone else) bore a responsibility for all his fellowmen. However suspect the emotional origins of so cosmic a sense

99 *The Words*, pp. 253–254.
100 Jeanson, "Un quidam," p. 345.

of responsibility—however it might lend itself to the urbane mockery of his educated countrymen—this sense was the legitimate heir of that aspiration to universal values that had long been the characteristic mark of the French intellectual. In expressing it Sartre aligned himself with the tradition of the great moralistes; he took his place in the lineage of French classicism. Yet he did so with a difference which to him was capital: Sartre thought of the universalism he espoused as something quite new, as an articulation of the longings of the non-European world, only very lately released from the domination of Westerners like himself.

Herein lay the pathos of Sartre's position. For all the generosity of his gestures to the world overseas, he himself remained incorrigibly Cartesian-French. The very manner in which he espoused the cause of the oppressed in Asia or Africa or Latin America betrayed him to be an old-style European intellectual, perhaps the last truly great one that the twentieth century was to see. At bottom he belonged with the ideologists of the previous century—although he angrily rejected the identification—pronouncing as an amateur on the variegated subjects his restless mind encountered. In the second phase of his intellectual endeavors, Sartre succeeded in illuminating no significant facet of human society; his "search for a method" ran into the sands. Sartre's striving toward universalism had the opposite of the effect he had desired: his impassioned revolutionary rhetoric, far from opening up new vistas, cut him off from the mainstream of contemporary social thought.

Sartre's analysis of ethical ambiguity had liberated a whole intellectual generation from facile moralizing. Yet the philosopher "who could unmask the deep bad faith behind the complicated network of individual motives with flawless lucidity, became paradoxically naïve each time he dealt with institutions, political parties, techniques of organization or social structure. . . . On the level of structures, Sartre made the black and white judgments that he—more than anyone— eliminated on the individual level. The subtle, complicated,

supremely comprehensive man that he tried to become . . .
reverted to an ideological bourgeois, peremptorily distinguishing between good and evil."[101] If the premature death of
Merleau-Ponty was a tragedy for French intellectual life, the
ideological adventures of the later Sartre reinforced the loss.
After the mid-1950's Sartre "brutalized" his own thought to
the point of caricature. He turned it to ends that were far
removed from disinterested inquiry. The fact that the most
powerful and original among the French thinkers of the mid-
century chose to pursue so eccentric a course could not fail
to retard the efforts of his countrymen to break out of their
self-imposed confinement.

[101] Michel Crozier, "The Cultural Revolution: Notes on the Changes
in the Intellectual Climate of France," *A New Europe?* edited by
Stephen R. Graubard (Boston, 1964), pp. 614–615.

CHAPTER
6

The Way Out

IN THE DECADE and a half following the war, France experienced three intellectual enthusiasms that both paralleled and contradicted the continuing influence of Jean-Paul Sartre. In intrinsic terms the successive recipients of the public's favor—Albert Camus, Pierre Teilhard de Chardin, and Claude Lévi-Strauss—had little in common. The first was a man of letters in the classical tradition, the second a scientist-priest and cosmological visionary, the third an anthropologist with irreproachable technical credentials; their writings were in totally different genres, and their explicit ideas seldom met. As social thinkers, their influence was equally diverse: while Camus and Teilhard were exemplary figures rather than rigorous theorists, Lévi-Strauss was a social scientist of major international influence, the first of such stature France had produced since Durkheim. Initially it might seem that the only attribute the three shared was the acclaim their work inspired, their situation at the origin of a cult which went far beyond what they themselves had written.

In addition to this, however, and directly relevant to the conclusions of the present study, Camus and Teilhard and Lévi-Strauss had in common an exotic strain that in itself was responsible for much of their popularity. No one of them conformed to the standard model of the French intellectual;

each drew his material and inspiration from outside France. And all enjoyed at least as great a reputation abroad as at home. This atypical quality, this ability to speak to the concerns of Frenchmen and foreigners alike, suggests the role they shared in the contemporary intellectual history of their country: they were the champions of France's return to a wider community, the men who reached out beyond the confines of their countrymen's cultural fortress. What Camus had discovered in North Africa, or Teilhard in China, or Lévi-Strauss in Brazil became the point of departure for a renewed search for a frame of social discourse wide enough to accommodate the French alongside and in sympathy with their counterparts abroad.

1. *Albert Camus: Sunlight and Exile*

To Camus most of his mature life was exile—exile from the Algerian sun that had nourished him. It was a familiar experience in France for a boy from the provinces to go to Paris to make his intellectual fortune. It was something quite new that a young man born across the Mediterranean should become a major figure in French cultural life: in France there were few parallels to the familiar British practice of assimilating promising "colonials" from overseas. During the period of his worldwide fame Camus might seem to have become a Parisian like any other. Yet what was deepest within him refused to be assimilated to the French norm; to the end of his life a nostalgia for North Africa dominated his thought, giving the key both to his philosophical pessimism and to his unshakable conviction that life was worth living.

Like most of the three-quarter million Europeans who once lived in Algeria, Camus was of mixed origin—his mother Spanish, his father descended from Alsatians who had left their native province on its annexation to Germany in 1871. The family was of the working class: besides his exotic birth,

Camus, in common with Péguy, was distinguished from the intellectuals with whom he was later to associate by the poverty in which he grew up. Born in 1913 in a village near the city of Constantine, Camus never knew his father, who died of wounds he had suffered at the Battle of the Marne. After her husband's death, his mother moved to Algiers, which from then on was to be the boy's home. Deaf, inarticulate, worn down by the domestic service with which she kept the family alive, Camus's silently suffering mother was one pole of the emotional experience that Algiers became for him; the other was the freedom and the joy of life under the Algerian sun—the "pagan" delights of young people tanning themselves on the beaches or splashing in the sea during a summer that stretched on almost without an end. Here lay the earliest and simplest of Camus's ethical dilemmas—how to reconcile his exultation in life itself with his sense of solidarity for the miseries of the poor.

From one standpoint—from the standpoint of European settlement—Algeria was a new, almost a frontier community comparable in its society, as it was in its climate, to California or Australia. Camus spoke of the beautiful city in which he grew up, and of Oran, its ugly sister, the home town of his wife and the setting for his most influential novel, *The Plague*, as cities without a past. Certainly the Algerian youth whom Camus knew, absorbed in physical pleasure, were as untroubled by history as they were by religion. But behind them were the Moslem masses, who had been in the land for centuries or millennia before the Europeans and who far outnumbered them, and behind the tradition of Islam the memory of Rome and Carthage—and more distant still, to the east and across the Mediterranean, Greece itself. As a young man, Camus was to extend his definition of Algeria's meaning for him beyond the beauty of landscapes and young bodies under the eternal sun to embrace the "North African" variant of Greek wisdom exemplified in the Neo-Platonism of Plotinus.

Whether he would have gotten that far without the ex-

perience of personal suffering is certainly open to doubt. In
his early adolescence, although Camus had been discovered
by his teachers and was being given the moral and financial
encouragement that enabled him to go on to the lycée and
the university, his dominant concerns remained those of the
young people he knew: his greatest pride was his skill as the
goalie of his soccer team. Then at the age of seventeen he
was stricken by tuberculosis; months of enforced inactivity
and the menace hanging over him prompted long reflections
on the tragedy and absurdities of man's lot. For the rest of
his life, although he led a very active existence and seldom
spared himself, Camus's health was to be precarious. His
illness also barred him from the career of teaching in the
French educational system for which he had earlier been
destined.

In the end, this disappointment may have been for the
best. For a man whose gravest intellectual weakness was a
tendency to moralize it was perhaps fortunate that he never
became a pedagogue. He had instead an opportunity to explore several different paths and to make his own mistakes.
Among the latter were a brief marriage at the age of twenty
and a somewhat longer period of membership in the Communist party. From 1934 to the outbreak of the war, Camus
led an extraordinarily varied and dynamic life, whose focal
points were journalism, directing an experimental theater,
and a share in founding a new review, *Rivages*, which was
intended to be the voice of "Mediterranean culture." In this
last venture Camus found himself associated with the small
but congenial literary elite of his native city—men who were
just becoming conscious of their special cultural situation as
Algerian-French and who recognized in him a leader and
companion of surpassing talent.[1] Again it may have been

[1] On Camus's Algerian youth, see Germaine Brée, *Camus*, revised,
Harbinger paperback edition (New York, 1964), Chapters 2 and 3, and
two articles in the special edition of *La table ronde*, No. 146 (February
1960), published on the occasion of his death: Jacques Heurgon,
"Jeunesse de la Méditerranée," pp. 16–21; Armand Guibert, "Limpide
et ravagé . . . ," pp. 26–29.

fortunate that Camus spent his early twenties in a milieu
where he was appreciated and encouraged to the full, far
from the literary cliques and the ruthless intellectual com-
petition of Paris. In Algiers he had a chance to write as he
chose and to absorb the example of his French predecessors
—Gide, Malraux, and the rest—through a screen of protective
distance. Hence a characteristic detachment and abstraction
in his writings, hence the severe classicism of a prose he had
purged of local eccentricity.

Two events brought to a sudden and brutal close this
passionate idyll under the Algerian sun. First there was the
approaching war. In the summer of 1939, the twenty-five-
year-old Camus, who thus far had traveled only as far as
Marseilles and Spain and Italy, was obliged to give up his
cherished dream of a trip to Greece.

> I had planned to make the voyage of Ulysses again . . .
> but I did as everyone else did: I did not sail. I took my
> place in the shuffling queue standing in front of the open
> door of hell. Little by little we entered. And at the first
> scream of assassinated innocence, the door slammed shut
> behind us. We were in hell, we have never quite come
> out of it again.[2]

When the war broke out in September, Camus tried to
enlist, not for reasons of patriotism or ideological conviction
but through a simple sense of solidarity. Quite predictably
he was rejected on grounds of health. Meantime his personal
situation in Algiers had become impossible. The second
painful sequence of events in this grievous year was the
reaction to a series of articles that Camus had published on
conditions among the Kabyle population of the neighboring
mountains: totally without racial and religious prejudice himself, he had described in unsparing terms the misery of the
native people and had proposed a set of reforms leading to

---

[2] "Prométhée aux enfers" (originally published in 1947), *L'été*
(1954), *Essais*, Pléiade edition (Paris, 1965), p. 842. I have quoted
Germaine Brée's translation.

self-administration. The result was something of a local
scandal: the authorities in Algiers gave Camus to understand
that his presence there was no longer appreciated. Camus
took the hint: he moved first to Oran, later, during the
winter of the phony war, to Paris. Ironically enough, he had
arrived at last in the French capital only just in time to
witness the great defeat.

Evacuated to the Unoccupied Zone with the Parisian
newspaper for which he was currently working, Camus
stood the fogs and gloom of France as long as he could. In
company with the girl from Oran whom he had married—
and who was to bear him twin children after the war—he
returned to Algeria in early 1941. For one more year, the
Indian summer of Camus's happiness, the idyll resumed.
Then his tuberculosis flared up: in the summer of 1942 he
was obliged to go to the mountains of central France to take
care of his health; the following November the full occupation of the country cut him off from his wife and from North
Africa. Although he was to revisit his homeland more than
once after the war, the Algerian phase of his career had come
to an end.

By the same token the "historic" period of Camus's life
began, as he enrolled in the Resistance, working first in
Lyons and later in Paris. As editor of the clandestine newspaper *Combat*, Camus became one of the most influential
of the Resistance journalists. In the last months of the
German occupation, he led the double life peculiar to the
underground: besides his perilous activity as a résistant, he
carried on a perfectly open existence in the literary and
theatrical milieu of Paris, installed in Gide's apartment and
already well known as the author of two noteworthy books,
his first novel, *The Stranger*, published in 1942, and a collection of essays, *The Myth of Sisyphus*, which had followed
a year later. Not until the end of August 1944, as Paris
rose in revolt and the clandestine press came out into the
open, did the general public learn that the successful young
novelist and the author of the nobly phrased editorials in

Combat were one and the same person. From that moment on, Camus's fame was established; he was only just over thirty, and his name was already a byword throughout the Western world—the first of his generation of writers to achieve international renown.

Camus's experience in the Resistance was the origin of much subsequent misunderstanding—a misunderstanding which clouded his memory even after his death. The commanding position he had won and the editorship of *Combat* that he continued to hold for three years after the liberation made him a public figure. Against his natural inclination, he felt obliged to pronounce on all topics of public controversy, many of which lay far outside the sphere of his natural interests. By temperament and training, Camus was anything but an ideologist or political commentator: he was primarily a literary craftsman, and after that a philosopher, but of the poetic and intuitive type. His ethical generosity had naturally drawn him to the Left, an inclination reinforced by his firsthand experience of discrimination against the native peoples of his homeland. The crimes of the Nazis had turned to passionate revolt this latent anger and hatred of oppression: the scandal of "assassinated innocence" had mobilized his energies for the underground struggle. But his sense of moral outrage gave him few cues for a political program: most of the time it found its outlet in categorical condemnation of cruelty and injustice.

As though unable to believe that Camus's ethical reasoning was in fact that simple, the public searched his writings for an attitude to which a philosophical label could be attached. Unaware that he himself thought of these works as a series of experiments with human and literary material, no one of which fully expressed his own views, his readers found in them a logical progression from a detached to a committed morality. *The Stranger*, the story of an unmotivated murder and of the murderer's indifference to his own crime, seemed to epitomize Camus's original philosophical universe of the absurd. *The Myth of Sisyphus* could similarly be interpreted as a celebration of the value of human existence pitted against despair. Finally, when Camus's greatest novel, *The Plague*, the account of a long, heartbreaking, virtually hopeless struggle against disease and death, appeared in 1947, the public was only too happy to discover in its author a lay saint, a man of modest but surpassing virtue. Unquestionably *The Plague* could be read as an allegory of fascism, the German occupation, and the quiet heroism of the Resistance, but in point of fact Camus had begun to write it in 1941 before his return to France, and its theme had a universal quality that eluded any single line of interpretation.

The most tenacious of the legends which gathered around Camus in the period immediately following the liberation was that he was an existentialist and the comrade-in-arms of Sartre. True, the two had become friends in 1944 and had subsequently seen a great deal of each other. And in some very broad, nonsectarian sense of the word "existentialism," Camus's writings, more particularly his essay on Sisyphus, might fit under the rubric—although he himself later insisted that this very essay was explicitly directed against the reigning philosophy. The almost universal coupling of his name with that of Sartre was based on little more than the personal association of the two and the fact that they were the most prominent pair of writers to have emerged from the French Resistance.

Sartre himself well understood the temperamental differences that separated them. In his own mind the Resistance had inaugurated a lifelong struggle on behalf of the oppressed: there would never be such a thing as a postwar situation of normalcy; the worldwide battle for freedom and equality had only begun. To Camus the experience of war, occupation, and Resistance was something hellish beyond the human norm; he yearned to find his way back to the universe of light from which he had been exiled. To commit oneself totally to an ideological cause he thought of as an emergency expedient, justified and even required in extreme circumstances, but in no sense the way to realize man's full capacities. In the war and immediate postwar period, Camus had of necessity become a political militant, but he hoped that he would not have to remain one forever. Those of his countrymen who were disappointed by his definition of ideological commitment as a limited liability failed to appreciate that for Camus, however profound his compassion for the poor, the joy of living remained the supreme human value.

Thus as Sartre grew more militant and peremptory—and concomitantly drew closer to the Communist party—Camus began to relax the either-or fashion in which on the morrow of the liberation he had separated the just from the unjust and to rediscover the Western tradition of tolerance and free institutions. To Sartre the terrorist practices of Stalin's last years were phenomena that had to be "understood" in terms of the Soviet Union's beleaguered situation; this was the lesson that Merleau-Ponty—the original Merleau-Ponty of *Humanisme et terreur*—had taught him. To Camus such political devices were identical with what he and Sartre and their comrades of the Resistance had loathed and combated in Hitlerism; when applied by the Russians they deserved exactly the same reprobation. As early as 1947, he had quarreled with Merleau-Ponty on this very score. Sartre had tried in vain to prevent the rupture: as he recalled the incident with bitter resignation fourteen years later:

> I was to the right of Merleau, . . . to the left of Camus. What perverse humor prompted me to become the mediator between two friends, both of whom, a little later, were to reproach me for my friendship for the Communists, and who are both dead, unreconciled?[8]

By 1949, the issue of forced labor camps in the Soviet Union was splitting apart the left-oriented writers of Resistance origin. While the Communists blandly lauded the

[8] Jean-Paul Sartre, "Merleau-Ponty" (originally publshed August-September 1961), *Situations*, IV (Paris, 1964), translated by Benita Eisler as *Situations* (New York, 1965), p. 254.

educational merits of such penal service, Merleau-Ponty and
Sartre followed an intermediate line: they recognized the
abuse but deplored its exploitation in the service of anti-
Soviet propaganda. Camus took his stand with those who
believed that the camps were an outrage against humanity
deserving the fullest publicity, and in so doing he further
strained his already precarious relations with Sartre. Then
came the Korean War, in which he and Sartre chose opposite
sides. By 1952, scarcely anything of their former friendship
remained. In that year it vanished entirely, with an angry
exchange of open letters prompted by the publication of
Camus's *The Rebel*, the longest and most important of his
speculative essays.

This book, on which Camus—constantly interrupted by
the pressure of his public role—had worked slowly and pain-
fully for a full half decade, was both a philosophical and a
political tract. On the level of ethics it tried to formulate
more precisely the Stoic protest against mass suffering that
had been the central theme of *The Plague*. As a political
polemic, Camus's book dealt with the two characteristic
attitudes of the French Left which were also the targets of
Aron's *Opium of the Intellectuals*—its worship of history and
the absolutist intransigence it brought to its ideological concerns.

As the writing of *The Rebel* progressed and the Cold War
grew more intense, the past crimes of Hitler began to take
second place to the present and now quite visible crimes of
Stalin. In its simplest form, Camus's essay was an attempt to
convince his fellow intellectuals that the great revolution of
the twentieth century had been perverted to ends nearly the
opposite of those its progenitors had had in view. For an
English-speaking public, with its tradition of philosophical
empiricism and common-sense argument, a citation of the
bare facts of Stalinist terror and oppression would have sufficed. For the French, a more elaborate train of reasoning

was required; Sartre and his like had to be answered on their own philosophical grounds and in their own vocabulary.

So Camus chose to begin his argument in typically Gallic fashion with a Cartesian formula—"I rebel—therefore we exist." The experience of personal rebellion against oppression, Camus argued, founded "its first value on the whole human race."[4] From Rousseau through the regicides of the French Revolution to Marx and Lenin, he outlined the thought of the great rebels who had tried to extend to all humanity their personal vision of a new universe. This was familiar ground. It was only in his parallel account of "metaphysical" rebels that Camus introduced his special abstract twist.

Among the latter he numbered the Marquis de Sade—whose fantasies of torture in closely guarded fortresses offered a microcosm of the future world of the concentration camp—the Romantic poets, Nietzsche, and the French Surrealists. The metaphysical current, he found, fused with the earlier "historical" one in the Russian terrorist of the late nineteenth century, "the cruel high priest of a desperate revolution." And from there it was only a step to "state terrorism"—the "irrational terror" of the Nazis, a "primitive impulse" whose ravages had been "greater than its real ambitions," and the still more fearful "rational terror" of Communism, under which "slavery . . . becomes the general condition, and the gates of heaven remain locked."[5]

By this double route, Camus arrived at a surprisingly mild conclusion. Since rebellion had reached an extreme point of nihilist self-contradiction, its tradition must either disappear or find a "new impetus." Yet when Camus came to define the new source of moral energy, it proved to be very old and very familiar. It was, he asserted, simply moderation—

---

[4] *L'homme révolté* (Paris, 1951), translated by Anthony Bower as *The Rebel: An Essay on Man in Revolt*, Vintage paperback edition (New York, 1956), p. 22.

[5] *Ibid.*, pp. 160, 186, 219.

mesure—something that was second nature in the Mediterranean world, where he had discovered through his own
experience that intelligence was "intimately related to the
blinding light of the sun." Moderation, Camus hastened to
add, was not "the opposite of rebellion. Rebellion in itself"
was the moderation which held the excesses of mankind in
tense equilibrium. In the "savage, formless movement of history," moderation alone could dethrone nihilism and restore
respect for the value of human life.[6]

Such was the weary, live-and-let-live wisdom that Camus
had derived from nearly a decade of participation in his
country's ideological struggles. Stated in bald terms, it would
have sounded commonplace and, still worse, conservative. So
Camus was virtually obliged to dress up his results for the
benefit of his public. Living as he did in an intellectual community in which some brand of leftism was de rigueur, he
could save his standing and self-respect only by the gym-
nastic feat of equating ancient common sense with the new
imperative of rebellion. And the same was true of the more
formal aspects of his presentation: for intellectuals of a
special sort a specialized literary argument was required.
Hence Camus grafted on to his unexceptionable but routine
account of "historical" rebellion the "metaphysical" branch
that gave it a loftier look—and in so doing failed to establish
any real link from the Marquis de Sade and his spiritual
descendants to the world revolution of the twentieth century.
By this literary device, Camus rescued his essay from banality.
But he also weighed it down with philosophical paraphernalia which barely escaped pretentiousness.

In taking a political stand that was unpopular among most
of his associates—however orthodox it might be in the rest
of the Western world—Camus apparently felt under a compulsion to vindicate his own position as an intellectual. And
at the same time he tried to prove his unshaken loyalty
to the tradition of revolt. The result was a disappointing

[6] *Ibid.*, pp. 300–301.

work. Despite the eloquence of its concluding pages and the moral passion that had gone into it, Camus's most extended effort at discursive prose only proved his inaptitude for such a venture. He had already given his personal ethic a classic formulation in *The Plague*. As a novel, *The Plague* had kept the moral precept on the level of metaphor—which was where it belonged. Camus's attempt to explain his meaning more precisely simply weakened the effect of what he had written earlier and brought down upon him a host of critics.

Most of the French read *The Rebel* in terms of their own presuppositions and judged Camus's work accordingly. It was more often outside France that the book was assessed without prejudice: in Britain and America, in fact, it was generally overpraised. In situating *The Rebel* in its intellectual context at home, it is instructive to juxtapose the contrasting objections that Gabriel Marcel and Jean-Paul Sartre lodged against it.

Marcel, while generous in extending his personal respect to the stand Camus had taken, could not accept certain of his formulations, which he found "soft and insufficient." He refused to endorse Camus's contention that risking one's life in rebellion "purified" such an action. For a Christian, Marcel asserted, revolt and the violence that went with it were by their very nature morally equivocal. Nor was the attitude of passive resistance a satisfactory response: under contemporary conditions, it was little better than "hypocrisy" in the face of evil. To the ethical problems Camus had raised, no simple answer could be given; each successive movement on behalf of freedom or humane behavior had to be judged on its own merits. To the Christian conscience, Marcel concluded, revolt could never have "the last word": it would remain a "crucifying" dilemma through all time.[7]

[7] Marcel's essay, entitled simply "L'homme révolté," after being delivered as a lecture in 1951, was subsequently published in the special number of *La table ronde*, finally figuring as an appendix to the new edition of his *Homo viator* (Paris, 1962), pp. 348, 351–353, 364–366, 368.

Sartre's reading of *The Rebel* prompted no such moral fastidiousness. What annoyed him in Camus's work was the way the latter tried to have the best of two worlds—to deliver ethical judgments while remaining personally unengaged. Recalling with nostalgia the Camus whom he once had loved, Sartre dwelt on the meaning his younger friend had had for him in the period of their close association at the end of the war: both résistant and advocate of personal happiness, still more, a man who taught his readers their "duty to be happy," Camus had offered "the admirable conjunction of a personality, an action, and a work," had summed up in his own person the conflicts of the epoch and gone beyond them by the intensity with which he lived them. But such a fortunate equilibrium—such a tenuous reconciliation of contrasts—Sartre lamented, could occur only "a single time, for a single moment, in a single man." The human struggle had progressed beyond the events of 1944 and 1945, leaving Camus far behind. He who had once been the exemplar of a whole generation now sounded like a voice from the past. The ideal for which he stood had become quite simply obsolete.[8]

Pondering what his critics had written, deeply wounded by the virulence of their attacks against him, Camus might well have wondered whether perhaps Sartre was right. The three years following the publication of *The Rebel* were the most difficult of his mature life: ideologically isolated, weakened through a recurrence of tuberculosis, and torn by conflicting emotional attachments, he was unable to make much progress with his writing; between 1951 and 1956 no major work of Camus appeared. He returned instead for spiritual refreshment to his early avocation of theatrical directing.

In 1954 a further torment descended upon him—the revolt of the Algerian Moslems and France's protracted war of repression against them. For most of Camus's fellow intellectuals of the Left, whether democrats or communisants, Algeria presented no serious moral or political dilemma:

[8] "Réponse à Albert Camus" (originally published in August 1952), *Situations*, pp. 91–92, 97, 100–101.

personally uninvolved, they found little difficulty in sympathizing with the movement of liberation. For Camus it was quite different: his own people, the Algerian-French with whom he had gone to school, played soccer, and swum in the Mediterranean, the people among whom he felt far more at home than with the Parisian sophisticates he had subsequently come to know, this people was fighting with its back to the wall for a land it regarded as its own. And the irony of the matter was that Camus was one of the small band of Algerian "liberals" who had understood and sympathized with the plight of the Moslems, and who, if they had been listened to in time, might have staved off the worst. Now it was too late. When at the start of 1956 Camus went to Algiers to appeal for a truce to the fighting, he was shouted down by the very people whom he thought he knew so well. Two years later he again proposed a peace of compromise—and again to no avail. After that, he fell into mournful silence, his thoroughly human and understandable refusal to take sides having alienated nearly everyone.

Camus did not live to see the end of the war and Algeria's liberation. But he must have known that he had lost his radiant home forever. As though with a premonition of what was coming, just before the outbreak of the struggle he had published a collection of essays and notes of travel about Algeria entitled simply *L'été*—Summer. In it he announced his joy at the discovery that the "invincible summer" he carried within him was stronger than the spiritual cold which had nearly destroyed him during his years of ideological altercation in Paris. And to underline what he meant—and perhaps to suggest that he had taken his leave of moralizing —in his last novel, *The Fall*, he abandoned the Algerian cities in which his earlier work had been set and plunged into the mists of Amsterdam. From the standpoint of craftsmanship *The Fall* was a tour de force, the finest thing Camus ever wrote. The five-day monologue of a "judge-penitent," a former magistrate turned self-accuser, it was a pitiless, unremitting revelation of man's hyprocrisy, pursued with psy-

choanalytic thoroughness into the depths of a hell that for
Camus was of necessity cold and wet.

The year following the publication of *The Fall*, Camus
received the Nobel Prize for literature; at forty-four he was
the youngest of the nine Frenchmen who had been thus
honored. With the prize money he was able to buy a house
in a village in Provence, where he planned to retire for long
periods of writing. By the end of 1959, his health seemed re-
established and he was hard at work on another novel that
was larger and more ambitious than anything he had written
before. A new life and a new burst of creation were beginning when in January 1960 Camus was killed, with heartbreaking irrelevance, in an automobile crash.

Sartre's reaction to the event was characterisically generous.
Although he and Camus had never been reconciled, the older
man mourned in the former friend, now doubly lost to him,
the "heir of that long line of moralistes whose works . . .
constitute what is most original in French letters. His stubborn humanism, narrow and pure, austere and sensual, waged
. . . dubious battle" against the formless events of our time.[9]
For Sartre, in common with so many of his countrymen,
Camus was primarily that Gallic brand of essayist known as
moraliste—an observer of mankind, detached and emotionally
concerned at the same time. Abroad he was more usually
esteemed as a novelist. Camus himself apparently could not
quite decide in what genre he wrote most comfortably. In
contrast to Sartre, who moved with rapidity and ease from
one kind of writing to another and seemed thoroughly at
home in all of them, Camus never ceased experimenting
with his own talent. Perhaps he was at his most natural in
the combination of journalism, narrative, and reflection with
which he recalled his native land.

As an Algerian, Camus had won his position in French
letters through a severe self-discipline. Like David Hume,

9 "Albert Camus" (originally published January 7, 1960), *Situations*,
pp. 109–110.

sedulously ridding his English prose of Scotticisms, he wrote
a French which was all the purer for the fact that it was in
part a learned language and not, as with Sartre or any other
Parisian from the educated classes, the speech he had heard
about him as a child. One of the baffling problems in arriving at an estimate of Camus—a problem neglected by most
of his critics, who take his language for granted—is to penetrate the screen of his noble diction to the human being
behind. A man of romantic temper and strong, direct emotions, Camus trained himself to write with classic simplicity.
His literary universe was "stripped to the fundamental"—
thus making it practically impossible for him "to draw upon
the wealth of comedy, tenderness, and infinite variety inherent in human living to which he himself was not insen-
sitive." In each of his novels he created a closed world which
recalled the "self-contained universe of classical tragedy."
Each was a separate and distinct stylistic feat: each was so
perfect as to hover on the edge of monotony.[10]

Camus was only too glad to recognize his debt to his
predecessors among the novelists of heroism. He wrote a perceptive and laudatory introduction to the collected works of
Martin du Gard, and he is reported to have remarked on hearing of his Nobel Prize that he personally would have voted
for Malraux. He was similarly open in his comments on what
he had learned from Greek literature, from the French seventeenth century, from Nietzsche, and from such nineteenth-
century novelists as Melville and Dostoyevsky. But the first
third of his own century passed him by: he had no time for
the psychological refinements of the generation of Proust and
Mann and Pirandello.[11] He was just reaching intellectual
maturity when Hitler came to power, and from then on he
was obsessed by the miseries of the era into which he had
been plunged. A man who had lost his father in the First
World War, Camus seemed destined from childhood to be

[10] Brée, *Camus*, pp. 85, 104, 110.
[11] R.-M. Albérès, "Albert Camus dans son siècle: témoin et étranger,"
La table ronde, No. 146 (February 1960), p. 13.

the voice of the desperate years, whose course exactly coincided with the three decades of his education and glory as a man of letters.

It was virtually inevitable, then, that Camus should have been put on a pedestal and canonized within his own lifetime. His reaction to his fame was predictably ambivalent. At times he reveled in it; more often he was harassed and annoyed by the miscellaneous demands his admirers made upon him, and distressed by the gap between his real personality and his public image. He who in his editorials or in the political debates he conducted with his fellow intellectuals could be haughty and almost priggish, in his moments of relaxation was not ashamed to show his boyish, comical, plebeian side whose existence most people never suspected. Camus knew very well that he was no saint: among the many excellences of his final masterpiece, *The Fall*, was that it closed at last the gulf between an impossible ideal figure and the very human and fallible individual that lay behind.[12]

At all costs Camus wished to remain true to the double lesson his Algerian childhood had taught him. "There is beauty and there are the humiliated," he wrote. "However difficult the enterprise, I should like to be unfaithful neither to the one nor to the others."[13] His effort to maintain a balance between his joy in the glory of creation and the compassion for suffering he had derived from an equally direct experience was doomed from the start to public misunderstanding. Camus was not even spared the ministrations of the well-intentioned religious who searched his writings for hidden traces of Christianity. In fact, Camus was in no sense a Christian. He was proud to be a pagan: the guiding concepts of Christianity—sin, grace, redemption, atonement, and the rest—had no meaning for him.[14] Nor did he fit into the

[12] See the comments of Simone de Beauvoir in *La force des choses* (Paris, 1963), translated by Richard Howard as *Force of Circumstance* (New York, 1965), pp. 53, 349.

[13] "Retour à Tipasa" (written in 1953), *L'été: Essais*, Pléiade edition, p. 875.

[14] Henri Peyre, "Camus the Pagan," *Yale French Studies*, No. 25 (Spring 1960), pp. 21, 23.

other schemas in which his critics tried to confine him. We
have noted already that he was far from being an existentialist in the manner of Sartre. Neither was he a hedonist
on the model of Gide: sensual enjoyments had come so
naturally to Camus that they did not have to be learned or
intellectually celebrated. Finally he was no junior Malraux
dedicated to the cult of the heroic: for Camus heroism was
bitter, unavoidable necessity, not a way of life to be sought
out for its own sake.

Thus all the commentators who found an ethical or philosophical system in Camus's work eventually proved to be in
error. And every time he himself tried to put his understanding in logical order—as in *The Rebel*—he ended by
distorting it. At the center of Camus's moral universe was
nothing more complex than a tremendous revelation of light
—the power of the sun, "not as a distant purity, but as a fe-
cundating bath . . . the unifying force of the cosmos." This
was the primal intuition of his childhood which his reading
of Plotinus had subsequently confirmed.

In contrast to the fundamental experience described in
most contemporary philosophies, he had a certain happy
experience of being which appeared basic to him: he
passed it on to us. Around him and in history he sees the
consequences of uprooting: he tells us about them.
Camus, who is a thinker though not a philosopher, in-
stinctively perceives certain truths. They had escaped
minds dialectically better prepared than his own, but
minds that did not know how to extract consequences
from these truths or . . . did not wish to extract them.
He recalls these consequences inexorably, monotonously.
He rediscovers the values of life and happiness lost in the
tumult and terrors of our age.[15]

For something over a decade Camus's shock and scandal
at what he had understood made him seem rigid and preachy.

[15] Serge Doubrovski, "La morale d'Albert Camus," *Preuves*, No. 116
(October 1960), translated by Sondra Mueller and Jean-Marc Vary for
Camus: A Collection of Critical Essays, edited by Germaine Brée
(Englewood Cliffs, N.J., 1962), pp. 73–74, 76–77, 83.

Later, as he saw more deeply into the ambiguities of his own life, his judgments became less categorical. Camus was in fact the exemplary figure his readers took him to be, but not in the way they imagined. He was neither a rigorous thinker nor the agonized symbol of the years of desperation. He was rather a spokesman for sunlight and joy ceaselessly protesting against desperation as a human norm—a stranger arrived from across a mythic sea to expose in unsparing terms the unholy mess that the Europeans, shrouded in mists of hatred and deception, had made of their Mediterranean heritage.

The protagonist of *The Fall* was called Jean-Baptiste Clamence—the name unmistakably suggesting a voice clamoring in the wilderness. And Camus himself was something of a John the Baptist. As a prophet of reconciliation, he came too early: in the 1950's the French, still torn by ideological strife, were not yet ready to listen to the man of good will who told them that their squabbling was a sordid blasphemy against nature. Had he lived into the 1960's, had he been able to see the end of the Algerian War and the beginnings of cordial understanding between France and the Soviet Union, Camus's public torment would have been infinitely mitigated, and his subsequent writing might have been more in tune with the attitudes of his countrymen. As it was—after Camus's career had been cut off in mid-course—it appeared in retrospect that his fame and the flowering of his talent had been premature: within a half decade of his death his prose was already beginning to sound dated.

However the intellectually sophiscated might belittle Camus, the young continued to read him with rapt attention. For them, particularly in the Anglo-American world, his voice was eternally fresh and alive. The young took Camus to their hearts and made him one of their own. And each successive generation read in terms of a renewed understanding the words with which he had accepted the Nobel Prize on behalf of all those who had come of age as he had in the shadow of approaching war:

For more than twenty years of absolutely insane history, lost hopelessly . . . in the convulsions of the epoch, . . . those of my age . . . had to fashion for themselves an art of living in times of catastrophe in order to be reborn before fighting . . . against the death-instinct at work in our history.

Probably every generation sees itself as charged with remaking the world. Mine, however, knows that it will not remake the world. But its task is perhaps even greater, for it consists in keeping the world from destroying itself. As the heir of a corrupt history that blends blighted revolutions, misguided techniques, dead gods, and worn out ideologies, . . . that generation, starting from nothing but its own negations, has had to re-establish . . . a little of what constitutes the dignity of life and death. . . . Perhaps it can never accomplish that vast undertaking, but most certainly throughout the world it has already accepted the double challenge of truth and liberty and, on occasion, has shown that it can lay down its life without hatred.[16]

11. *Pierre Teilhard de Chardin: Vision of the Future*

By calendar reckoning, Teilhard de Chardin belonged with the generation of Febvre and Bloch, Maritain and Marcel, Martin du Gard and Bernanos. Indeed, he was very nearly the oldest of the lot, having been born in 1881, the same year as Roger Martin du Gard. But the slow pace of his intellectual growth and the exceptional circumstances that held up the publication of his writings until after his death made him the contemporary, rather, of Sartre and Merleau-Ponty and Camus. He was almost unknown in France until 1946; his most influential work did not appear until 1955; his tremendous vogue was a posthumous phenomenon of the

[16] *Discours de Suède* (Paris, 1958), translated by Justin O'Brien as *Speech of Acceptance upon the Award of the Nobel Prize for Literature* (New York, 1958), pp. x–xii.

late 1950's. In this context, Teilhard's influence can be treated as post-existentialist, post-Sartrian, impinging on French cultural life at a time when even Camus was past the point of maximum public favor.

Born in the Massif Central of aristocratic lineage, Teilhard de Chardin grew up in a serious-minded provincial household where the Catholic religion went unquestioned. His family was also of the strenuous, outdoors variety, rooted in a region whose extinct volcanoes and bizarre rock formations could tempt the imagination of a curious child. The boy Pierre early discovered a vocation for geology. For the rest of his life the link between science and religion was to be both his torment and his joy.

By the time Teilhard began the long course of training for the Jesuit priesthood, the Church in France was entering on the most difficult period it had known since the eighteenth century. The clergy's obstinate alignment with the cause of reaction and untruth in the Dreyfus Case brought down upon it the revenge of an anti-clerical government and the suppression or exile of the militant teaching orders. And as though this were not trial enough, the condemnation of Modernism by Pius X demoralized the forces of Catholic renovation. The young Teilhard could not fail to be aware of such a stirring and distressing sequence of events; but they found little reflection in his subsequent writings. As a fledgling Jesuit, he seems to have been a docile pupil: throughout his life he was to combine personal and intellectual adventurousness with an uncomplaining obedience to his religious superiors. The chief effect on him of the tumult within the Church in the early twentieth century was that it obliged him to go for part of his training to England, where he acquired a fluency in the English language which subsequently gave him easy access to the world of international science.

It was the First World War, rather, that awakened in Teilhard the vision of his future course. He did front-line service as a stretcher-bearer, giving the comfort of religion to countless soldiers at the moment of death. When offered promotion to the position of divisional chaplain, with the rank of captain, Teilhard characteristically refused: he felt he could be more useful if he remained with the enlisted men. Without question, he saw his full share of the filth and horror of the trenches. Yet he managed to distill from the experience something beyond agonized participation in the suffering of his fellowmen. He who until his early thirties had lived the sheltered life of a scholarly priest was thrust by the war into close, promiscuous contact with humanity in its raw mass. Whatever his personal fastidiousness—and he remained an aristocrat in manners to the end of his life—Teilhard was not revolted by what he saw around him. On the contrary, he found his soul uplifted by a mighty realization, cosmic in scope, that mankind was one.[17]

When the war was over, Teilhard was free once more to pursue his studies. He took his doctorate in palaeontology and began teaching, as Maritain had done a decade earlier, at the Institut Catholique in Paris. By 1926, however, his evolutionary interpretation of the doctrine of original sin had alarmed his religious superiors. Three years earlier he had made an initial trip to China, where he had joined an expedition exploring the Mongolian desert. Now, with teaching forbidden and further residence in Paris inadvisable, Teilhard returned to Asia as to an intellectual refuge. His second period of work in China little by little extended into a twenty-year exile, lasting from his mid-forties to the age of sixty-five. Here he lived most of the time in Peking, where he soon became quite at home, partly pursuing his own researches and partly serving as scientific adviser to the Chinese government. Field expeditions alternated with the quiet work of writing and classifying: Teilhard's greatest discovery was the remains of Sinanthropus, a Neanderthal-type predecessor of Homo sapiens. As the years went by,

---

[17] For Teilhard's early years, see Claude Cuénot, *Pierre Teilhard de Chardin: les grandes étapes de son évolution* (Paris, 1958), translated by Vincent Colimore as *Teilhard de Chardin: A Biographical Study* (London, 1965), Chapters 1 and 2.

Teilhard's name became respected among palaeontologists, and he himself a familiar, well-loved figure within the international group of scientists who based themselves in China.

Although he was permitted to return to France at intervals, he never stayed there very long, and this absence from his native land proved particularly painful during the Second World War, when he and the small band of Frenchmen stranded in Peking were virtually the prisoners of the Japanese. Hence it was with a sense of tense anticipation that Teilhard finally reached Paris in the spring of 1946 after a seven-year absence. He had grown old in exile: now was his last chance, he realized, to introduce his countrymen to the meditations he had been elaborating during his two decades in China. Thus far his strictly scientific articles had alone been published: his larger, more speculative works had circulated only in typed or mimeographed form among his friends and associates (we have seen that Saint-Exupéry had some of them). During the five postwar years he spent in Paris, Teilhard worked patiently, tenaciously to break down the ecclesiastical barrier which cut him off from his prospective public: he circulated in high society; he lectured to small, selected groups—he was forbidden large meetings—debating on one occasion with Gabriel Marcel himself; and he made a special trip to Rome to plead for permission to publish his most important work, *The Phenomenon of Man*.

Teilhard was disappointed on every score. Despite changes he made in the text, his book remained under ecclesiastical ban. He was similarly not allowed to be a candidate for a chair at the Collège de France, where the faculty was prepared to vote in his favor. In 1951, he was obliged to leave Paris once more. His "underground" popularity had become too much for Teilhard's religious superiors, who intimated that exile was again in order. The last four years of his life he spent in New York, cherished by his American friends, who were both numerous and faithful, and devoting himself to the twin tasks of getting abreast of the latest theories in evolutionary geology while trying to persuade the anthropological profession as a whole to become more conscious of its ties to physics and palaeontology.

When Teilhard died on Easter Sunday 1955, few in either New York or Paris noted the event. But by the end of the year his posthumous fame had begun. An international committee undertook the publication of his complete works. In December 1955 the appearance of *The Phenomenon of Man* produced a literary sensation; within a short time 100,000 copies had been sold. In the next half decade the rest of Teilhard's semi-clandestine corpus saw the light. By 1960, "Teilhardism" had itself become an intellectual phenomenon of major dimensions.

In attempting to assess what mushroomed into an organized cult, with its devotees and special publications, it is necessary to stress at the start that in the strictly scientific sense Teilhard was a geologist or palaeontologist and nothing more. In the two aspects of his work which most engaged the general public, evolutionary biology and Catholic theology, he ranked as an amateur. What we know of Teilhard's reading suggests that little of it was theological. When Maritain first met him, he was surprised to discover that his colleague either had never known anything about Thomism or had forgotten what he had once learned.[18] His intellectual allegiance had gone, rather, to French neo-idealist philosophy and more particularly to Bergson, whom he revered as a "kind of saint." References to Bergson crop up constantly in Teilhard's writing, and it is quite apparent that this was the strongest and most persistent influence on his thought. Yet the views of the two men on evolution were far from identical. Where Bergson had seen a divergence between reason and intuition, or matter and spirit, Teilhard found all nature converging in one tremendous synthesis in which such philosophical distinctions disappeared.[19] The

[18] Jacques Maritain, *Le paysan de la Garonne* (Paris, 1966), p. 173.
[19] Madeleine Barthélemy-Madaule, *Bergson et Teilhard de Chardin* (Paris, 1963), pp. 9, 639.

great novelty of Teilhard's thought was that it totally abandoned the old dichotomy between the material world and the realm of consciousness, discovering the latter already present as potentiality for the future within brute matter itself. Little wonder, then, that Teilhard early fell under the suspicion of heresy.

From the standpoint of evolutionary biology, Teilhard's work descended from Lamarck rather than from Darwin. Although at the end of his life he tried to bring his theories closer to the Darwinian-Mendelian tradition of natural selection and heredity cultivated in Britain and the United States, he remained at heart a Lamarckian: he was convinced, as so many French scientists and philosophers had been before him, that there was an immanent "intention" to the evolutionary process which the human mind could discern. And he was similarly convinced—and thought it his mission to persuade others—that this understanding of evolution was compatible with revealed religion. Thus Teilhard took up within the ranks of Catholicism a battle which the Protestants had fought out a couple of generations before. Originally—in the third quarter of the nineteenth century—Catholics had remained calmer than Protestants in the face of Darwin's *Origin of Species*. Less dependent on "natural theology" as an argument for the existence of God, Catholic intellectuals had been inclined to keep their religion in one compartment of their minds and their scientific work in another.[20] Through this politic device, evolution had gradually been able to find a place within Catholic education without kicking up too much fuss. Teilhard, however, scorned such evasions. He wanted to bring the whole matter into the open, to prove to the religious that the evolution of the cosmos was by its very nature a manifestation of the glory of God, and at the same time to lead the unbelievers along with him in his search for traces of the divine intent.

In pursuit of the latter aim, Teilhard steadfastly insisted

[20] Stephen Toulmin, "On Teilhard de Chardin," *Commentary*, XXXIX (March 1965), 53–54.

that even his larger speculative works were "purely and simply" scientific treatises. He kept out of them any explicit theological references, introducing the deity solely in the guise of a cryptic "Omega Point." Such was notably the case with Teilhard's most influential book, *The Phenomenon of Man.*

Originally written in China between 1938 and 1940 and revised during its author's residence in France in 1947–1948, *The Phenomenon of Man* was a detailed, highly organized demonstration of Teilhard's central contention that the historical development of the cosmos displayed a rational order.[21] The species known as man, Teilhard observed, was by its very nature the "center of perspective" on the universe. But it was more than that: man was also its "center of construction"— the "axis and leading shoot of evolution" which gave the entire process its final meaning. Even before the appearance of Homo sapiens—or of life itself—there had existed within the "biosphere" enveloping the earth the prerequisites for human consciousness. Thus there was an inherent solidarity to all life on the planet: both structurally and genetically, living things followed a single line of progress which could be defined as a "rise of consciousness."[22]

The decisive step in the evolutionary ascent, then, was the emergence of "reflection." As Teilhard never tired of repeating, an animal only "knows" while a man "knows that he knows." Or—to introduce some of Teilhard's special vocabulary—the jump from instinct to thought or from animality to the potential for civilized society could be defined as a process of "hominization." And with this process, evolution entered the "noosphere," the sphere of the soul in which man could begin to communicate with the divine.[23]

From the strictly biological standpoint, Teilhard recog-

[21] *Ibid.,* p. 51.
[22] *Le phénomène humain: Oeuvres de Teilhard de Chardin,* I (Paris, 1955), translated by Bernard Wall as *The Phenomenon of Man* (New York, 1959), pp. 33, 36, 72, 96, 142, 148.
[23] *Ibid.,* pp. 165, 180.

nized, Homo sapiens had made no progress since the Cro-
Magnon epoch. At the same time man's contemporary situation opened up totally novel perspectives of evolutionary
adaptation. Modern man suffered from anxiety on a cosmic
scale: the new relationship between space and time that
technology had created gave him a sense of desperate vertigo;
the linking together of the continents into one world civilization produced a feeling of compression and heightened intensity. Under these unprecedented circumstances, man had
no recourse except to lie down on the job—which would be
unthinkable—or to press on to the realization of his full
evolutionary potential through a "mega-synthesis." If they
chose the latter, it was incumbent on all men to push forward
together, to advance in pursuit of the complementary ideals
of science and humanity to a "super-consciousness." Then
would be achieved at last a hyper-personal order in which
individual wills would be merged into a wider spiritual unity.
In the conjunction of reason and mysticism, science and religion, mankind would penetrate beyond the barrier of the
phenomenal world to a culminating "ecstasy."[24]

In a series of essays and lectures written over a period of
three decades and published after his death under the title
The Future of Man, Teilhard specified more precisely what
he meant by these predictions and applied them to the har-
rowing circumstances of his own day. Human progress, he
explained, was not the comfortable and comforting doctrine
its vulgar votaries imagined. It was a strenuous ideal, laden
with peril. Its "source of life" was a steady increase in
scientific knowledge, its social manifestation a growing pressure toward collective existence. Thus regarded, the frightful
events of the 1930's and 1940's in Teilhard's eyes lost some
of their terrors: the Second World War itself figured as the
birth pangs of a new human order; modern totalitarian movements were "neither heresies nor biological regressions" but
"rough drafts" in the direct line of cosmic evolution. Col-
lectivization was inevitable: the question rather was whether

[24] *Ibid.,* pp. 225–233, 244, 251, 284–285, 289.

it would come about through external compulsion or through an inner work of unification in which the value of the individual personality would be preserved. The first process would be merely mechanical, the second a union of souls inspired by fraternal love.[25]

Similar dizzy options faced mankind with respect to its biological future on the planet. A world that had taken ten thousand years to create had changed more in two centuries than in all the millennia which had gone before. What would it be like in another million years? One possibility was that the intense concentration of human life on the globe would create a cosmic explosion in which mankind would disappear utterly. Alternatively—if spiritual values were to come to predominance—the physical cooling of the planet might be matched by a psychic heating-up that would finally lead to a detachment of humanity from the earth and a reuniting of souls in Omega Point itself. Such was Teilhard's vision of the ultimate "ecstasy"—an "eruption of interior life," the merging of man's spirit in the divine toward which the Christian mystics had aspired through two thousand years of contemplation.[26]

To try to epitomize in a few sentences hundreds of pages of prose that leap without warning from a dryly scientific to a visionary tone and back again is to suggest the overwhelming difficulty in arriving at a fair-minded judgment on Teilhard de Chardin. No figure in contemporary French culture has prompted more divergent assessments. For his votaries Teilhard ranks as the most potent intellectual force of the century: his scientific detractors curtly dismiss him as a mystagogue and charlatan. Indeed, some readers may be surprised that he appears in the present study at all. What is the intellectual historian to do with so perplexing a cultural phenomenon?

[25] *L'avenir de l'homme: Oeuvres de Teilhard de Chardin*, V (Paris, 1959), translated by Norman Denny as *The Future of Man* (London, 1964), pp. 19, 46, 54, 74, 117.
[26] *Ibid.*, pp. 71, 122–123, 307–308.

At the very least it is only reasonable to separate the man himself from the movement that gathered around his name after his death. The latter is irrelevant for our present purposes: as a phenomenon of what used to be called middlebrow culture, it has no place in a study of intellectual leadership. We can simplify the problem further by dealing only in passing with the much-vexed question as to whether Teilhard is to be read—as he himself wanted to be—"purely and simply" as a scientist. Whatever Teilhard's scientific merits —and we may recall that he was known in scientific circles exclusively as a palaeontologist—the passages in his works that gripped his readers' attention and that aroused the greatest subsequent controversy were not those in which he was speaking as an expert. They were his predictions about the future, his charting of the unsuspected evolutionary possibilities that were open to mankind. And these could by no stretch of vocabulary rank as scientific in the customary meaning of the word. It was impossible either to prove them or to disprove them by any experimental procedure. One could simply apply them as a stimulus to the scientific or the religious imagination. And the same was true of Teilhard's idiosyncratic vocabulary. How was the reader to understand such terms as "biosphere" and "noosphere"? Was he to think of them as physically existent strata enveloping the earth? Or was he to regard them as spatial metaphors describing successive stages in the ascent of life on the planet? The latter appears the more probable. Teilhard's language as a whole is so heavily metaphorical, so consciously literary, that the scientific origin of his thought soon becomes lost in the mists of prophecy.

We can similarly dismiss as of concern to only a minority of Teilhard's readers the suspicion of heresy which overshadowed the last thirty years of his life. Unquestionably there was much in Teilhard's writings that exposed him to such a charge: passage after passage seemed to echo Spinoza's pantheist identification of God and nature. On the occasion

of his trip to Rome in 1948, Teilhard did his best to reply
to his theological enemies. While accepting the term "pan-
theism" in its "etymological meaning," he argued that his
particular version of it was "legitimate" from the Christian
standpoint. He also reminded his readers that he was dealing
with no more than the phenomenal aspect of nature; be-
lievers were free to posit divine intervention as a supplement
to his account.[27] After Teilhard's writings finally appeared
in print, their mounting popularity brought the very real
danger that they would be put on the Index. But when the
Second Vatican Council met, "Teilhardism," either pro or
con, never figured on that body's agenda: the assembled
Church fathers passed it over in silence. And in the wake of
the Council the Index itself for all practical purposes ceased
to function. By the mid-1960's the legacy of Teilhard de
Chardin, whatever the theological doubts it continued to
arouse, was no longer threatened by ecclesiastical censure.

Among Teilhard's contemporaries as thinkers "who were
Catholics," Gabriel Marcel and Jacques Maritain in characteristic fashion fixed on widely contrasting aspects of his
work. The former was deeply suspicious of a theory which
tried to explain away the horrors his generation had witnessed
by ascribing them to the "coming into being of a planetary or
cosmic consciousness," or by depicting them as "in some
sense the price mankind" had "to pay for establishing itself
on a new and superior level." Marcel thought that such a consciousness was a "mere fiction," and he accused Teilhard of
having destroyed his own ability to conceive the "unspeakable
and intolerable reality of the suffering of the single person"
by "thinking in terms of millions and multiples of millions."
When the two held their debate in Paris in 1947, no meeting
of minds occurred. Marcel was obsessed with the "dehumaniz-
ing" effect of collective living and the machine. Teilhard had
no fear of technology as such, and he was confident of man's

[27] *Phenomenon of Man*, pp. 169n., 308.

ability to master the forces his ingenuity had unleashed and
to direct them to beneficent ends.[28]

Maritain dealt with Teilhard more charitably. While he
was surprised that the scientist-priest should be so ignorant
of formal theology, and repelled by the intellectual confusion of his popularizers, he found in Teilhard's own career
more matter for admiration than for reproach:

> The solitary, painful, obstinate search of Father Teil-
> hard, his patient courage in face of the ignoble obstacles
> raised against him, his passion for truth, his total com-
> mitment to a mission he considered prophetic, the pure
> sincerity which shines throughout his work, and the
> extraordinary and entirely personal experience he lived
> through and which might have torn asunder someone
> less steeled against adversity, are things that deserve the
> most profound respect.

At the origin of Teilhard's thought Maritain found a "poetic
intuition" of the sanctity of "created nature." This poem
which he might have written, and which he delivered over
to his readers in a "kind of disguise," was the "true work"
that remained after one had sloughed off the scientific trappings and the popular cult with which it was surrounded.[29]

Maritain's characterization of Teilhard as a poet in scientific disguise comes closer to the mark than any alternative
interpretation and has the advantage of combining critical
rigor with a personal generosity of judgment. Few who encountered Teilhard failed to be attracted by the directness
and charm of his manner. One traveling companion described
him as "vibrant as a flag fluttering under the Asian sky,
energetic, lively, . . . tireless, greeting each day with a burst
of joyous enthusiasm." Another spoke of his being "very
handsome," with a "matchless style of an . . . irresistible

28 Gabriel Marcel, *Les hommes contre l'humain* (Paris, 1951), translated by G. S. Fraser as *Men against Humanity* (London, 1952), pp.
122, 124, 198; Cuénot, *Teilhard de Chardin* (English translation), pp.
251–253.
29 *Paysan de la Garonne*, pp. 172, 175, 186.

distinction. . . . There was nothing obtrusively clerical about
him; in gesture and deportment he was as simple as could be.
He was gracious and obliging, yet . . . as unyielding as a
stone wall." Teilhard's fellow-scientists found him splendid
company; but under the courtesy and fascination of his
manner they felt a "disarming loneness."[80]

In an intellectual sense he was equally alone. In his early
and middle years, he was only rarely able to share his
cosmological speculations with his colleagues in the priesthood or in the geological profession. Not until the last decade
of his life—after his return from China—did he encounter
in Julian Huxley a visionary scientist who agreed with him
that man was capable of taking over his own evolution. Outside the ranks of natural science Teilhard had a natural
affinity to such "meta-historians" as Spengler and Toynbee,
both of whom he studied and admired. Like them he sought
to find an underlying design in man's adventure on the planet.
But he protested against their "barren cyclism," arguing that
it was the long-term "drifts" rather than the "rhythms" that
were most important in human history. His optimism about
the future of mankind—his effort to expand the confines of
a cyclical interpretation—put him closer to Toynbee than to
Spengler.[81] Similarly—and predictably—he expressed a preference for Camus over Sartre, and for Jung over Freud.

Once one has charted a few such connections, the basic
fact remains that most of the leading thinkers—whether in
France or abroad—who encountered Teilhard's work, while
granting him their personal respect, refused to take his speculations seriously. Again—as in the case of Spengler or Toynbee—his true following was recruited among those of mid-
dling education. These found in Teilhard a kind of super-
ecumenicism, preceding by only a few years the Johannine
revolution in the Catholic Church and reinforcing the great
Pope's message. Teilhard's vision of human unity burst upon

[80] Cuénot, *Teilhard de Chardin* (English translation), pp. 130–131.
[81] *Ibid.*, pp. 237, 345. These connections have been charted by Frank
E. Manuel in *Shapes of Philosophical History* (Stanford, Calif., 1965),
pp. 145–151, 159–161.

the world just as the Cold War was lifting and peace seemed
within reach at last. Those who absorbed his teaching
could view all mankind's conflicts as ultimately reconcilable,
and the antagonism between Europe and Asia or between
Communism and Western democracy as capable of being
transcended in a higher synthesis. Although Teilhard had
only a superficial understanding of Asian religions and never
learned the Chinese language, he taught his countrymen and
Westerners as a whole to find spiritual value in alien cultures. In similar fashion he urged them to seek out what was
positive in Communism—its faith in man and in the future
of the world. And the less dogmatic among the French Communists were ready to grasp the hand he had extended to
them, stressing Teilhard's agreement with them in his joy
and confidence in humanity, in his celebration of action,
labor, and the material world, and in his anticipation of a
"humanism of the total man."[82]

Such expressions of opinion, however well taken, belonged
more to the category of poetry than to that of science or
rigorous reasoning. Teilhard's hymn to humanity brought
tidings of good cheer to a tormented planet: it seemed to
put man back where he felt he belonged—at the center and
summit of creation from which the science of a Darwin or a
Freud had deposed him. (But at this summit, how many of
man's usual attributes would remain, after he had been
stripped to his divine core?) For assertions like these, Teilhard's technical credentials appeared more relevant than they
actually were: his readers saw in him an expert replying to
his scientific predecessors—denying that nature was necessarily "red in tooth and claw" as the late nineteenth century
had believed, or that there was an ultimate irreconcilability
between that nature and the culture which man had imposed
upon it, as Freud had lamented in his *Civilization and Its
Discontents*. What Teilhard's readers seldom noticed was

[82] *Future of Man*, pp. 191–192; Roger Garaudy, *Perspectives de
l'homme: existentialisme, pensée catholique, marxisme*, 2nd ed. (Paris,
1960), pp. 193–194.

that his more far-reaching statements were almost totally without scientific buttressing: when evidence was lacking, his prose simply took off into rhapsody.

As poetic insight, however, Teilhard's writings gave his countrymen something they needed very badly. His work opened vistas on the world outside France, challenging the central assumptions of French ethnocentricity. As a prophet of universal love and reconciliation Teilhard will doubtless continue to be read long after his meta-science has been either refuted or absorbed into a more systematic inquiry concerning the future of man.

III. *Intermezzo: The New France*

Whatever date one selects—the mid-1950's and the beginnings of prosperity, 1958 and the advent of De Gaulle, or 1962 and the end of the Algerian War—it is apparent that sometime around 1960 French society underwent a profound change. In his last published work Merleau-Ponty, with his customary sensitivity for psychological nuances, began to ruminate on the altered ideological climate he found about him. It was an emotional atmosphere, he surmised, in which the old appeals to "history" had lost their force—in which conservatives could concede the innocence of Captain Dreyfus as a "commonplace" and remain conservatives just the same. The verities of the postwar Left, the passionate belief in "revolutionary heroism and humanism," had "fallen into ruin." Merleau-Ponty's own generation was filled with remorse for speaking about such matters "too dispassionately."

> But we should be careful. What we call disorder and ruin, others who are younger live as the natural order of things; and perhaps with ingenuity they are going to master it precisely because they no longer seek their bearings where we took ours. In the din of demolitions, many sullen passions, many hypocrisies or follies, and many

false dilemmas also disappear. Who would have hoped
it ten years ago?[33]

Where Merleau-Ponty remained hesitant and reserved,
younger observers—and particularly those from the Anglo-
American world—were quite sure that the change was for
the best. These were happy to find that as old-line Communism sank into irrelevance, the more flexible Socialists
were coming into their own as the advocates of economic
planning within a pluralist society. And they also had nothing against the ascension of power of a new class of
planners: people of this sort were the bearers of "middle-
middle" class values which had traditionally been slighted
in French social attitudes; the emergence of middle-range
technicians and managers was bringing a new directness to
interpersonal relations and an emphasis on competence as
the criterion of prestige.[34]

In this new atmosphere, the intellectuals themselves were
coming closer to the middle-middle norm and differentiating
their standards and way of life less sharply from those of
physicians, engineers, or administrators. The loosely-organized
political associations, like the Club Jean Moulin, which had
become a characteristic mark of the Fifth Republic, provided a common ground on which bureaucrats and intellectuals could exchange views as equals. The mandarin, like
the revolutionary, was succumbing to irrelevance. In the new
France of public optimism and confidence about the future,
the apocalyptic rhetoric of the immediate post-liberation era
rang hollow; intellectual life had lost both its fervor and its
special prestige.

The liberation—as Sartre put it—had been the intellectuals'
"perfect moment": with the traditional powers in collapse

[33] Introduction to *Signes* (Paris, 1960), translated by Richard C.
McCleary as *Signs* (Evanston, Ill., 1964), pp. 4, 22–23.
[34] George Lichtheim, *Marxism in Modern France* (New York,
1966), pp. 51, 144; Jesse R. Pitts, "Continuity and Change in
Bourgeois France," *In Search of France* (Cambridge, Mass., 1963),
p. 300.

or disarray, the mandarinate had enjoyed an unexampled public eminence; its every word seemed laden with portentous meaning. Yet it had never succeeded in defining a content for its doctrine of universal responsibility: it had oscillated erratically "between the total liberty of the individual revolutionary and the total constraint of Stalinism." By the 1960's such preachments had lost their vertiginous appeal. The younger French intellectuals—more especially the younger social scientists—were renouncing their "excessive ambitions"; their research was becoming "more positive and cumulative"; no longer claiming "to deal with everything at once," they were far more conscious than before of the relation of their work to practical action. As early as 1954 the brief, abortive premiership of Pierre Mendès-France had given the cue for a new public attitude of sober expertise and of reform through "concrete commitment."[85]

Yet if the old questions had been "too big, too vague, too murderous," there now loomed the danger that there would be no questions at all. If Sartre and his like had sacrificed the present to the future, the younger generation of French intellectuals seemed tempted to make a similar sacrifice of ethical aspiration to the acceptance of existing society as a going concern. The young were interpreting Camus's or Aron's pleas for ideological modesty as an "appeal against intellectual probing."[86] They were very nearly as suspicious of the older generation's ambitions as they were of its rhetoric. In putting so heavy a stress on the concrete and the nonrhetorical, the younger writers and social scientists were inclined to lump together the literary vices of the French tradition and the moral seriousness which had given that tradition its characteristic flavor; in the pursuit of a rigorous nominalism of method, they threatened to abandon the old

[85] Michel Crozier, "The Cultural Revolution: Notes on the Changes in the Intellectual Climate of France," *A New Europe?* edited by Stephen R. Graubard (Boston, 1964), pp. 602, 611, 613, 624–625.
[86] Stanley Hoffmann, "Europe's Identity Crisis: Between the Past and America," *Daedalus*, XCIII (Fall 1964), 1262.

quest for ethical norms and for universal statements about human society.

Once again, then—and at least as acutely as at any previous point in the century—a conflict of generations separated those who thought of themselves as the young from those who in fact were not so many years their seniors. Just as the men coming to maturity in the 1930's had been impatient with the refinements of the "last generation of French classicism," so those who grew up in the 1950's failed to understand their elders' absorption with ideology and revolutionary rhetoric. In this situation of mutual incomprehension, a mediator was required; and it was fortunate that the man who emerged as Sartre's rival and successor as France's intellectual laureate was ideally equipped to perform the role.

Claude Lévi-Strauss was only three years younger than Sartre; but his fame had come more than a decade later than that of the author of *Being and Nothingness* and in an atmosphere in which the attractions of both existentialism and Marxism were already on the wane. In his personal style, Lévi-Strauss combined the rationality and humanism of a philosophe in the great tradition with a thorough grasp of the latest techniques in social science. He was close enough to the familiar pattern of French thought to be able to lead along with him the more adventurous of those who still dwelt in that intellectual universe. Yet in recasting the pattern of thought in a new terminology, he in effect exploded it.[87] And in so doing he accomplished the feat of reuniting his countrymen with the world of social speculation beyond France's borders and of epitomizing in his own person the fact that France had finally produced a social theorist who was universally acknowledged as a master.

IV. *Claude Lévi-Strauss: Structure and Society*

With Lévi-Strauss, contemporary French thought was back where it began—in the sphere of social science, international

[87] Crozier, "Cultural Revolution," p. 628.

in scope, and with Frenchmen taking the lead. Like Bloch
and Febvre, Lévi-Strauss was deeply, almost obsessively, concerned with developing a type of study that would render
the "human" in all its infinite variety. He differed with them,
however, in finding in structure rather than in flow the
metaphor best adapted to convey what he had understood;
indeed, he pushed the notion of structure further than any
of his predecessors in this type of social inquiry. Nor did he
limit his work, as Bloch and Febvre had done, to the analysis
of Western societies. He took up the challenge with which
imaginative writers such as Saint-Exupéry and Malraux had
already engaged themselves, of combatting French ethnocentricity by an open-minded confrontation with the values
of alien peoples overseas. Like Malraux, Lévi-Strauss tried
to understand what it meant for non-Western societies to live
"without a history." But he went far beyond the novelists of
heroism in the rigor of his method and in the thoroughness
with which he shared the life and thought of the "primitives"
who were to become the protagonists of his subsequent
anthropological studies.

Which is all to say that Lévi-Strauss' intellectual antecedents were inordinately complex and reached back both to
his immediate predecessors of the 1930's and to the pre-First
World War generation of French social theorists. Among the
latter Durkheim and Bergson naturally loomed the largest.
Toward Durkheim, Lévi-Strauss' attitude was of necessity
ambivalent. As a young man he had been in "open insurrection" against Durkheim's precepts or any comparable "attempt to put sociology to metaphysical uses." Yet as his
professional career went on, he gradually discovered a lingering affinity to the Durkheimian tradition that set him apart
from English and American anthropologists.[88] By 1958—
the centenary of Durkheim's birth—Lévi-Strauss was ready
to dedicate to his predecessor, in the guise of an "inconstant
disciple," the series of essays he had collected under the title

[88] Claude Lévi-Strauss, *Tristes tropiques* (Paris, 1955), translated
(and slightly abridged) by John Russell under the same title, Atheneum
paperback edition (New York, 1963), p. 63.

Structural Anthropology. And he was frank in recognizing his own debt to the kinship and language studies of Marcel Mauss, the most influential of Durkheim's heirs. Toward Bergson, Lévi-Strauss took a more informal tone. In no sense a Bergsonian himself, he nevertheless made a point of recognizing where the philosopher of the élan vital could come to the aid of the student of primitive societies. With characteristic urbanity—and a hint of patronizing—Lévi-Strauss congratulated Bergson on being an "armchair philosopher" who in certain respects reasoned "like a savage," since "his own thought, unbeknownst to him, was in sympathy with that of totemic peoples."[89]

A second of Lévi-Strauss' major works, *The Savage Mind*, was dedicated to the memory of Merleau-Ponty, who had died in the year before its publication and had been its author's friend and colleague at the Collège de France. In this book, as throughout Lévi-Strauss' later production, one finds echoes of Merleau-Ponty, notably in the concern for man as "speaking subject." Yet the minds of the two friends —who in age were only a few months apart—worked in radically different fashions. Where Merleau-Ponty preferred to leave his thought open and elusive, Lévi-Strauss strove for closed formulations that had the precision of crystal. Each faced the same methodological problem: where was the study of man to go, once it had absorbed the teachings of Max Weber? Merleau-Ponty's choice was to push Weber's work to its logical consequences by "relativizing" still further the relativist implications in the ideal-type method—that is, by recognizing even more radically than Weber had done, the subjective and unverifiable character of the ideal types in question. Hence the floating, unstable intellectual universe of Merleau-Ponty's later thought. For Lévi-Strauss such indeterminacy was intolerable. As convinced as was his friend of the instability of the ideal-type method as currently under-

[89] *Le totémisme aujourd'hui* (Paris, 1962), translated by Rodney Needham as *Totemism*, Beacon paperback edition (Boston, 1963), pp. 98–99.

stood, Lévi-Strauss wanted to redefine and to tighten that method by eliminating its ambiguities.

In so doing, he took up the word "model" that in the meantime had come into currency among American social scientists, equating it with the older term "structure" to which he now gave a more precise significance. For Lévi-Strauss a structure was a model that conformed to several specific requirements:

> First, the structure exhibits the characteristics of a system. It is made up of several elements, none of which can undergo a change without effecting changes in all the other elements.
>
> Second, for any given model there should be a possibility of ordering a series of transformations resulting in a group of models of the same type.
>
> Third, the above properties make it possible to predict how the model will react if one or more of its elements are submitted to certain modifications.
>
> Finally, the model should be constituted so as to make immediately intelligible all the observed facts.[40]

Thus the model (or group of models) had an internal consistency that gave an initial guarantee of its validity. But even this progress over Weber was insufficient to satisfy Lévi-Strauss' thirst for certainty. Despite his agnosticism about the values—whether religious or ideological—ordinarily professed in his own society, he refused to remain in a similar state of suspended judgment about the nature of man: the overriding aim of his career as a social scientist was to dig below every theoretical level yet discovered and to come at last to a basic structure of the human mind which would at once cancel out and reconcile the countless explanations of

[40] "La notion de structure en ethnologie" (originally presented in English at a symposium in New York in 1952), *Anthropologie structurale* (Paris, 1958), translated by Claire Jacobson and Brooke Grundfest Schoepf as *Structural Anthropology* (New York, 1963), pp. 279–280.

their behavior that men had offered through all ages and all
types of savagery or civilization.

A breath-taking quest—as ambitious as that of any twentieth-century investigator—and one which a half century
earlier would have been totally unfeasible. For Lévi-Strauss
enjoyed advantages denied to the generation of Weber or of
Freud: in the meantime the study of man had evolved in
two new directions which opened up unsuspected vistas of
intellectual certainty.

The first was Lévi-Strauss' chosen discipline of anthropology. The latest arrival among the social sciences, anthropology as a clearly delimited field of study was only a quarter
century old when he encountered it in the early 1930's. At
that time its first great generation of field workers was still
alive and active. The leaders of this generation, which included Bronislaw Malinowski in Britain and Alfred L.
Kroeber in America, were of an age to be Lévi-Strauss' fathers,
as the generation of Freud and Weber ranked as his intellectual grandfathers. Certain of them he treated with filial respect, others with an equally filial combativity. Much of Lévi-
Strauss' work was a polemic against the underlying conviction of Malinowski and the British school that the rites and
myths of primitive peoples could be understood in terms of
a social function. His admiration, rather, went to such Americans as Kroeber and Franz Boas in whom he discovered an
optimum combination of empirical method and a gift for
synthesis.

By the very choice of anthropology as a field of study,
Lévi-Strauss was led in a double sense outside France's cultural fortress. The contact with pre-literate societies was the
more obvious of these outlets; equally important was the fact
that the discipline as a whole was dominated by the Anglo-
Americans (many of whom, however, had Central or Eastern
European origins) and employed English as its international
language. Thus, as a cursory sampling of his footnotes revealed, Lévi-Strauss worked at two removes from the familiar

idea-world of his countrymen: he dealt with exotic peoples whose customs were for the most part interpreted in a Western language that was not his own.

The fact that the only anthropologist since Sir James Frazer to achieve general public renown was a Frenchman rather than an Englishman or American gave Lévi-Strauss' work an extra dimension. He brought to his labors a characteristic French conviction that cultural phenomena obeyed an immanent law. And more rigorously than his English-speaking colleagues, he insisted on a standard of objectivity in anthropological study which set this discipline apart from the other social sciences. Every social scientist, he recognized, strove to be objective in the sense that he tried to rise above his own value system; yet the anthropologist alone went one step further and questioned the entire method of thinking which permeated Western civilization. The anthropologist in effect jumped backward through time to the moment in pre-Socratic Greece when the canon of logical reasoning had first been established, and then took off from this point to a systematic investigation of how the mind of primitive man worked. Only by divesting himself of the methodological prejudices, scientific or philosophical, that were second nature to Europeans and Americans, could the student of pre-literate societies hope to discover the fundamental patterns of human thought that underlay its overwhelming diversity of expression.

In this quest, Lévi-Strauss brought to bear the second—and still more recent—of the new methods of study developed since the time of Freud and Weber, the technique of structural linguistics. Since the original pioneering work of a Swiss scholar, Ferdinand de Saussure, before 1914, linguistics had in a single generation become the most sharply defined of the sciences of man. Having totally separated meaning from sound in their study of language, the structural linguists were free to concentrate their attention on the phoneme, the basic unit of human speech. And once they

had done so, they found that the possible combinations of
phonemes were finite in number and followed rules which
were statistically predictable. Such combinations, since they
occurred at the unconscious level and were quite innocent of
subsequent policing at the hands of grammarians, had the
advantage of being value-free and devoid of meaning. The
lesson for anthropology seemed clear:

> If . . . the unconscious activity of the mind consists in
> imposing forms upon content, and if these forms are
> fundamentally the same for all minds—ancient and
> modern, primitive and civilized . . . —it is necessary
> and sufficient to grasp the unconscious structure under-
> lying each institution and each custom, in order to ob-
> tain a principle of interpretation valid for other institu-
> tions and other customs. . . .[41]

What Lévi-Strauss learned from the structural linguists
was to think of his subject in terms of a net of relationships,
all of which, if reduced to their essentials, had something in
common. In this view, the task of the anthropologist became
one of first drawing up an exhaustive inventory of such relationships and then establishing their necessary connections.
And the area in which Lévi-Strauss himself chose to illustrate
his theory seemed at first glance the most difficult of all—
the realm of myth, where the human imagination was com-
monly supposed to wander untrammeled. If in *this* domain,
he argued, the mind could be shown as "bound and determined in all its operations, a fortiori, it must be so everywhere."[42] If the systematic study of myth would bear out
his basic contention, then he could "buckle together" the
untidy loose ends in the study of man and forge a new positivism more potent and more sophisticated than the nineteenth-century positivist teachings which the generation of

[41] "Introduction: Histoire et ethnologie" (originally published in
Revue de métaphysique et de morale, LIV, 1949), *ibid.*, p. 21.
[42] "Réponses à quelques questions," *Esprit* (special issue on Lévi-
Strauss), XXXI (November 1963), 630.

his intellectual grandfathers had thought they had dis-
credited forever.[48]

Although, as we have seen, Lévi-Strauss was the chronological contemporary of Sartre and Merleau-Ponty, he was
launched onto the French intellectual scene later than these
two, since he abandoned philosophy for the slow and round-
about path of becoming a field anthropologist. His reasons
for so doing epitomized his entire intellectual endeavor:
"With philosophy I had a sense of stopping half-way, of
stopping at certain types of thought . . . which were those
of our Western society, . . . whereas anthropology gave me,
rightly or wrongly, an impression of going to the farthest
limits of what was possible in the exploration of philosophy's
goal."[44]

Like Bergson and Durkheim and Bloch, Lévi-Strauss was
of Jewish origin. But no more than for these three was Juda-
ism a living reality to him. (The eminence of this succession
of names—as influential a quartet as one can find in the
history of twentieth-century French thought—suggests religious agnosticism against a Jewish background as an optimum point of departure for social speculation.) In the case of
Lévi-Strauss, the Jewish tradition was attenuated in the extreme: his only memories of the ancestral religion derived
from the years of the First World War, when, already past
his early childhood, he lived with a rabbi grandfather whose
formal and desiccated practice of his faith was hardly of a
kind to stir the emotions. Ten or fifteen years later, Lévi-
Strauss found his philosophical studies equally unappealing:
although he did everything expected of him, passing the
agrégation at an early age and even beginning the normal
course of academic advancement by teaching in a lycée, he
felt that he was simply playing an established set of rhetorical

---

[48] Marc Gaboriau, "Anthropologie structurale et histoire," *ibid.*,
p. 595.
[44] Claude Lévi-Strauss, "A contre-courant," interview published in
Le nouvel observateur, No. 115 (January 25, 1967), p. 30.

games which bore little relation to "truth." Even the newer
forms of philosophical inquiry held no appeal: Lévi-Strauss
was suspicious of the phenomenologists' claim to have found
a basis for reality in the minute data of experience and of
the "indulgent attitude" of existentialism "towards the illusions of subjectivity."[45] Hence it was with a sense of deliver-
ance that in the autumn of 1934, when he had just turned
twenty-eight, he accepted, quite literally on three hours'
notice, the chance to go to São Paulo as professor of sociology.

The better part of the following five years Lévi-Strauss
spent in Brazil. Although sociology was his designated subject and although he was fascinated by the fast-growing,
chaotic metropolis in which he taught, his real purpose in
leaving France was to pursue the anthropological interests
to which he had already been drawn in amateur and unsystematic fashion. Now he was resolved to make himself a
professional: at home base in São Paulo, he read the literature of the field; in vacation time he ventured ever farther
into the Brazilian interior to study the Indians at first hand.
The last and longest of such expeditions, lasting a full year
and unprecedented in its scope and hardship, took him all
the way across the center of the continent through endless
wastes of scrub growth to the valley of the Amazon. By mid-
1939, when he returned to France, Lévi-Strauss had become
a seasoned anthropologist.

By the same token he had become a stranger to France and
had fallen out of the customary sequence of university promotion. The tumults of the late 1930's had passed him by:
perspiring and struggling through the desolation of central
Brazil, he had sometimes wondered ruefully whether it was
not quixotic to follow so eccentric a course rather than getting
ahead in the academic world as a fledgling French intellectual
was supposed to do. And these biographical anomalies were
reinforced after the outbreak of the war. In early 1941, having
finished his military service and feeling threatened (as was
only sensible) by the Vichy government's cooperation with

[45] *Tristes tropiques* (English translation), pp. 61–62, 215.

German anti-Semitic measures, Lévi-Strauss embarked for the
United States, where a group of American anthropologists, to
whom his name was already known, were prepared to take
care of him. For the remainder of the war years he taught
in New York, at the New School for Social Research and at
the Ecole Libre des Hautes Etudes founded by other Frenchmen stranded overseas, notably Jacques Maritain. Here Lévi-
Strauss acquired the fluency in English and the familiarity
with American anthropology that were later to rank among
his most valuable assets. But he also remained conscious of
his role as a *French* intellectual: it was as cultural counselor
of the French Embassy, a position he held from 1946 to
1947, that he presided over a lecture delivered by Albert
Camus at Columbia University.

Back in France at last—and this time for good—Lévi-
Strauss brought to completion the anthropological studies he
had been working on for more than a decade. In 1948 the
publication of his first book, a study of family and social life
among the Nambikwara Indians, established him as a leader
in his profession. A year later the first of his more speculative
works, on the "elementary structures of kinship," brought
him to the attention of a wider circle of intellectuals. Finally
in 1955—the year of Teilhard de Chardin's death and of the
posthumous publication of *The Phenomenon of Man*—the
appearance of *Tristes tropiques* made Lévi-Strauss almost
overnight a celebrated author in the eyes of the general reading public.

Although it was totally different in style and conception
from *The Phenomenon of Man*, Lévi-Strauss' book derived
its popularity from a similar quality of extending the frontiers
of a scientific treatise far beyond the usual professional concerns. Besides giving a systematic account of what he had
learned about four different South American Indian peoples
among whom he had dwelt, *Tristes tropiques* was at once an
autobiography and a philosophical reflection on travel in the
manner of an eighteenth-century moraliste. Its tone (more
nuanced than Teilhard's) alternated like his between the

dryly factual and the lyric. Its underlying mood, as its title
implied, was of restrained elegy. Subtle in phraseology, dense
in thought, *Tristes tropiques* offered the extended meditation
of an ultra-civilized Gallic mind on the ways of "savages"
whom he had found to be not nearly so unsophisticated as
their nakedness and destitution might suggest.

With the publication of his *Structural Anthropology* in
1958, the theoretical outlines of Lévi-Strauss' position had
been established; the following year he received a newly-
created chair at the Collège de France. It now remained for
him to make fully explicit what he had earlier sketched out
and to reply to the impatient critics who stood ready to trip
him up. This process he began with a small book entitled
Totemism, the prologue to the most important of his theoretical writings, *The Savage Mind*, published in 1962.

If *Tristes tropiques* had made Lévi-Strauss famous, *The
Savage Mind* made him controversial. As the sharpest expression of his views he had yet set forth, it aroused passionate
discussion among social scientists, philosophers, and men of
letters. For its combination of ultra-relativism and the new
dogmatism of the structural method had something in it to
upset or displease almost every French school of social speculation.

The mind of the savage, Lévi-Strauss argued, was neither
so simple nor so wayward as it was ordinarily supposed to be.
In point of fact primitive man thought in an exceedingly
complicated fashion; his logic was merely of a different order
from the logic of abstract science to which Western man had
become accustomed. Still more, the savage thirsted for objective knowledge and was adept at observing the concrete;
the systems by which he classified plants, animals, and
natural phenomena were detailed and sometimes even intellectually elegant. The results of his speculations were preserved in a "science of the concrete"—the "memory bank" of
techniques in agriculture, pottery, and the domestication of
animals which had made possible the beginnings of settled

habitation in neolithic times. After that enormous cultural revolution, mankind had stopped in its tracks—and most cultures had remained there. Even in the West, thousands of years had gone by before the advent of modern science: the scientific speculation of classical antiquity and the Middle Ages was still neolithic in temper. The only way to explain this "level plain" of "stagnation" was to postulate "two distinct modes of scientific thought"—"one roughly adapted to that of perception and the imagination: the other at a remove from it." The former—the "primitive" science of the concrete—had to its credit the achievements secured ten thousand years ago which still remained "at the basis of our own civilization."[46]

Having thus established the credentials of the savage way of thought, Lévi-Strauss went on to point out the vestiges of such thinking in contemporary Europe and America. These vestiges were of the sort that the Freudian school of therapy condemned as magical—that is, the conviction of hidden affinities and sympathies between human actions and the world of nature. But the word "magic"—like everything else in the mental universe of primitive man—held no terrors for Lévi-Strauss. Magic too had its logic: it would be better, he maintained, "instead of contrasting magic and science, to compare them as two parallel modes of acquiring knowledge"; the former, unlike abstract scientific thought, postulated a "complete and all-embracing determinism." And once the principles of such determinism had been fully understood, they were found to work rather like a kaleidoscope: they reshuffled bits and pieces of traditional lore into endless variations of basically similar structural patterns; they displayed both "internal coherence" and a "practically unlimited capacity for extension."[47]

The magical—or totemic—way of thinking was by its nature anti-historical. But it did not deny the category of

[46] *La pensée sauvage* (Paris, 1962), translated as *The Savage Mind* (Chicago, 1966), pp. 3, 15–16, 42.
[47] *Ibid.*, pp. 11–13, 36, 217.

time: the savage mind simply could not bring itself to believe that anything really changed. Nor did the lack of a sense for history denote some ineradicable inferiority of feeling: an "obstinate fidelity to a past conceived as a timeless model," Lévi-Strauss argued, "betrayed no moral or intellectual deficiency whatsoever." As opposed to the usual "clumsy distinction" between "peoples without history" and those who thought of themselves in historical terms, he preferred to speak of "cold" societies that tried to stay in equilibrium and "hot" ones that were forever on the move.[48] Thus a thoroughgoing ethical relativism lay at the end of Lévi-Strauss' search for the principles of primitive thought: in their acute understanding of the plant and animal world, in their sense of an overarching cosmic harmony, those who dwelt in the "cold" cultures displayed a nobility of temper that the super-heated West had long ago forgotten.

Finally, the structures the mind of primitive man revealed could be presumed to be universal. Under the lofty scaffolding of modern science, the mental patterns of the contemporary city dweller in the West were much like those of his neolithic ancestor. The task of the anthropologist was to find those patterns—proceeding on the principle that "either everything, or nothing, makes sense." And when they had been sufficiently understood, Lévi-Strauss concluded, "the entire process of human knowledge" would assume "the character of a closed system."[49]

The completion of *The Savage Mind,* by Lévi-Strauss' own account, marked a pause in his thought. But the task he had set himself was far from accomplished. He had affirmed the existence of basic mental structures: now he had to prove it. He had declared that myths were capable of structural analysis: to date he had given only a few scattered examples. The purpose of the four-volume series entitled *Mythologiques* which he launched in 1964 was to show the structural method

[48] *Ibid.,* pp. 233–236.
[49] *Ibid.,* pp. 173, 269.

in action—to derive from an exhaustive "coding" of mythic material a "picture of the world already inscribed in the architecture" of the human mind.[50]

Drawing his data from the Indians of South America whom he knew at first hand, Lévi-Strauss focused his attention on myths dealing with food, tobacco, and the transformations raw meat and plants underwent in being prepared for human use. The first volume analyzed how the practice of cooking had altered man's relations with nature; the second traced the more complex symbolic significance of smoking and eating honey. In the remote past, the mythic material suggested, men had simply laid out their food on stones to be warmed by the heat of the sun: the sun's rays had united heaven and earth in a harmony in which mankind felt itself to be in no way separate from the world of nature. With the change to cooked food, these relations were profoundly altered: the introduction of cooking was the decisive step in the passage from nature to culture; man was cut off both from the gods and from the animals who ate their food raw. In consequence his world became problematic and threatening. Only through the mediation of friendly and helpful animals—the tapirs or jaguars or opossums who were the protagonists of the major myths—could a precarious cosmic order be restored.[51]

In his first volume Lévi-Strauss set up a series of opposites which were simple and tangible: the raw as against the cooked, the fresh as against the rotten, the dry as against the humid. In his second volume—the one which dealt with honey and tobacco—the contrasts were more abstract and equivocal: "empty and full, container and contained, internal and external, included and excluded," plus variants in between.[52] This procedure by pairs was the key feature of Lévi-Strauss' coding: it constituted his method of reducing myth to its component parts, "retaining . . . only a small number

[50] *Le cru et le cuit* (*Mythologiques*, I) (Paris, 1964), p. 346. An English translation, under the title *The Raw and the Cooked*, is scheduled for publication in 1968.
[51] *Ibid.*, pp. 172, 295, 333.
[52] *Du miel aux cendres* (*Mythologiques*, II) (Paris, 1966), p. 406.

of elements suitable for expressing contrasts and forming pairs of opposites." Such codes, he argued, were capable of transformations from one into another. Among them there were no "privileged semantic levels."[53] In a universe of concepts liberated from the "servitude" of "concrete experience" all relationships were equally meaningful—or perhaps equally lacking in significance.[54]

The work of coding and transformation—carried out in meticulous detail—made *Mythologiques* exceedingly difficult to read. It also raised the central problem of meaning in Lévi-Strauss' whole enterprise which will occupy us shortly: what was one to make of an endeavor which the author himself described as a kind of mythologizing of mythic material?[55] Moreover, all question of meaning aside, certain peripheral features of these volumes were sufficiently extraordinary to suggest both the fascination his work exerted, particularly on the young, and his reputation as an elusive and hermetic thinker.

In *Mythologiques* the mannerism that had always been latent in Lévi-Strauss' prose became explicit and obtrusive. The work was quite unnecessarily precious in tone, and the first volume was organized around a labored (and frequently inappropriate) analogy with musical composition, its chapters including an overture, theme and variations, sonata, symphony, cantata, and fugue. Evidently the author enjoyed playing cat-and-mouse with his readers. As one British critic put it, half admiring and half exasperated:

> The prose of Lévi-Strauss is a very special instrument. . . . It has an austere, dry detachment, at times reminiscent of La Bruyère and Gide. It uses a careful alternance of long sentences, usually organized in ascending rhythm, and of abrupt Latinate phrases. While seeming to observe the conventions of neutral, learned presentation, it allows for brusque personal interventions and

[53] *Le cru et le cuit*, p. 347.
[54] *Du miel aux cendres*, p. 407.
[55] *Le cru et le cuit*, p. 14.

asides. Momentarily, Lévi-Strauss appears to be taking the reader into his confidence, . . . making him accomplice to some deep, subtle merriment at the expense of the subject or of other men's pretensions in it. Then he withdraws behind a barrier of technical analysis and erudition so exacting that it excludes all but the initiate.[56]

Thus a writer who ostensibly made no claim to being a literary figure in fact very consciously contrived his work for its effect as literature. And the stance he adopted toward his subject matter was equally ambivalent—stoicism and disengagement alternating with warm human sympathy. If on the one hand he ruthlessly saw through all meanings and directed his attention to structure alone, he was not ashamed to give voice to his own values when his emotions were stirred: he could write with transparent anger of the ravages of a Western technology that converted South Sea islands into "stationary aircraft-carriers" and threw its "filth . . . in the face of humanity"; he could bemoan the irony of his profession that condemned him to hasten "in search of a vanished reality."[57] He loved his métier; yet it brought him to near-despair as he watched how contact with "advanced" societies dissolved his subject matter before his very eyes. To the young French of the 1960's such reflections carried the ring of truth: in France too the achievement of technical modernity was being purchased at a painful psychic cost. In sum, the secret of Lévi-Strauss' immense influence lay in his talent for "carrying out a rigorous and strictly scientific work, while at the same time reflecting on this work, examining its method, extracting the philosophic elements from it, and remaining through it all a kind of Rousseau, both misanthropic and a friend of mankind, who sometimes dreams of reconciling East and West by completing the economic

[56] "Orpheus with his Myths," *The Times Literary Supplement,* LXIV (April 29, 1965), 321.
[57] *Tristes tropiques* (English translation), pp. 39, 45.

liberation inherent in Marxism with a spiritual liberation of Buddhist origin."[58]

The relation to Marx was one central problem that Lévi-Strauss' work raised. The relation to Freud was another. Beyond these lay the question of his attitude toward his own contemporaries—more particularly Sartre—and toward the high valuation they placed on historical understanding. Finally, and most troublingly, loomed the problem of meaning, the ground on which compromise between Lévi-Strauss and his adversaries was next to impossible.

Marx he encountered early in life, when as a boy of about seventeen he met a young Belgian Socialist.

A whole world was opened to me. My excitement has never cooled: and rarely do I tackle a problem in sociology or ethnology without having first set my mind in motion by reperusal of a page or two from the *18 Brumaire of Louis Bonaparte* or the *Critique of Political Economy*. Whether Marx accurately foretold this or that historical development is not the point. Marx followed Rousseau in saying—and saying once and for all, so far as I can see—that social science is no more based upon events than physics is based upon sense-perceptions. Our object is to construct a model, examine its properties and the way in which it reacts to laboratory tests, and then apply our observations to the interpretation of empirical happenings.

No more than Merleau-Ponty in his final guise, could Lévi-Strauss be called a Marxist in any simple meaning of the term. It was rather that for him, as for so many of his French contemporaries, Marxism remained a source of inspiration and a point of departure for social-science method.

It was comparable, Lévi-Strauss found, both to geology

[58] Jean Lacroix, *Panorama de la philosophie française contemporaine* (Paris, 1966), p. 222.

and to psychoanalysis in that all three tried to reduce an obvious reality to a less apparent one which took care to "evade our detection." In all three cases the problem was the same—"the relation . . . between reason and sense-perception"—as was the goal pursued, which could be defined as a *"super-rationalism,"* an integration of sense-perceptions into reasoning in which the former would "lose none of their properties."[59]

Yet if Lévi-Strauss was convinced that Marx had been on the right track, he was less sure about Freud. One senses that psychoanalytic theory was a point of special difficulty for him: of the various "codes" his predecessors had offered, it was the most recalcitrant to the universal relativizing process at which he aimed. Much of what he wrote in *Mythologiques* about the trauma mankind had undergone in tearing itself loose from the world of nature seemed of a piece with Freud's own musings in *Civilization and Its Discontents*. But this was Freudianism in its speculative and quasi-anthropological manner: toward its clinical claims Lévi-Strauss was more severe. He warned against the possibility that psychoanalytic therapy might result in no more solid a "cure" than a conversion on the part of the patient to the particular and limited mental set of the therapist himself. This was substantially what sorcerers and shamans had always done—and in a tone of scarcely veiled patronizing Lévi-Strauss remarked that the psychoanalysts of today might learn something from comparing their methods and goals with those of their "great predecessors."[60] Such tolerance for magical procedures, however, did not extend to the work of Jung. Whatever superficial similarities their common interest in the realm of myth might suggest, Lévi-Strauss found Jung's "obscurantism . . .

[59] *Tristes tropiques* (English translation), p. 61.
[60] "Le sorcier et sa magie" (originally published in *Les temps modernes*, IV, 1949), "L'efficacité symbolique" (originally published in *Revue de l'histoire des religions*, CXXXV, 1949), *Structural Anthropology*, pp. 182–185, 201–204.

quite abhorrent." Still more, the latter had committed the supreme methodological error of directing his attention to the content of myth rather than to its form.[61]

The emotions, Lévi-Strauss argued, explained nothing; they were "consequences, never causes." These latter could be sought only in a biological investigation of the organism, or in the intellect, which was the "sole way offered to psychology, and to anthropology as well."[62] Lévi-Strauss' own method of coping with the emotions was to intellectualize them. He reduced subjectivity to its "intellectual laws," proposing a "sequence of constantly narrower definitions of the unconscious."[63] The result, as the philosopher Paul Ricoeur complained, was an unconscious that was "rather . . . Kantian than Freudian," an unconscious that dealt in categories and combinations—a formulation of his own thought to which Lévi-Strauss in the end was quite willing to assent.[64]

This process of intellectualization, in terms of method and sympathy, put him closer to Marx than to Freud. While the accusation of hostility to psychoanalysis seems to have bothered him very little, he was quick to reply to the Marxist charge that he was a foe of progress.[65] A lingering affinity for Marxism kept him safely within the camp of France's left-oriented intellectuals and helps explain the surprisingly respectful attention he gave to the work of Jean-Paul Sartre.

Lévi-Strauss regarded the *Critique of Dialectical Reason* as a sufficiently important cultural phenomenon to warrant his devoting to it a special and concluding chapter of his *Savage Mind* and to linking up with it his own reflections on the study of history. Sartre was right, Lévi-Strauss agreed, in dis-

[61] George Steiner, "A Conversation with Claude Lévi-Strauss," *Encounter*, XXVI (April 1966), 35.

[62] *Totemism*, p. 71.

[63] Emilio Renzi, "Sulla nozione di inconscio in Lévi-Strauss," *Aut Aut*, No. 88 (July 1965), pp. 57–58.

[64] "Structure et herméneutique," *Esprit*, XXXI (November 1963), 600; "Réponses à quelques questions," *ibid.*, p. 633.

[65] *Structural Anthropology*, Chapter 16; see also Edmund Leach, "Claude Lévi-Strauss—Anthropologist and Philosopher," *New Left Review*, No. 34 (November–December 1965), pp. 17–19.

tinguishing the dialectical from the analytic method, but he refused to accept the former's sharp separation of the two. Rather than being of a different logical order, the dialectic was a prolongation of analysis onto new and risky territory. Moreover, Sartre had muddled his account by equating dialectical reasoning (in its "true" form) with the historical consciousness of the West, while describing such a procedure among "primitives" as a merely repetitive process which was close to the biological level. Nor was this the end of Sartre's confusions. "In his manner of invoking history," he had mixed up three common but quite distinct meanings of the term— the "history men make unconsciously," the "history of men consciously made by historians," and the subsequent interpretations philosophers put on the two previous types of activity.[66]

Most of the time, Lévi-Strauss found, Sartre's work fell within the third definition; he was the architect of a grand historical design in the Hegelian manner. And as such, what Sartre had offered ranked as a "first-class ethnographic document" (again the note of patronizing) which could claim the dignity of myth. Indeed, Lévi-Strauss seemed to suggest, the nobility of Sartre's attitude lay in the intense fashion with which he lived his own myth—the myth of the French Revolution and its thunderous twentieth-century successors. Lévi-Strauss personally had nothing against this way of thinking—as a part-time adherent of the Left he even shared in it —he simply maintained that "in a different register" of their consciousness people like Sartre and himself should recognize that their ideological notion of historical meaning did not constitute eternal truth and that posterity would regard things quite differently.[67] Moreover, they should take care, as Sartre had not done, to distinguish their reflections on history from the second meaning of the word, that is, the history of the historians.

The accusation of anti-historicism lodged against Lévi-

[66] *The Savage Mind*, pp. 246, 248, 250–251.
[67] *Ibid.*, pp. 249n., 254–255.

Strauss almost invariably referred to the speculative, Hegelian activity which exerted so strong an attraction on postwar French intellectuals. And in such a form he was perfectly willing to accept the charge: he had no use for historicity as the "last refuge of a transcendental humanism."[68] The majestic type of history with a capital "H" was quite foreign to his own concept of social science. But for what the professional historians did he voiced real sympathy. He referred to it as a type of study complementary to anthropology, which organized its data "in relation to conscious expressions of social life," while anthropology proceeded by "examining its unconscious foundations." Nor could even this division be airtight. "To an increasing degree," Lévi-Strauss found, the historian was calling "to his aid the whole apparatus of unconscious elaborations. . . . Any good history book" was "saturated with anthropology"—Lucien Febvre's study of sixteenth-century disbelief offering an illustrious example.[69] Throughout the inaugural lecture he delivered at the Collège de France in 1960, Lévi-Strauss scattered conciliatory remarks in the direction of his historical colleagues. And six years later in his *Mythologiques,* he repeated the reassurance: far from refusing to recognize the claims of history, structural analysis granted it a position of first importance—the position that belonged "by right to the irreducible contingency without which necessity would not even be conceivable."[70]

So much seemed clear: the contingency that historians studied was the indispensable prerequisite to Lévi-Strauss' own efforts to establish the basic categories of human thought and action. In such a methodological program Bloch and Febvre might well have concurred. Or at the very least they would have been willing to give the new procedure a fair hearing. This was the line their successors on the *Annales* took in assessing Lévi-Strauss' work: as long-time proponents of a unified study of man, they were bound to welcome it—

[68] *Ibid.,* p. 262.
[69] *Structural Anthropology,* pp. 18, 23.
[70] *Du miel aux cendres,* p. 408.

if only as a "cathartic" which forced them to question the very language of their craft.[71] Yet with whatever good will historians might greet Lévi-Strauss' attempt to find structure in history, the type of analysis to which he was inviting them to adjust was not always clear. In his methodological state-ments—as in his *Mythologiques*—he seemed to be proposing a reduction (or coding) of historical material on a mecha-nistic model; in the bulk of his published work he proceeded in the more conventional anthropological fashion of trying to understand an exotic society in its own terms.[72] The latter was approximately what the school of Bloch and Febvre had been doing all along. The former was a program so alien to the historian's mentality that he had no choice but to watch its development from a respectful distance.

However polite Lévi-Strauss might be to the professional historians—however carefully he distinguished their work from the ideological exploitation of history which he criti-cized in Sartre—on one point he refused to compromise: he was unwilling to accord history the status of a privileged order of knowledge that constituted the special cultural su-periority of the West. To have done so would have been inconsistent with the radical relativism of his approach and with the equal weighting he gave to the values of "cold" societies as against the "hot." In this final sense there re-mained an irreconcilable incompatibility between Lévi-Strauss and those who thought in primarily historical terms.

By training and temperament historians were more con-cerned with the content than with the formal characteristics of their subject. They were similarly inclined to take the values they studied "straight"—rather than trying to con-vert them into an abstract and universal code. What Lévi-Strauss was after was precisely the opposite: he believed that content in itself had no meaning; it was only the way in

[71] Roland Barthes, "Les sciences humaines et l'oeuvre de Lévi-Strauss," *Annales: économies—sociétés—civilisations*, XIX (November–December 1964), 1085–1086.

[72] Gaboriau, "Anthropologie structurale et histoire," pp. 592–594.

which the different elements of the content were combined
that gave a meaning.[73] But once meaning had been drained
of content, what was left? This was the ultimate question
historians and philosophers and social scientists proposed:
was there in fact any meaning to Lévi-Strauss' infinitely ingenious constructions?

The basic trouble with his method—quite aside from the
closed conceptual universe it presupposed—was that it made
no value distinctions among the coded relationships it established. Nor could it even lay claim to an exhaustive process
of coding: the elements that went into it, as in the performance of a computer, were limited to the small number
that were capable of unambiguous manipulation. The result
was perhaps no more than a glorious cerebral game. Or, in
terms of formal philosophy, it amounted to a "discourse" at
once "fascinating" and "disquieting"—an "admirable syn-
tactical arrangement" that said nothing.[74]

Thus in one guise Lévi-Strauss could be considered the
most extreme and consistent of the students of society who
in the 1940's and 1950's—throughout the Western world—
were inaugurating a new and more sophisticated positivist
method. He was convinced that he had fulfilled—or was
about to fulfill—the social scientist's eternal dream of in-
tegrating method and reality.[75] He had re-established the
structure of the mind as basically rational; he accepted the
word "determinism"; he was unafraid of materialist explanations. In so doing, Lévi-Strauss accomplished the extraordinary feat of carrying out a universally-applicable and intellectualist program in the dominant French tradition while
at the same time linking up with the work of other neo-pos-
itivists outside France who were attracted by the rigor and

[73] Steiner, "Conversation with Lévi-Strauss," p. 35.
[74] Paul Ricoeur in "Réponses à quelques questions," p. 653.
[75] *Totemism*, p. 91. This universalist claim provides the point of
attack for Clifford Geertz's expert and ably-reasoned critique: "The
Cerebral Savage: On the Work of Claude Lévi-Strauss," *Encounter*,
XXVII (April 1967), 25–32.

elegance of his method: he broke out of his countrymen's cultural confinement while remaining authentically and recognizably French.

But there was also Lévi-Strauss' second guise as moraliste and philosophe, the heir of Montaigne, Montesquieu, and Rousseau. If his first incarnation was of greater interest to the world of science, the second was the source of his prestige among the general public. For it was here that in true eighteenth-century manner he held up the cultural universe of the "primitives" among whom he had dwelt as a mirror in which the French (and Westerners as a whole) could find a critique of their own society. He grieved over the defenseless savages whose way of life stood condemned by material "progress." In a tone of lyric pathos he had written in his travel notebook of the 1930's a passage on the tiny remnant of the once great Nambikwara people, which he was to publish two decades later and which may stand as a sample and symbol of this elegiac aspect of his thought:

> The camp-fires shine out in the darkened savannah. Around the hearth which is their only protection from the cold, . . . beside the baskets filled with the pitiable objects which comprise all their earthly belongings, the Nambikwara lie on the bare earth. . . . When they lie entwined together, couple by couple, each looks to his mate for support and comfort and finds in the other a bulwark, the only one he knows, against the difficulties of every day and the meditative melancholia which from time to time overwhelms the Nambikwara. The visitor who camps among the Indians for the first time cannot but feel anguish and pity at the sight of a people so totally dis-provided for; beaten down into the hostile earth . . . by an implacable cataclysm; naked and shivering beside their guttering fires. . . . Laughing whispers can still make light of the Nambikwara's poverty. Their embraces are those of couples possessed by a longing for a lost oneness. . . . In one and all there may be glimpsed

a great sweetness of nature, a profound nonchalance, an
animal satisfaction as ingenuous as it is charming, and,
beneath all this, something that can be recognized as
one of the most moving and authentic manifestations of
human tenderness.[76]

During his stay with the Nambikwara, Lévi-Strauss had
discovered a "society reduced to its simplest expression"—a
society in which "nothing but human beings" remained. It
was perhaps a "vestigial version of what Rousseau had in
mind" when he spoke of a state of nature. As he had proceeded with his field investigations, Lévi-Strauss' respect for
Rousseau had steadily grown. The author of *Emile* and *The
Social Contract*, he surmised, had seen the necessity of setting up a model—based on an exact correspondence to no
existing social state—which would orient future investigations
by "enabling us to distinguish the characteristics common
to the majority of human societies." And Lévi-Strauss was
"inclined to think" that Rousseau "was right" in believing
that the "image nearest" to this model "was what we now
call the neolithic age." For the author of *Tristes tropiques*,
as for the philosophe he hailed as his "master" and "brother,"
the neolithic was the norm.[77]

We who dwell in "hot" societies, he constantly implied,
could well take lessons from those who have no truck with
change. And in an interview he gave after the publication of
the second volume of his *Mythologiques*, he made this injunction, and with it his own attitude, explicit at last:

> I have little taste for the century in which we live. What
> seems to me the present tendency is on the one hand
> man's total mastery over nature and on the other hand
> the mastery of certain forms of humanity over others.
> My temperament and my tastes lead me far more toward
> periods which were less ambitious and perhaps more
> timid but in which a certain balance could be maintained

[76] *Tristes tropiques* (English translation), p. 285.
[77] *Ibid.*, pp. 310, 389–390.

between man and nature, among the various and multiple forms of life, whether animal or vegetable, and among the different types of culture, of belief, of customs, or of institutions. I do not strive to perpetuate this diversity but rather to preserve its memory.[78]

Thus—despite the contradictions he recognized in such an attitude—Lévi-Strauss found that an anthropologist like himself almost inevitably became a "critic at home" and a "conformist elsewhere."[79] Abroad he resented the inroads of "civilization" on his "primitives." In his own country he saw more starkly than his fellow-citizens what was out of the human scale in modern industrial society. The same range of sympathy came into play in both cases. In this perspective it was perfectly consistent for Lévi-Strauss to preserve an attachment to the ideological Left; it was thoroughly understandable that he should have joined Sartre and the other members of the celebrated "121" in their opposition to the Algerian War.

Yet with Lévi-Strauss—whether in his mood of conservation or with his voice of protest—there was a difference of "register," as he would put it, from other intellectuals of his generation. There was a tone of acceptance, of cosmic resignation in the face of nature reminiscent of Buddhism. "The world began without the human race," he declared in one of his most quoted utterances, "and it will end without it."[80] Lévi-Strauss was anything but a doctrinaire opponent of progress; his outlook necessarily made him favor the kind of change that would reduce human want and suffering. But he was far more aware than the run of his contemporaries of the enormous price in ugliness and cultural dislocation which progress entailed. His conception of freedom, alternately elegiac and utopian, was authentically of the late twentieth century in that it looked beyond the liberal or radical or

[78] "A contre-courant," p. 31.
[79] *Tristes tropiques* (English translation), p. 384.
[80] *Ibid.*, p. 397.

Marxist ideology to a time which Saint-Simon had glimpsed
in his prediction that humanity would finally pass "from the
government of men to the administration of things." Lévi-
Strauss yearned for that distant era when the imperative of
progress would have ceased to operate—or better, when
machines would have taken over the task of social improve-
ment—and when the characteristics of the hot and the cold
cultures would be gradually fused, until humanity was
liberated at last from the "age-old curse which forced it to
enslave men in order to make progress possible."[81]

v. Conclusion: History, Anthropology, and Poetry

In French intellectual life of the 1960's Lévi-Strauss
found no lack of counterparts or imitators. By the middle of
the decade "structuralism" had become the mode—the word
was discussed everywhere, whether or not those who spoke of
it had any precise idea of its meaning. Most of them probably
did not: the writings of the leading "structuralists" were
austere, hermetic, and difficult to follow. Such was notably
true of the work of Louis Althusser on Marxism and of
Jacques Lacan on psychoanalysis. Both of these emptied the
original teaching of its humanist content and recast it in the
form of a rigorous logic; in both cases the structural interpretation relentlessly emphasized a single aspect of the
theory in question. In an ironic sense, psychoanalysis might
finally be said to have become acclimatized in France since
it had produced in Lacan its own indigenous heretic.

Most broadly, the philosophical turning-point of the 1960's
could be defined as a concerted attempt at the liquidation
of traditional humanism. Lévi-Strauss' successors let drop
the moraliste content in his work and devoted their exclusive
attention to his structural method. In this new perspective,
the three decades 1930–1960 began to look like a transition

---

[81] Collège de France, Leçon inaugurale faite le mardi 5 janvier 1960
par M. Claude Lévi-Strauss, pp. 43–44.

era in which a succession of thinkers—often against their announced intention—had tried to salvage whatever items in the classical humanist baggage could still serve the needs of heroism or despair. The structuralists of the 1960's banned both humanism and the starker attitudes that had issued from it: all smacked of a subjectivity that was no longer tolerable. Whether Catholic or Marxist, existential or Weberian, the thought of the previous generation stood condemned as irremediably subjectivist and amateurish. The new stress was on the formal aspects of syntax and of thinking itself. It was symptomatic that the most influential of the younger structuralists, Michel Foucault, composed an "archaeology of the human sciences" delineating the successive abstract categories in which man's reflection on his own works had expressed itself since the sixteenth century.[82]

Language, logic, and coding having become ends in themselves, French thought was undergoing, "with thirty years delay, its crisis of logical positivism."[83] It was experiencing the sort of change that had occurred in Anglo-American philosophy a generation earlier. From this standpoint, structuralism might have been expected to provide a bridge to the world of speculation abroad. But it came too late to perform such a role: by the time the structuralist onslaught hit France, the British and Americans were having second thoughts about logical positivism and linguistic analysis and were becoming more tolerant of other types of philosophical discourse. Furthermore, it came encumbered with characteristically French accretions that made it difficult to export. The writing of the structuralists lacked the literary leanness and colloquial manner of the best English work in analytic philosophy. It was over-argued and over-sophisticated, affected, pretentious, and given to esoteric word-games—"mandarin"

[82] *Les mots et les choses* (Paris, 1966); see also Lacroix's comments in *Panorama de la philosophie française contemporaine*, pp. 8–9, 209.
[83] Lecture by Mikel Dufrenne at the annual congress of the review *Esprit* at Melun, December 4, 1966. For a fuller statement see his "La philosophie du néo-positivisme," *Esprit*, XXXV (May 1967), 784.

in the most unfavorable meaning of the term. In respect to
the rhetoric of social thought, the structuralist revolution had
had the melancholy effect of reintroducing, under the guise
of philosophical rigor, the age-old vices of the Gallic mind.
And these weaknesses obscured the richness and originality
of what someone like Foucault had to offer.

As the century reached the two-thirds mark, the self-
confidence of the French, whether in international affairs
or in the realm of the intellect, had quite apparently been
regained. But it had been restored at a heavy cost. Although
the elections of 1967 seemed to announce the twilight of De
Gaulle's regime, the experience of Gaullist rule was likely
to leave its mark for a long time to come. In the intellectual
sphere the counterpart to the pride—the orgueil—that the
General-President had taught his countrymen was the re-
surgence of a cultural nationalism against which writers as
diverse as Camus and Teilhard and Lévi-Strauss had warned
in vain.

With the twentieth century two-thirds past, of fourteen leading thinkers of the contemporary era eight were dead.
Three more—Marcel, Malraux, and De Gaulle—for a number
of years had published little major writing. Of the three
remaining, Lévi-Strauss alone—with half his *Mythologiques*
still to go—seemed to be in full course. Sartre was evidently
pausing for breath: the public was still waiting for a second
volume of the *Critique of Dialectical Reason* he had promised.

Maritain was old enough to be the father of these two, and
the fact that he felt sufficiently vigorous to publish a substantial work was the great philosophical surprise of the
year 1966. From the monastery in Toulouse to which he had
withdrawn after the death of his wife, Maritain issued a book
of essays in the form of a self-interrogation on his own time.
Much of it recalled the militant Thomist of the interwar
years—the polemical vigor, the spare style, and the carefully
articulated arguments. But there was also a new tone of

informality, of indulgent amusement at his earlier incarnations, as when he recalled the time that he had "gently entreated his gray matter" and it had obliged him by producing the "personalist" formula. And in a retrospective passage in which he surveyed his philosophical reading over nearly seventy years, he characterized with generous understanding the masters against whose example he had fought or who had brought him intellectual sustenance: Descartes was an enemy who had aroused his liveliest interest; Hume's "implacable bitterness" had won his admiration; he was even grateful to Comte for the "uncharitable joys" he had given him. Then had come Bergson, who had tried to break off the whole philosophical succession; but he had failed—after him everyone went back to Cartesianism, or on to Husserl, for whom, "despite the catastrophe he caused," Maritain entertained a "great intellectual respect"; even Sartre, who was too "cunning" by far, had "borne witness" to something "which one would be very wrong to neglect."[84]

Thus the "old layman," as Maritain now called himself, ruminating on his illustrious antecedents and successors, suggested that his philosophical track was not so rigidly marked out as his earlier writings might have led his readers to suppose. At eighty-four the senior figure among France's social thinkers, he could afford to grant himself the indulgence of a slackening of intellectual tension. And he could at last give voice to the lyricism in his temperament that he had earlier held in check.

Maritain had always been more of a poet than he had permitted himself to appear. He might well have applied to his own work what he had written of Teilhard de Chardin, that he had clothed his vision of the universe in a "kind of disguise"—a Thomist disguise, where Teilhard's had been scientific. And the same had been true of a succession of younger men. These had done their best to cast off the straitjacket of Cartesianism. But they had not allowed themselves to enjoy their liberty for long: they had hastened to

[84] *Paysan de la Garonne*, pp. 82, 151–152.

embrace the new servitude of Hegelian or phenomenological discourse or of structural method. Still more, they were prone to falling back into the familiar Cartesian formulas. Writer after writer who had at some point experienced a burning intuition felt obliged to discipline that illumination in an accepted philosophical form: the author of *The Plague* went on to write *The Rebel*; the author of *Tristes tropiques* would not rest content until he had begun his *Mythologiques*.

Most of the time between 1930 and 1960 French social thought had had poetry at its core. Writers who had thought of themselves as rigorous theorists had been poets without knowing it. And this "disguise" slowed their coming to full awareness of what they were about. Their problem was not so much one of making contact with the world of discourse in which Anglo-American and Central European thought had fused—although that was part of it—as of extricating themselves from the intellectual confinement of their own tradition. By the 1960's this liberation was still far from accomplished. But a few pathfinders had shown the way.

In the process the French had once more proved to be fearless explorers of the moral universe. Novelists and philosophers alike had probed the mortal anxiety, the bad faith, and the ever-disappointed yearning for human solidarity that had engaged the thoughts and emotions of their contemporaries. In the very act of breaking with the French classic tradition, they had maintained and reinforced the heritage of the moralistes whose work had been an integral part of that tradition. Such explorations, however, were by their nature fragmentary and frequently amateurish. In the more "scientific" aspects of social thought, the originality of the French was not yet apparent. So much of their energy had been absorbed in catching up with methodology abroad that it was not until the 1950's that they began to devise in structuralism a new procedure of their own. A decade later the future of the structural method was still an unknown quantity. It was perhaps just another of those fragile constructions—those untenable syntheses—which had punctuated the years of desperation.

Meantime in the study of history alone—in the discipline which was the closest to poetry of the social sciences—the pre-eminence of a handful of the French had been universally recognized. It was here that what was still viable in the example of both Durkheim and Bergson had produced its finest results. In historical study redefined as retrospective cultural anthropology, the French had pointed the way to a broader and more "human" understanding of the life of man in society. By the 1960's it was symptomatic that Foucault's work, although formally labeled psychology, was in fact a kind of anthropological history which combined the insights of Febvre and Lévi-Strauss—the former's feel for the mentality of past ages and the latter's structural method.

The social thought of the desperate years began with history and ended with anthropology. It was in the dialogue between these two that French speculation of the era just past produced what was most compelling and of greatest interest to the world outside.

Index

304

Index

Schelling, Friedrich Wilhelm Joseph von, 84
Schweitzer, Albert, 62, 172
Schweitzer, Charles (Karl), 172–74
Seignobos, Charles, 23–24
Sex and sexuality, 5, 37, 38
Sillon, the, 71
Simon, Pierre-Henri, *quoted* 104
Socialism, 76, 100, 115, 118, 154, 157, 158, 161, 189, 262
Sombart, Werner, 32
Sorbonne, 14, 40, 72, 193, 208
Sorel, Georges, 14, 144, 157, 190, 220
Soviet Union, 142, 164, 165, 170, 200, 202, 212, 213, 235, 236, 237, 246
Spanish Civil War, 69, 70, 118, 123, 125–26, 135, 139, 142
Spencer, Herbert, 82
Spengler, Oswald, 141, 145, 259
Spinoza, Baruch, 256
Spoerri, Theophil, *quoted* 183
Stalin, Joseph, 165, 190, 201, 205, 213, 235, 236
Stalinism, 190, 199, 200, 217, 263
Stendhal, 10, 31, 138
Stoicism, 236, 279
Strasbourg, University of, 29–30, 39, 50, 62
Structuralism, 269–70, 274, 276, 284–86, 290–92, 294, 295; *see also* Lévi-Strauss
Suhard, Cardinal (Archbishop of Paris), 98
"Super-rationalism," 281; *see also* Rationalism
Synthesis, 4, 26, 43, 45, 53, 260, 295

Taine, Hippolyte, 82
Teilhard de Chardin, Pierre, 17, 137, 227–28, 247–61, 292, 293
L'avenir de l'homme (The Future of Man), 254, 260
Le phénomène humain (The Phenomenon of Man), 250, 251, 253, 273
"Teilhardism," 251, 256

Temps modernes, les, 177, 199, 202, 216
Third International, 191, 205; *see also* Communism
Tolstoy, Leo, 108
Toynbee, Arnold, 259
Trotsky, Leon, 205
Turin, 189

"Ultra-Bolshevism," *see* Bolshevism
UNESCO, 56
United States of America, 8, 9, 12, 14, 21, 63, 66, 75, 76, 79, 80–81, 84, 91–92, 103, 163–70, 190, 191, 202, 212, 213, 222, 239, 250, 252, 262, 265, 267–69, 273, 291, 294
Universalism, 225, 276, 281
USSR, *see* Soviet Union

Valéry, Paul, 2, 3, 5, 103, 119
Vatican, *see* Papacy
Vatican Council, Second, 67, 81, 95, 96, 100, 130, 257
Verstehen, 195, 217
Vichy government, 79, 87, 97, 113, 136, 154; anti-Semitism of, 50, 56, 272
Vico, Giambattista, 21
Vidal de la Blache, P., 24
Vietnam, 213
Vigny, Alfred de, 150

Wagner, Richard, 31
Weber, Max, 9, 12, 14, 32, 53, 61–62, 196, 204, 206, 209, 220, 266–67, 291; and religion, 35; and Marxism, 190
Weimar Republic, Marxism in, 189
Weisman, Avery D., *quoted* 185
Wilkinson, David, *quoted* 151
Wilson, Edmund, *quoted* 21
Worker-priest experiment, 98–101
World War, First, 5, 12, 118, 148, 153, 192, 243, 248
World War, Second, 6, 69, 132, 139, 192, 231, 250, 254

Zola, Emile, 31